CW01678342

OVER

& US

18+ stories, anecdotes
and more to remove
overwhelm from your door

Compiled by Carolyn Street

2022 Youier Media

Copyright © 2022 by Carolyn Street

All rights reserved. This book or any portion thereof may not be reproduced or used in any manner whatsoever without the express written permission of the publisher except for the use of brief quotations in a book review or scholarly journal.

First Printing: 2022

ISBN 978-1-8382248-7-5

Youier Media
The Blue House
Queen Victoria Road
Llanelli, SA15 2TH
YouierMedia.com

Contents

Foreword

by El Edwards, Youier Media

Over the course of the last eighteen months, it's been my absolute joy and privilege to publish the *And Us* series of "self-help" books - although a more accurate description would be "community-help" books since the real power of this series has been the vast array of stories, insights and methodologies presented by scores of contributors.

One size does not fit all and so you have in your hands a guide that offers you the opportunity to explore the issue at hand from various directions. And our sixth book in the series, Overwhelm & Us, is no exception.

Long time readers will be familiar already with my personal soapbox around the "shoulds" of life. Short version: They are bad for you and are the stuff of overwhelm!

How many times have we found ourselves over-burdened by a list of things stuffed inside our minds that we allowed to be put there in the service of a "should"? What if we shoved all the "shoulds" and instead embraced a life that allowed us to simply be who we were created to be?

- *How* you do that is the subject of this book. As with previous titles, you don't need to read the book from beginning to end. Instead, launch in as you feel led. I mention that specifically with this title because with so much wonderful, juicy content on offer, there is a chance you might start to feel overwhelmed by the goodness before you even get started - and that would totally defeat the purpose of this book!

Remember, no matter where you've come from, regardless of the story that's led you to today, you have the opportunity to grow and develop from where you are right now.

The relatively new field of neuroplasticity, our understanding of the brain's ability to modify, change and adapt, has exciting implications for any of us who've ever fallen for the lie "I am what I am". Your mind can adapt and take on new learnings. You're not "stuck" with your lot.

Jump into this vast collection of learnings with an open mind and prepare to say goodbye to overwhelm, once and for all!

Introduction

by Carolyn Street

Dear Reader,

First off I'd like to say welcome to this curated collection of stories and sharings all to do with how we have encountered and go about handling overwhelm in many of its forms. We hope that you find resonance and encouragement as well as useful insights into how you or your dear ones and peers or clients can adopt or adapt the contents for when things get a bit much.

As El mentioned in the foreword, this book is designed for you to read at your own pace and leisure. We are most mindful that we are here with rich, substantial content on Overwhelm, a subject on which there is so much input available. It is our wish that in the pages that follow, you will find abundant food for thought and many interesting and even edifying sections.

A quick word on what this book is not - it is anything but the sort of 'x number of guaranteed steps to manage your time'. Nor is there any hint of psychobabble as we value the effectiveness of down-to-earth, empathetic sharing from the heart. The value is in the way each of us has written and shared with a view to meeting the reader where he or she is or they are at. We have not held back from getting into the truth and tell-it-like-it-is aspects where clarity, transparency and honesty warrant it.

You will see that writings we call 'Interludes' are interspersed among the chapters. These are short sharings in different styles, genres and formats which add variety to the whole compilation.

We, the team of writers, each have our own personal approach to the subject and we have retained our own flavour and communication style which means that each chapter is fresh and refreshing and has its own unique appeal. Some writers use British English and others, US English. Some are native English speakers, some not and we are as diverse as any group of souls can be. You might play the 'guess where the author is from' game. Here are some clues: the countries represented are Singapore, South Africa, Germany, Spain, England, Scotland, Wales, The United States, Nigeria and Canada. That is semi-superficial information as some of us have homelands that differ from the lands we call home.

We all have one thing in common - a spirit of 'sharing is caring' and a desire to facilitate healing, learning and recovery for the benefit of our readership. As the saying goes, a (solved) problem shared is a problem halved - though that only happens when one has truly emerged from the trauma and lived to tell the tale.

Some of the chapters and interludes feature content and experiences which might be overwhelming or intense to some; a feature of the rawness and realness of the narratives all of which come with solutions and learnings that are invaluable take-aways.

I will get straight into a brief overview of the chapters so you can take your pick; a little like the 'Choose Your Own Adventure' stories that were popular back in the day. That said, I will endeavour to avoid 'spoilers'.

Chapter One entitled 'Too Afraid To Turn On The Phone' by Anke Hermann compares and contrasts two situations many of us face; one relating to work and the other in which she faced the challenges of a major inter-country move and made a new start.

In Chapter Two 'Borderline Personality Disorder And I' Didi Kan narrates the birth, development and end to his own story of overwhelm. From the perspective of a child suffering culture clash and discrimination in a foreign country, mental and emotional illness in his family, and 25 years of addiction and self destruction, to an inspired human being and empathetic mental health professional today.

Kellie Ahl's Chapter Three,'Painting My Way Out Of Overwhelm' is a personal sharing of her encounters with overwhelm paired with some beautifully doable and richly engaging guidance on how to engage with paint and your senses.

There's more at Four:'A Hero's Overwhelm' by Martin Seville features precious insights into overwhelm in a corporate setting and his discovery of his true purpose and role. Invaluable for those with work pressure and overwhelm.

Chapter Five comprises Annemarie Wilson's awesome insights and discoveries on her own approach to enabling the transition 'From Overwhelm To In-Powerment'.

In Chapter Six 'Chasing My Tail, Dropping Balls, Managing It All' Parul Banka shares how a multitude of individual, significant events all going on at once amounted to overwhelm and how she came through unscathed to tell the tale along with her go-to strategies.

'A Posy Of Resources' features a selected but not exhaustive shortlist of remedies, processes and healing actions which have helped me, loved ones and clients move through overwhelm. The sharings keep coming in a heartfelt account of how my paternal Grandfather equipped me with wisdom, strength and strategies that I have and often remember to use - smile.

Chapter Eight is Debbie George's piece 'Create A New Beginning'. It illustrates the value of seeing expectations as they are and of managing them with sensitivity to our needs and self-love.

In Chapter Nine, 'The Last Straw That Breaks Us, And the One After That', Gali Rosas gets personal, sharing just 3 of her most transformative dealings with capital "O" Overwhelm, and following each with just one tactic, to help lighten your load, protect yourself and your loved ones from the worst of it, and heal when the episodes inevitably end. She encourages that if you, like we, have too much on your plate right now, and are maybe looking for a quick fix, start with just one story, just one strategy, and just one moment at a time.

'How Overwhelm Affects the Chakras' - Zeeba Khan's Chapter 10 is a goldmine of Ayurvedic wisdom and some uncommonly-known information on how we can help ourselves, our fellow humans and the planet.

In Chapter 11 'Seven Hidden Treasures Within Empath Overwhelm' Johannah Stirzaker encourages us to consider a unique form of overwhelm. To lean into it with bravery and curiosity. To embrace the opportunities it gives us for growth, compassionate connection and resilience.

Chapter the Twelfth, penned by Adriann Meyer is a hugely generous and brave set of insights into the challenges and upheaval faced by a person who has been at the receiving end of a narcissist's behaviour. It is highly personal, as all the chapters are, and really speaks to the issues he himself faced, having been in that situation.

In Chapter Thirteen: 'Cool At The Pool: Filtering Out The Noise So The Show Can Go On', Wiwiek Najihah - Singapore's first female contestant at the World Championships Of Public Speaking Finals - recounts how she made the near-impossible happen in August 2018 in Chicago, Illinois.

Chapter Fourteen, intriguingly entitled 'There Is No Such Thing As Overwhelm', Morag Shaw poses a challenge and deftly takes us through her rationale for this assertion, with highly effective reflections, mores and points of view, much to our - her readership's - edification.

'Burnout And Me' shines a light on this very real group of experiences as we see through the lenses of Ina Leitner, an amazing coach and thought-leader in the field of entrepreneurial business whose learnings and insights are invaluable for those of us who find ourselves in positions of vulnerability where self-sufficiency is our only recourse for survival.

Majero Bouman's essay and sharings on the practice of truly being in a body is a wealth of precious tools for self-discovery and finding our own personal path to finding our innate abilities while discovering how our own mindset and the body-mind-soul trifecta factors in resilience-building.

In Chapter Seventeen, Jenny Schmal shares with us her experiences with the overwhelm that accompanies grief and her lived experiences along with her own 'Journey Of Healing' and how she found equilibrium, equipoise and excellence along with her own brand of elegance that make her the quintessential relationship and life-coach she is.

In 'The Fatigue Trap' Rachpal Kaur Tulsi shares her hard-won learnings on the path through overwhelm from the perspectives of a wonderfully-rounded coach with delightfully-formed perspectives on the components of overwhelm and strategies to tackle it feasibly and practically.

So, dear reader, we all invite you to have at it; take a dive into these specially-crafted and humbly-offered pieces.

Too Afraid to Turn on The Phone

By Anke Herrmann

I hadn't turned the phone on in days. I hadn't had a full night's sleep in weeks. In a desperate attempt to get enough caffeine into my body to get through the day, I popped across the road to the "Café 4 Gatos" ("4 Cats" because that's how many souls fit into the cosy space). The mild morning sun throwing warm shadows onto the small wooden tables, relaxed chatter from moms who'd stopped for breakfast on the way back from the school run, the smell of freshly ground coffee, the familiar friendly face of the owner behind the counter gave me a sorely missed sense of normality.

"There you are! I've been trying to get hold of you for days! Why don't you pick up the phone? When are you coming for a fitting? The performance is next week! What do you expect me to say to the parents of the girls? Do you realise how many calls from anxious moms I've had to deal with while you're sitting here sipping coffee?" The dance teacher's rage washed over my sleep deprived face, leaving me unable to breathe. It was springtime - "crazy season" in my sewing business. Dance schools were preparing for their yearly end-of-course performances and I had more costume orders than I could cope with.

I didn't have a sewing business, I WAS the sewing business. Talking on the phone to clients wanting to know when their costumes would be ready would take up precious time I didn't have, and the best solution to the problem I could come up with was to turn off the phone. I'd call them when I had something positive to tell them. Not communicating at all until then isn't a great idea, you might think. And you'd be right. But overwhelmed people don't make good decisions.

When the client's wave of anger had run its course and she eventually looked at me, expecting an answer, I burst into tears. Shame, exhaustion and a blank mind lost for words came out through my eyes. I knew how bad it looked for her to find me in a coffee shop when she'd travelled across town to come and see me, after I hadn't answered her calls. There was an explanation for the ridiculous time pressure. It had nothing to do with her, it wasn't her concern and she didn't care.

Eventually, we both calmed down and found a solution. We asked someone to take the dresses to the dance studio for a fitting while I kept working to finish the rest.

In the end, the girls enjoyed their dance performance without delay. Nobody knew or cared about the sleepless nights I'd gone through to get their costumes ready in time. But my body let me know that enough was enough - dark rings under my eyes, hair falling out, cold sores on both sides of my mouth, clothes hanging off me. Overwhelm isn't healthy.

But a lot of work that needs to get done by a certain time doesn't automatically lead to overwhelm.

An Effortless Move

When the office door in Central London closed behind me on a cold February Tuesday evening at the usual time, a new chapter of my life had begun. It was the last day at my software developer job and it was my last day in the UK. My one-way flight to Spain left the next day.

I was ready to embark on the biggest adventure of my life after leaving East Germany. I'd quit my job to start my own business in the sunny south of Spain. I was excited, not sure if my crazy idea to open a sewing studio specialising in flamenco dance costumes would take off or flop, but I was ready to give it a go.

If you had walked into my London flat that night, you wouldn't have believed that I'd leave the country for good the next day. No boxes, no suitcases packed. Everything was as it had been for the last few years.

Moving to Spain had been a spontaneous idea but not a rushed decision. For a couple of years, I'd prepared. I'd taken sewing classes with a well-known London tailor and dressmaker. I'd spent countless hours studying Spanish. I'd gone on trips to Spain as often as I could to familiarise myself with the place and eventually started looking for a place to live. I'd found and rented a lovely attic in the historic heart of Granada, with a beautiful view of the Alhambra, got a bank account and resident's card. I'd researched the best way to move all my belongings from the UK to Spain and hired a removal company. I'd put into practice my new Spanish skills to find and hire a local transport company to arrange a place for the removal truck to drop off my boxes, and for a small local van to take over and deliver them to my new home.

But I hadn't had time to pack. The removalists offered a "we pack for you" option and I took them up on that offer gratefully. At 9am the next morning, a small team arrived, armed with boxes, bubble wrap and duct tape, and we got started. Forming a smooth assembly line, I put my belongings on the dining table and they expertly packed everything up. At 2pm they left with a truck full of boxes and I shut the apartment door behind me for the last time. An hour later I made my way to the airport to start my new life in Spain.

I slept in my new Granada apartment that night. My boxes arrived a couple of weeks later.

Turns out the large, heavy TV set I'd paid to bring over didn't work in Spain. There had been a misunderstanding over a CD player that got packed even though it wasn't mine and had to be sent back. A couple of months later, I had to fly back to the UK in order to get my deposit back from my London flat. The real estate agent had tried to take advantage of me being out of the country and I had to show up in his office to get things resolved. Not everything went smoothly but there was no overwhelm at all involved in that move.

Burnout

For the first 8 years of running my sewing business, I experienced overwhelm every spring, working through nights and getting ill as a result of it. It didn't occur to me that 4 months of overwhelm each year wasn't the only or best way to run a business. I thought having too much work was a luxury problem. In 2012, I hit my limit. The last project of the season involved me making over fifty costumes for a dance school, with 8 additional outfits thrown onto my already overloaded cutting table at the last minute. I ended up working through 4 days and 3 nights without sleeping, apart from 20 minutes on the tiled floor next to Leo, my dog. I was afraid that I wouldn't wake up in time if I got just a little bit more comfortable. I finished the last stitches by hand in a dressing room in the theatre, while dancers were already stepping out onto the stage.

The day after that performance, two of the dancers left to go on holidays without paying what they owed me. That's when my long overstretched patience snapped. I was ready to throw in the towel. I had enough of "living the dream". If it meant spending spring time in permanent overwhelm I wanted nothing to do with it anymore. For the first time since starting my sewing business, I took time out to reflect about how I'd gotten myself into that situation and how I wanted my business and life to be instead. Eventually, I saw through the misunderstanding of what serving my clients meant that had led me to saying yes to everything they asked of me. I often wish I'd realised sooner that there was another way but I needed the total burnout to open my eyes.

A few years later, I decided that it was time for another pivot. I didn't want to still sew for dancers when I reached my sixties, with dwindling eyesight and aching back. I qualified as a coach so I could support others through the business building journey our upbringing leaves us so entirely unprepared for. Soon, fellow coaches asked for tech help, knowing about my background in software development and ongoing passion for the online world. Now, I use everything I've learned about business, creativity, psychology and tech to help my clients grow their businesses online. And I get to witness plenty of overwhelm.

Sinking in Online Tech Quicksand

"Your FREE registration includes access to over 60 transformational gifts from female leaders, coaches, creatives, healers, authors and visionaries in the fields of: Personal Transformation | Wisdom & Self-Growth | Parenting & Relationships | Health & Wellness | Spiritual Development | Success & Mindset | Divine Feminine | Parenting & Relationships | Intuitive Development | Conscious Business | and many others," the registration page for an online giveaway promises.

"20 Heart Centred Leaders help you launch profitable programs, products and memberships that serve your communities without having to sacrifice your values" if you register for the summit and free up at least an hour a day for a week to listen to all the experts. Of course you can buy the VIP pass to access everything later, but it doesn't get any less, especially if you go on to sign up for the speakers' free gifts.

What if one of these gifts contains the golden nugget that will make all the difference to your business? It's a possibility but how much of your time will it take to find the needle in the haystack of videos, books, or events on offer?

What about social media? The moment you turn on your phone or computer the notifications flood in, fighting for your attention, oh so hard to ignore. Direct messages don't just beg for your attention, they demand it. Inboxes are designed in a way to keep you worried you might miss something important, so you better make sure you reply to your messages before you lose sight of them.

Are you feeling overwhelmed just reading all of this? My guess is that several notifications of new emails, messages or other "important" events on social media have distracted you in the few minutes it took you to read this far. It's a jungle.

The good news is, you can ignore giveaways, summits and even social media. But what about the platforms and strategies you need to build your business online?

If you're looking to offer your services online, you're bombarded with often conflicting advice: You need a website. You can build a thriving business without a website. You need an online course. Nobody finishes online courses. You need a high-ticket offer. You need to sell something affordable first. Webinars are the best way to get clients. Webinars don't work anymore. All-in-one platforms make tech easy. All-in-one platforms make you pay a lot for features you don't need and will spend ages trying to understand. Email marketing, funnels, memberships. Each strategy, each platform is a world of its own. It's a rabbit hole - easy to slide into, much harder to avoid than giveaways, summits and social media.

If you feel a sense of overwhelm wrapping itself around you like a heavy blanket every time you turn on the computer, trust me, you're not alone. I meet my clients on Zoom, so I see their frowns and tense shoulders as they hop from one tab to the next, clicking on links before the page has time to load, now heading off to places they have no intention to go to. Sometimes the last bit of patience gets killed by an unexpected error message.

"I wish I could just find a 25 year old who does all that for me," a friend burst out in frustration. "All I want is to get people to sign up for my free thing on my website and get their names into Mailchimp." She'd googled how to do that and found a tutorial, promisingly titled "How to Integrate Mailchimp with Squarespace". But the tutorial didn't make sense to her. The instructions included a step involving an "API key". She had no idea what an API key is, where to find one and what to do with it once she had it. When she googled that, she sunk further and further in online tech quicksand, without getting any closer to her original goal. It's when frustration and overwhelm set in. Can you relate?

Error Messages Are My Friend

For many of my clients, error messages are frustrating - yet another thing that isn't working, yet another problem to deal with, yet another can of worms where one answer raises three new questions. An error message feels like confirmation that tech is just too hard, that they don't have what it takes to make an online business work.

For me, error messages are an invitation - an invitation to explore, to get curious, to problem solve and troubleshoot, to get creative and think outside the box. One error message - two entirely different perceptions and reactions.

So, What's Behind Overwhelm And How Can You Overcome It?

Quitting a job, moving to a different country and starting a business or two, figuring out online tech - there is certainly a lot of work to do. It'd be easy to think that overwhelm would be inevitable. But sometimes we're overwhelmed, sometimes we're not. Why?

In my experience, overwhelm sets in when you:

- face more than you think or know you can handle in the time you have available,
- think or know that there is no help available, and
- cannot see a way out of the situation.

When I calculated how many hours I needed to finish the dance costumes on time and realised that I'd have to work 18 hours a day for 2 weeks, overwhelm took over. I was already tired and the thought of another two weeks at that rhythm felt too much to bear. I couldn't move the performance date. The theatre had been booked months in advance and tickets had been sold. Nobody would agree to changing the date because of the dressmaker. I didn't know anyone else who knew how to sew well enough to take some of the load off my plate. Even if I'd known someone, I wasn't charging enough for my work to be able to afford help. And I couldn't just cancel the project and pull out. My reputation was on the line. Who would hire a dressmaker who'd left a dance group without costumes for their end-of-year performance?

There was no deadline for my move to Spain. I could see solutions for the issues I could potentially face. If I hadn't found an apartment in Granada in time to move in once I'd given up my place in London I could have stayed in a hostel for a few weeks. Packing up in half a day was no problem with the help of the removal company. Everything felt doable, that's why there was no overwhelm.

What about Online Tech?

When clients first come to me they often experience tech overwhelm because they know that an online business can give them the flexibility, location independence and scalability they're looking for but it won't be possible without the use of online tools. They feel out of their depth, facing too steep a learning curve and not enough time. So there is more than they feel they can handle and there is no way out. What about help? That's available, isn't it?

Well, asking for help isn't as easy as it sounds. I remember sending a survey to people in my community asking about their challenges and frustrations relating to online tech. The answers to the question, "What's one thing, if you knew the answer, that would make a big difference to you and your business?" surprised me. They were either vague or too specific to be useful. I couldn't make sense of it until the topic came up in a conversation with a client and she said, "Oh, I remember that survey! I felt really stupid. I didn't even know what to ask or where to start." You can't ask for what you don't know exists.

But that's not all. When you feel like a tourist in a big city without a map in the digital space, it's hard to know who to trust. When you don't know enough to be able to judge whether a recommendation makes sense or not, you're easy prey for pickpockets and unethical salespeople, and you know it.

If you're anything like me, when overwhelm hits, you freeze. Maybe you procrastinate, maybe you "throw money at the problem" trying to buy yourself a way out.

Whatever you do, when you're overwhelmed you're not operating at your best. Chances are you're not making the best decisions. Chances are you can't see the solutions that are available to you.

What To Do?

Stop the hustle long enough to reflect and plan and come up with solutions before it's too late. If I had calculated the time I needed to finish the dresses a couple of weeks earlier, I would have become aware of the issue two weeks earlier and had more time to find help.

Find the map. Invest time to understand the big picture of the task or project at hand. It helps you find your bearings. When you have a map, the distance from one place to another doesn't get smaller, but you won't get lost or waste time with unnecessary detours. When you don't feel lost, you're more relaxed, and when you're more relaxed you learn and do better.

Be discerning about who and what you allow onto your calendar or to do list. Run every task through the "4xD filter" first:

- Delete: Does it have to get done at all? Do yourself a favour and don't brush over this one!
- Delegate: Does it have to be you doing it? Find creative ways to get help.

- Do: If it takes longer to think about when to do it than to do it, just do it now and save yourself having to deal with it again later
- Delay: Do you have to make a decision now? It's amazing how many tasks become obsolete when you just sit on them for a while. I call it conscious procrastination and it's very effective.

Get organised. Find a way to keep track of everything you're doing. It took me a long time to find a tool that worked for me, one that's easy enough to feed so that it does in fact contain all my tasks. It's made a huge difference in several ways:

- It frees up headspace - no more nervous undercurrents, worrying that I might drop the ball on something;
- Tasks get done faster - no more scrambling to find the information needed to get something done;
- Things get done in a more efficient manner after consciously thinking through what needs to get done and how;
- Saying NO becomes easier - I don't overbook myself if I can see all my current commitments in one place.

Only deal with what's right in front of you. All other tasks don't exist until this one is done. Things get done faster when you don't distract yourself thinking ahead to other tasks instead of concentrating on the one at hand.

Use the "10 minute frustration rule": If you can't figure something out in 10 minutes, walk away or get help, rather than wasting hours and hours trying harder and harder to work it out. I call that "pitbull mode" and it makes you waste precious time you could use to do something else, rest or simply have fun. Nothing better to get the creative juices flowing and seeing new angles and solutions than disconnecting for a while.

Give yourself the gift of kindness. Pushing yourself to do too much too fast puts you on the path to overwhelm and nobody wins. Last but not least, work off the assumption that you have what it takes to figure things out. Because you do.

About Anke Herrmann

Anke Herrmann is a business coach, mentor, online tech expert, and author of Taming the Tech Monster. She started her entrepreneurial journey in 2004 when she quit her software developer job in the UK, moved to Spain and started a sewing business.

She soon realised that building a business really is a creative process, the same as sewing a dress or developing software - a magical mix of vision, skill and soul.

She now brings everything she has learned about business, tech, creativity and psychology to help coaches and educators confidently build their businesses online, without losing their sanity over complex tools or mind-numbing admin tasks. Find out more at ankeherrmann.com and join the free community at Facebook.com/groups/businessbuildingformavericks

"There are no inherent bad thoughts, bad emotions, bad feelings or bad sensations, only information mismanagement"
Didi Kan

Overwhelm

We process and experience the world through thoughts, emotions, feelings and sensations. And because the universe is constant impermanence, just like with anything and everything else in the universe, thoughts, emotions, feelings and sensations are transient, ephemeral and transformative. They are meant to be experienced and processed in our mind and body, then released back into the universe, so that we can invite new thoughts, emotions, feelings and sensations, one moment at a time, and expand our human experience continuously. Being overwhelmed is being out of sync with the universal flow. Being overwhelmed is having hoarded, accumulated and being overloaded with too much information.

And Us

Overwhelm And Us is the last conclusion and brief recapitulation to all the chapters I have contributed in the And Us book series up till this point. With Anxiety And Us I address a mindset that believes that whatever hurt us in the past is doomed to happen again at some point in our adulthood. So we must hold onto the vibrations of fear in our body, like the sword of Damocles, constantly reminding us that being safe in a hostile world, therefore inner peace, is not available to us. With Sadness And Us I address a depression mindset that believes that belonging, being loved unconditionally, purpose and happiness are not available to us. With Anger And Us I address a reactive mindset that believes that division, judgement, scapegoatism and aggression is the only way to behave if we want to survive the others. With Fear And Us I address a scarcity mindset that believes that there is not enough goodness in the universe for all to share, and that we are not enough to deserve these good things without hardship and sacrifice. The fear of scarcity forces us to struggle and work hard if we want to get health, love or fortune, because luck, ease and enjoyment are not available to us. With Authenticity And Us finally, I suggest a flow mindset, so that people can replace all the disempowering mindsets I have addressed in the previous 4 books, and learn how to synchronise harmoniously with the pulse of the universe. The mindset we choose to operate within each moment and set of circumstances defines the nature of our relationship with all thoughts, emotions, feelings and sensations, and therefore subsequently the nature and quality of our life experience. A disempowering mindset is a mindset that works in a short circuit mode, and keeps repeating and regurgitating the same tedious informations in a sterile loop, like a broken record, like a stagnant putrid swamp. An empowering mindset is a growth mindset. And the ultimate mindset is the flow mindset. A mindset that operates through intuition.

The Power Of Letting Go

Because our brain is designed to prioritise survival, because our mind's nature is to constantly entertain thoughts, and because generational traditions of toxic beliefs are being perpetuated all over the world, letting go is probably the most difficult and alien concept for the vast majority of us. When we can understand the power of letting go and the freedom we get from it, we can start to empty our bags of old disempowering beliefs, and regain a light heart and mental clarity. We can reconnect with our intuition and access all the power, the intelligence, the support and the inspiration we ever needed, to become the person we were always meant to be. As opposed to being a pale copy of our parents, the impostor our teachers made us believe we should be, and repeating a cycle of unhappiness and limitations. It is important to highlight that letting go is not trying to let go. Letting go is a process that can not be forced, and requires an education of it. Trying to let go when we are not ready, just like trying desperately to be happy creates toxic positivity.

The Power Of Change

Next comes the concept of change, and the awareness that change is not only the essence of the universe, but also the best thing about that universe. It takes a lot for humans that have been brought up to recognise a sense of safety in what is known and familiar, to welcome change and its uncertainties. But if and when we are able to embrace change, there is nothing that can ever hold us back from expanding our unlimited potential, enjoying the most exhilarating life, and impacting the world positively, as a byproduct of our happiness.

It Was Always A Part Of Our Journey

The universe seems chaotic to our human intelligence. But everything has a place, a time and a reason. And so just like with all states, if we have felt and still feel overwhelmed at times, it is because it is a part of our journey, a part of our education, a part of our human experience.

Overwhelm is neither bad nor good. Overwhelm does not define us. Overwhelm is only a moment, telling us that we are being overloaded by information. And we can all learn how to let go, how to embrace changes, and how to eventually feel the flow, go with the flow, and even become the flow.

Borderline Personality Disorder and I

By Didi Kan

Every Story Has A Start

It all started with one word. One word that prompted a lifetime of overwhelm. One word that introduced me to homelessness, drugs, prostitution, alcohol, hatred, desperation and mental disorders. One word that invited into my life Bipolar Disorder, Borderline Personality Disorder, Attention Deficit Hyperactive Disorder, Obsessive Compulsive Disorder, Tourettes, Psychosis, self-destruction, suicide attempts, anger, violence... and rage against the whole of humanity, starting and ending with myself. A lifetime of depression, anxiety, addiction, self-sabotage, over reactivity and crippling insecurities. One word. Not even a sentence. One sole word. A magic spell, a curse that taught me that I was different, inferior, unworthy and unlovable ...

'Chink!'

A word charged with hatred, disdain, contempt, mockery and malice. A word that comes with insults, laughter, mimicking of stereotypes such as grotesque Chinese accent, slanting eyes making, and exaggerated Bruce Lee style Kung Fu moves, complete with faces and sound effects. A word that has been drilled into me relentlessly, like bullets from a machine gun I could not escape. This is the short story of one of the afflictions that used to affect my life until very recently. This is a story of Borderline Personality Disorder.

Little Me

I was 10 years old once. A shy Chinese boy born in France. Living with his parents who owned a Chinese restaurant, and his older brother, in a middle-class borough of Lyon.

Up until that point I had been a good son, a good brother, a good student and a good boy across the board. My main objective was to make my parents proud. They worked very hard to provide a decent life for my brother and I.

They came from Hong Kong to escape communism, with little money, little network, and no grasp of the French language, in a time when discrimination and prejudice were rampant. As a result my Dad was constantly working very hard, or being ill as a result of it. And my Mum was constantly worried for him, terrified at the prospect of a life without him, in such an alien place, with the burden and pressure of two kids at young ages.

And so I grew up with the belief that life was hard, and that my mission, priority and role in my family was to justify my parents' efforts by doing my utmost to make them proud. And so I was always battling at school to be the top of the class. Sometimes I was second. Most of the time I was first. But I was never third. Even in my everyday behaviours I would act like the perfect son my parents kept on saying I was. Because they decided I was the best looking son for instance, I was always posing, and aware of the importance of looking good in public.

Ironically, because my family endured severe scarcity the first years they arrived in France and when I was a baby, as we started to be able to afford it, my Mum's favourite spike of dopamine would be to watch me eating rich and luxurious foods. And so I became an obese child.

From a young age, like all of us, I started to experience the incongruity, contradictions, and inconsistency of the human mind.

Dark Clouds

And then one day, things started to shift in my reality. My sense of identity had been challenged and tarnished by the contact with kids at school, and my inability to understand and regulate that stress. It became increasingly harder for me to keep on being that golden child.

Progressively, relentlessly and mercilessly, sadness, fear and anger infected me from all fronts. I was bullied at school. French, white, beautiful and rich kids called me names. They picked up on my ethnicity, my obesity, and the clothes that I was wearing. I was also extremely spotty, my hair was greasy and infested with dandruff, and I had a collection of motor and verbal tics. I was the perfect target for bullies.

If some kids didn't know they were bullies yet, the mere sight of me would trigger that instinct in them. I was a terrified and defenceless mouse thrown into a snake pit, reminding the snakes of their nature.

And when I came home there was no one I could talk to about this. My parents worked so hard they were either at work or resting. My brother was going through and dealing with his own problems, suffering from a stutter, tics and anxiety. And all I can remember from our home was a thick, heavy and almost tangible silence, loneliness and emptiness.

In the afternoon I could only watch TV with little sound and in the dark, because my dad was sleeping during the breaks between the lunchtime and the dinnertime shift, and my parents' bedroom was adjacent to the living room, only separated by a room divider. Also my mum was always cold so the heating was always on and the windows were always closed. I remember either suffocating when they were home, or feeling immensely sad, lonely, and terrified of the dark when they were at work. I would see monsters everywhere. Even my distorted reflection in the mirrors would terrorize me.

My only solace every day was hearing them coming back from home after work. We lived two floors above the restaurant, so it was easy to calculate and anticipate their return, with the sounds of the restaurant closing and their steps climbing up the stairway. But of course I was not allowed to stay awake that late, so I had to pretend I was asleep in bed when my Mum smothered me with kisses as soon as she got home.

Even in those short moments of tenderness I was unable to fully connect with affection.

Darker Clouds

The bullying became worse and worse. Being insulted, spat at, threatened and publicly humiliated was my norm, punctuated by regular chasing, lynching and ruining of my belongings.

I remember my first significant possession. My parents started to do better financially, so my Mum bought me a platinum pendant of Tweety. Tweety the yellow canary from the Looney Tunes animated series. Because that was my nickname (Titi means little brother in Chinese, and Titi is also the French translation for Tweety). And so I owned a symbol of who I was. But most of all this was a symbol of all my parents' hard work, their love for me, and their pride in me.

The pendant didn't last a day. As soon as the kids saw it, they circled me, snatched it, snapped it in half, threw it back at my face, tripped me on the floor and kicked, spat and laughed at me for making a fuss over such a cheap and tacky pendant.

But the worst was when I came home. My mum would be off her head from the drugs she would take to alleviate her anxiety, because my dad was always ill from working so hard. Dad had his first cancer already and would have five in total by the end of his life, so I really didn't feel that I should burden my parents with more worries.

My need for love and comfort, it was obvious, was a luxury we couldn't afford.

And so my mum's behaviour would become more and more erratic, volatile and unstable day after day. My grades at school went from top to bottom. I stopped being happy. I stopped posing. I stopped being the golden child.

We would fight all the time over anything, my mum and I. Her level of hysteria and irrationality got worse and worse. Even my brother would use me as a punching bag occasionally. Not because he had any problem with me personally. Just because he could and I happened to be there.

Whether I was at school or home I seemed to be attracting that sort of energy. I was a beacon for anger, aggression and cruelty.

And then one day Mum really lost it. I remember her waving a kitchen knife at me in the kitchen. I remember my dad holding her back, yelling at me and telling me to leave. I remember my brother staring at me with contempt. I was twelve years old when that happened.

And this was the first time I ended up in the street.

The Court Of Miracles

On the streets I found a new family. My "Cours Des Miracles" (to use a French term), a place for orphans, ugly children, rejects, outcasts, unloved forgotten kids and freaks like me.

We lived from squat to squat, surviving from petty crimes, selling drugs and prostitution, and sharing a common passion for consuming heavy drugs on a daily basis. We would mix up heroin, cocaine, pills of all sorts: sedatives, stimulants, hallucinogenics… also LSD, opium, magic mushrooms, cannabis, alcohol, etc... and anything we could get our hands on that would entertain us away from the cruelty of our conscious reality. We would call our mixes "cocktails", and then see what doors those cocktails would open for us.

There would be dramas, chaos, hallucinations and total randomness. Sometimes violence. Sometimes comas. And more often than not waking up the next day in some strange places, with some strange people, and in the strangest situations.

I have witnessed overdose. I have witnessed death. I have witnessed extreme abuse, violence, manipulation, betrayal and the full range of psychotic states. Some of my friends were shot, crippled, found dead hanging at the end of a rope, or found dead in the back of a car. Some ended up in prison or mental institutions. Many caught AIDS. Few of us made it.

I have explored the depths and the true meaning of survival. And although that new "family" quickly became dangerously toxic, for a little while I fluctuated between my first family at home and my street family, because that was all I knew and had.

I went to and fro, depending on what was happening at home, and what was happening in the streets, and what was the least horrible option at that moment... until I stopped coming home.

My Dad

My Dad organised an expensive private school for me to attend, to maintain some sort of connection with me and not lose me completely. Chinese people traditionally communicate with gestures as they have little understanding of emotional intelligence. And so despite the rupture between my family and I, my dad put secret measures into place to keep an eye on me.

I was high or hungover most of the time, turning up at school with a gun or a knife hanging down my trousers, reeking of cigarettes and alcohol with coke all over my face, and sleeping on the desk during classes when I was not skipping them.

And the school would let me stay and continue the scholarship, because that is what expensive private schools were about in France back then.

Eventually, once I had failed all hopes of academic success my dad asked me to work for him. He was recovering from his second or third cancer and was not able to run his restaurant anymore, so I said yes for him.

I admired him. He was the only one I liked in my first family because he was the only one that didn't hurt me directly. He only hurt me indirectly. And that was still the best and most precious thing I had.

He did let me down. He chose my mum over me without a split second of hesitation that day in the kitchen when she tried to stab me with a kitchen knife, and allowed me to end up rotting in the streets with all the other unchosen and unwanted children. He always made it clear that the love he had for his wife would always come first, that everyone else came second, and that he would even support her unconditionally if she killed someone. I was no better than everyone else. I would never come first in my dad's heart. And his prophecy even fulfilled itself, when my Mum killed any remnants of love between her and I, and I was made an outcast.

But if it wasn't for those subtle connections he put in place, I probably wouldn't have made it either. My dad did his best to keep me alive and connected to the family, despite the madness of both my mum and me, despite his lack of emotional intelligence and his inability to communicate with me.

His best was good enough.

Mental Disorders

As I started to work for my parents and run their restaurant, I stopped all drugs, and I became a fully functional hard core alcoholic. I would get drunk and pass out not once but twice a day, every day, for months on end, until I would suffer alcohol poisoning, fall into a mini coma, wake up in a pool of my own vomit and urine, take a day off to recover, and then repeat the cycle.

I would speed drink to pass out after the lunch shift, in order to fall asleep during the break, and at night after work.

I would smoke 60 cigarettes a day and entertain a towering repertoire of addictions of all types and intensity, such as the addiction to sex, porn, television, theft, lying, crying, anger, anxiety, negative thoughts, paranoid thoughts, suicidal thoughts, etc... but the one constant was my addiction to hatred.

Hatred towards people, hatred towards life, and of course hatred towards myself. I was resentful and vindictive of all those who hurt me. I had a list of people I would hurt and kill just before killing myself. And I would play that movie in my head relentlessly.

I was jealous. Jealous of the beautiful and happy people. Every time I would see a couple in love in the street, that would make me want to cry and kill myself.

I was obsessed with death. I tried to kill myself many times.

And so my dad took me to a mental hospital. I was diagnosed and treated for suicidal manic depression (what we call Bipolar Disorder nowadays). But it is only in the last couple of years, thanks to the pandemic, and after working five years as a full time professional therapist, that I realised and understood that I also suffered all my life from Borderline Personality Disorder (BPD) and Attention Deficit Hyperactive Disorder (ADHD).

BPD

Borderline Personality Disorder, as with all personality disorders and mental conditions, can vary subtly from one individual to another.

For me, BPD was characterised by a profound and extreme sense of unworthiness, insecurity and reactivity, and the subsequent toxic side effects on my life, and for whoever crossed my path.

There was a constant crippling social anxiety, that could only be managed with alcohol, as a result of the obsession with abandonment, rejection, being inferior and being persecuted.

I was obsessed about what people thought about me, why they said the things they said to me, why they said those things the way they said it, and why they didn't say certain other things.

My mind was in overdrive 24/7. My body was a trigger-sensitive nuclear time bomb, ready at the first opportunity to explode, and unleash brutal, irrational and hysterical outbursts of toxic emotions, reactions and delusions. I was convinced for instance that I was not my parents' legitimate child because my mum told me repeatedly that she should have killed me when she found me as a baby. She used to abuse me verbally all the time with the nastiest, most inventive, cruel and vicious comments. She was my bully at home when I was a child, and I believed everything she said. I would believe anything that would confirm my inadequacy in this world.

I believed that happy and beautiful people in love would display and show off their happiness, beauty and love, just to remind me of my exceptional and spectacular unworthiness. And laugh at me. To humiliate me. Just like the bullies at school did when they broke my pendant. Because that is who I was and all that I will ever deserve.

I would cry every day and every night without fail. Wondering every night why I was so heartbreakingly lonely, unlucky and pathetic. Wondering every morning why I had to suffer another day.

There was delusion, grandiosity, and the desperate need to always lie and "bigger myself up", in order to be accepted by others.

And there was the paranoia, the hallucinations, the reactivity and the obsession for revenge. I would hear voices. I would see ghosts. I would display violence, stupidity and madness. I would transform into the Incredible Hulk or Mister Hyde, and create havoc around me.

There were always the regrets, the guilt, the apologies, and a terrible sense of not being in control of my life the next day, when I realised what I had done the night before.

And finally, there were the addictions. I would get exhilarated and high on joy, pleasure and instant gratification. Because BPD and Bipolar together offer the perfect ecosystem for addictions to thrive. And my addictions were the only things that justified my life and kept me alive.

Transformation

By this point I had been a physical, mental, emotional and social wreck all my adult life.

I moved to London in 1997, in the hope of making it in the music industry. Unfortunately, my afflictions consistently sabotaged all my attempts.

In 2008, at the age of 38 and out of nowhere, I was given a once in a lifetime opportunity. And many of my fellow peers dislike using the term "broken". But to me it is important to use that word, because this is exactly what I have been all my life. Broken. Nothing worked in my life. Nothing ever went well. And if ever there were some good things in my life, I would ruin them. I was broken. My mum was broken. And this was my chance to fix both of us.

She had been diagnosed with cancer, and tried to kill herself twice, my estranged brother told me on the telephone. And she wanted me to look after her, and be her sole full-time carer, or else she would kill herself for good. I followed my heart and my intuition. I left everything on the spot and took the first plane to Paris, where she lived with my brother and his family.

I stayed, and lived with them in that house, for nearly nine months. This was the most challenging decision I ever had to execute. I suffered from alopecia and lost my hair because of the stress, the cabin fever and the emotional rollercoaster. But eventually my mum got better. The mental clarity came back and the cancer went into remission.

So I came back to London. And a few days later my mum called me. "Thank you for saving my life" she said over the telephone. In those three seconds, a lifetime of addictions, suffering and resentment lifted out of my chest instantly and forever.

Three seconds is all it took for my transformation to happen.

Those three seconds were the culmination of my thirty eight years on this planet at that point in time. The fireworks that would reflect and celebrate my epiphany, and the new found inner peace and mind clarity. I realised in that moment that all that I ever needed was praise from my Mum. All that I had been craving desperately for all my life was a gesture, a token, an acknowledgement that I was still her golden child, her favourite son, her much loved little boy. I needed to be reminded that I was never alone. I was never abandoned. I was never unloved, unsupported nor forsaken. I believed I was.

And because I believed I was, I forgot that I wasn't.

And this is one of the most fascinating things about the human mind: when we choose to believe a belief, we only select the memories that support those beliefs. I had tons of happy memories from my childhood, and the love my mum gave me. But my mind blocked them all.

My mind chose to only remember the hurt, the bullies, the manic episodes and the hysteria.

And so I came to the conclusion that I was unlovable, ugly and despicable. It was an irreversible curse. I decided that because I was unworthy of my mum's love, I was also unworthy of anyone's love, starting with myself.

In that moment of bliss, when she said "thank you" to me, I was reminded that we were alike, that we have always been and we will always be alike. Not different. Not opposite. Not separated.

The same in our afflictions, imbalance, overwhelm and despair. The same in our fragility and humanity.

We were never separated because we both suffered in the very exact same way. And the moment I could see myself in her, and her in me, I remembered how much I loved her. We have never been able to acknowledge and express the love we had for one another, because of the overwhelm the Bipolar Disorder and the Bordeline Personality Disorder we both had in common brought between us.

There Is No Such Thing As 'Normal' Behaviour

Of course this is only my story. Some people suffer from parents who genuinely never had and never will have any love for them. Some never had any parents in any shape or form at all. But I have learnt as a therapist that there is a way for everyone.

We can all find solace, balance and sense. That does not mean that we will all choose to go this way, or are even able to make that choice just yet. But there is a way for all. Because we don't come from our parents. We come through our parents.

And despite all those years of extreme suffering I can honestly say that I feel like the luckiest person in the world today, with the best mother I could ever have, now that I understand that no one chooses to be broken.

No one chooses to hurt or hurt others. No one chooses to have a mental and emotional condition.

For years I blamed my mum for all the suffering. For years she has blamed me for hers. But it was never her fault nor mine. It was the fault of the belief that people must behave in a certain way. And if they don't behave in a certain way there is something wrong with them. They are selfish. They are lazy. They are stupid. They are bad. They are doing it on purpose and they must change or be punished.

And the moment we understand that there is no good or bad, only judgements we create out of expectations spawned from arbitrary beliefs, we can start the healing, the growth and the reconnection.

We All Have Something

We all carry baggage, or traces of scars of some sort in our system. Beliefs, traumas, triggers and habits of thoughts, emotions and feelings that affect our quality of life, and limit our potential for happiness, health, growth and connection.

We found out during the pandemic in my household for instance, that my husband has been on the Autism spectrum, and had Attention Deficit Disorder (ADD) all his life. We also found out that I used to suffer from BPD and ADHD too, and still carry some remnants of those conditions in myself.

We had no idea of it. And although I have personally transformed in 2008 and never had a bad day ever since, I still reacted to certain events, situations or things said, especially in my relationship with my husband Matt. There were no longer serious reactions, and we would always find a way to eventually talk ourselves out of them. But they were nevertheless reactions that would taint our happiness every now and then.

The self diagnosis of Autism for Matt, and BPD for me gave us freedom and empowerment.

Freedom from habitually blaming the other person in the room. And empowerment in the understanding that it was never my fault nor his fault.

It was always and only the fault of our not understanding that our personal perception and experience of the world were fundamentally diametrically opposite. We are literally the most incompatible people on paper. No one in their right mind would ever suggest putting someone on the spectrum, with someone who is Bipolar and has BPD in the same room. Yet we have been together for nearly seventeen years at the time I am writing this, and getting stronger as a couple all the time.

And this is due to the fact that we always knew, at some intuitive level, that there was more than meets the eye. Although Matt would drive me mad every day with his poor communication skills, the meltdowns, the frequent over reactivity and the cruel perceived absence of empathy, I always knew at an intuitive level that this was not Matt. This was the story of his traumas being reflected in his behaviour.

Although Matt would suffer my profusion of energy, my insecurities and my intense obsessive nature, and although he was convinced at the beginning of our relationship, when I was still drinking, that he would die at my hands one day, he stuck by me. Because he always knew at an intuitive level that this was not me. This was the story of my traumas reflected in my behaviour. And we both learnt that from our respective families.

We were connected at an intuitive level, yet we could never put our finger on it. And thanks to the pandemic and the self-diagnoses, we have discovered names, definitions and explanations. And now everything finally makes sense.

Because we were unaware of our respective conditions, I expected from Matt, and Matt expected from me, to be normal, to behave in ways that were unnatural to either of us. We would be disappointed by one another. We would take things personally. And we would react to each other's reactions increasingly, like a clueless, pointless and petty ping pong game.

Stop Judging, Start Understanding

Labels can be problematic when we identify with them and restrict our potential because of them. When used as indicators however, when we see them not as fixed traits, but rather like clues and traces from the past that can be absolutely processed, utilised and discarded, they can be liberating. Because if we recognise any condition in us, or with our close ones, we no longer need to blame self, others or bad luck.

We can understand. We can blame the condition. We can free ourselves from the burden of guilt, shame, judgment, assumption, frustration and scapegoatism. We can develop empathy, compassion, healing and reconnection. And we can organise strategies and a lifestyle that support our sensitivities and idiosyncrasies.

I for instance fully understand now the paramount importance of good quality sleep, physical training and reminding myself of my triggers. If I don't sleep enough, if I don't train regularly, and if I am not mindful of my level of energy in regards to the way I interact with people, with my conditions, it would be extremely challenging for me to function and connect optimally physically, mentally, emotionally and socially, and to keep overwhelm at bay.

Nowadays, thanks to the internet, we can all self-diagnose, and see if we own any elements of any condition at all. And that is the key word: elements. Some of us may suffer a condition full scale. Most of us only carry some degrees of them. But I truly believe that most of us would benefit from self introspective work and research.

Because traumas of any size and shape are information from our past. Information passed onto us generationally from our parents, and their parents before them. And since overwhelm is information overload, in order for us not to be overwhelmed anymore, all we ever had to do was to understand, and release that information back into the universe.

Every Story Has An End

The story I share with you in this book is a glimpse of my experience with the BPD. How it came into my life, how it affected it, and how I managed it.

This is the story of how one word thrown at me by bullies at school, just like one grain of sand would block the gear of a machine and sabotage its whole operation, would lead to the first disconnect between my family and me, and hurl me down a downward spiral of extreme depression, anxiety, addiction and self sabotage.

And so it is that story that comes to an end.

Because understanding my story allowed me to change the narrative. My conditions are no longer a problem. They have become my super powers. Thanks to the Bipolar and the ADHD I can obsess on things and become excellent at whatever I choose to obsess on over time.

Thanks to the BPD I am learning a depth of empathy and compassion few are able to explore.

Thanks to all those conditions and the thirty eight first years of my life, I was able to become the therapist, author and coach that I am today, and expand that obsession, passion and mission with no limit for the rest of my life.

"Didi is a kind boy, a very good boy, my good son"

Mama Kan

About Didi Kan

Didi Kan is an RTT transformational therapist, author and coach who specialises in depression, anxiety, addiction and self-sabotage.

Didi experienced his own transformation in 2008. Ever since he has been on a mission to help and teach people how to be happy and enhance all aspects of their life, by letting go of all disempowering habits of thought, emotion and feeling, that are creating suffering and limitations. Overwhelm And Us is his sixth collaboration in the And Us book series.

If you have enjoyed his contribution to the And Us book series, please feel welcome to find out more about him as a transformational therapist and coach, and follow his journey as an author and content creator on social media. All details and links are constantly updated and found on his website:
Didikantransformation.com

Painting My Way Out of Overwhelm

By Kellie Ahl

Overwhelm is something I have struggled to manage for much of my life. In Part 1 of this chapter I share with you my personal story of overwhelm and how discovering how to express my emotions with paint has helped me to move through it and build resilience. In Part 2 I guide you through my two-stage painting process so that you can experience its healing and transformative power for yourself.

Part 1

Overwhelm Creeps In

Here we go again… It's 2.33am and there is that feeling in the pit of my stomach. A deep quiet foreboding ache. I notice I'm holding my breath, pretending to sleep. Who am I trying to kid?! I'm actually trying to convince myself, my body, my brain that I am asleep and not lying here thinking, worrying and ruminating. So this is what has me now putting fingers to keyboard (finally) to write this chapter. What better way to write a chapter on overwhelm than to be experiencing the exact emotion in the moment.

Did I subconsciously leave writing this chapter long enough in order to feel overwhelmed? If I'm honest I do this every time I have a deadline approaching. I wonder if you can relate? I tell myself I work better under pressure but deep down part of me doesn't believe that, even though I do acknowledge that a deadline does focus my mind and helps me to slay my 'inner perfectionist'. I actually believe I'm a bad person for not being organised and getting it done early to take the pressure off myself.

The thought of having to write so many words and making it into a coherent and interesting story on top of my work and life challenges feels, well, overwhelming. I mean, I'm not a writer! Shall I just back out now? Every time I begin a new writing project I have to overcome the belief that I'm not a 'good writer'. I have my secondary school English teacher to thank for that! These old beliefs can have me procrastinating and finding excuses and so the feeling of overwhelm begins to creep in which only serves to compound this behaviour.

I have noticed that the mere hint of overwhelm rising in response to a trigger, causes me to doubt myself, my abilities and begin to question my worth. This raises my stress and anxiety levels, creating a negative feedback loop confirming my fears. In addition to this the numerous concerns in my personal and work life that are demanding my immediate attention, cause the overwhelm to escalate rapidly if I don't process it in a timely manner.

I guess it begins with having lots that I desire to create in my life and to grow from. I have always had big ideas and dreams but for much of my life I haven't been adept at breaking them down in baby steps and achievable goals so they feel too big a mountain to climb. I can wind up paralysed by overwhelm, feeling so exhausted and anxious that I can end up wondering if I have lost the passion for whatever I was reaching for and questioning if I should give up.

The Pattern, Purpose And Gift Of Overwhelm

Overwhelm is such an ingrained, conditioned behaviour for me, and a way of being that I identified with for a long time, not knowing how to effectively deal with it. Its familiarity brings a false sense of safety. I learnt the pattern of behaviour resulting in and in response to overwhelm from members of my family growing up but it only started to present itself in my life at secondary school. I would put immense pressure on myself to perform well academically, often beyond my realistic capabilities and together with my perceived expectations of others this would lead to anxiety, crippling my ability to concentrate and plan effectively to achieve my best. It wasn't until my undergrad degree did I understand how to revise effectively and break it down into manageable chunks and so I learnt to curb overwhelm through prevention.

However since then I have experienced a number of painful and difficult times in my life from trauma and grief and the resulting PTSD when my father was killed when I was just 22, to a marriage tarnished by financial debt, job loss, anxiety and depression and the stress of a challenging ADHD son. These have led to overwhelm once again becoming a feature of my adult life as I grappled to deal with processing these experiences and live an authentic life. Any one of these issues is stressful but this is multiplied when they overlap with each and overwhelm seems to rocket. I then conclude that I can't cope.

Even when things in my life feel calm or even good I have noticed that I will subconsciously add to my stress by being busy or what I call "comparisonitis". Very quickly I can lose sight of who I am, my uniqueness, gifts and talents and the simplest of tasks can feel too much. That's when the voice in my head gets louder, ultimately concluding that I am never going to amount to anything and that I can't be/do/have what I desire. I make cruel judgements about myself because I feel I can't do it all.

In the past I have tried to control my overwhelm by getting practical (brain-dumping, ticking things off the to-do list etc) but that doesn't appease the inner critic.

For much of my life I thought resilience meant to "keep calm and carry on" and that my purpose as a "good girl", then later as a woman, was to make sure others are happy. Now I realise these beliefs act as an internal pressure cooker squashing the truth of who I am. And they are a lie. Instead, what I need to do is be really honest with myself, express and release my emotions so that I naturally create space and calm to function effectively.

My experience of overwhelm when it takes hold is exhausting, stressful, debilitating and depletes my life force leading to doubt, anxiety, fear or making myself wrong, resenting and blaming others which impacts my relationships and my ability to ask for and receive support.

What this indicates is that I'm taking on too much and not honouring my "No's" and "Yes'" (hello boundaries!). In this way overwhelm is a gift; an opportunity to really meet myself where I am at and listen with compassion, giving myself the time and space to honour and express my feelings, to move them through and integrate the lessons. Then I have the energetic space within my being and mind to hear my truth and recognise where I am giving up myself instead of giving of myself in service to others. I can then reassess my to-do list, make plans, delegate and ask for support in alignment with my truth rather than attempt to control overwhelm through attempting these actions first.

Painting Is Medicine

Even now after all this time of using painting as a tool as medicine to process my emotions I can still forget. I end up stuck in my head trying to manage overwhelm with a checklist or plan my way out instead of releasing the feelings first.

At some point though I'll remember the catharsis from painting my emotions and the relief and clarity that follows. It helps me to ride the waves of overwhelm without getting caught in the swells. In staying with the process I feel soothed and receive clarity and deeper guidance as to what my priorities are and the direction I need to take. I am able to sift out the voices in my head and hear the truth of my heart revealing what is most important to me and create new beliefs that support my dreams and intentions, not sabotage them. I paint myself back to my truth. I can then look at my list of priorities through a different lens and can plan them more effectively as I am no longer in throes of overwhelm itself.

There is something so powerful about just being completely honest with how I feel, allowing it to be seen for its ugly and messy without trying to prettify it or convince myself that I've got this when inside I may feel like I'm crumbling. Can I just be honest with myself about that? The chances are I'm not really crumbling, it just feels like that because it's gone unacknowledged and been suppressed.

We live in a culture that expects us to be strong, independent and to do it all, where asking for help is deemed weak and sharing our problems and emotions isn't socially acceptable. The great thing about painting is we can be as socially unacceptable as we want in our honest expression of what we're feeling. It helps us to realise we are not our emotions but that our emotions are valid and certainly better out than in (when expressed in safe and healthy ways).

Painting has enabled me to be present with the feelings of overwhelm and seeing it in colour, texture and marks helps me to appreciate and accept what is and let go of the stories I'm holding on to and become aware of what it is trying to protect me from. The emotion can physically be moved through my body and the lessons become integrated. Through painting I can actively listen to and feel empathy for my overwhelm and soothe myself. It helps me to be my own best friend, parent and wise sage all in one, so building resilience in the process.

Here I am reminding myself of my own medicine to express and release overwhelm first! Otherwise it's like putting a plaster over a dirty wound. Paint the feelings, brain dump the thoughts then repeat until I come back to presence, calm and joy. When I remember this, it's such a relief! It's something I can use to be present and honest with my overwhelm for a short period of time. So excuse me while I stop writing and go paint this shit out…! You can do this with me in Part 2 of this chapter.

Part 2 - How To Use Paint To Move Through Overwhelm

My painting process will help you to consciously express overwhelm. To be present with the feeling in terms of body sensations as well as being an opportunity to express some of the thoughts that are driving it. Here I guide you through my two-stage process to help you open yourself up and allow the paint to work its magic.

Firstly you don't have to be feeling overwhelmed in the moment to paint it but it's great if you can! If not, you can recall when you felt overwhelmed just enough to tap back into the energy to paint from here. It will also help to "mop-up" residual unexpressed emotions related to it held in your cellular memory. You do not need to go into it deeply, trust the body knows and will release what needs to be released through the paint.

Paint allows you to be with your overwhelm long enough to feel it through to completion. You can stay with the feeling in your body and how it wants to express itself without getting caught up with the why in your head. The beauty is that it doesn't have to be beautiful! It simply doesn't matter what the painting looks like if it feels good in the moment to choose a certain colour / tool / make different marks or sounds as you move the paint around. If it feels as though overwhelm is being expressed to you, then it is. If it doesn't, try something else (suggestions are outlined in the process below).

No skill is required or assessed. It will be different as you move with your overwhelm in its various forms and each time you will transmute it through its expression coming back to the light and peace within. Know this is coming but please don't force this too soon. Allow the paint to hold your overwhelm and to dance with it for as long as it needs even if you use the same colour, same movement or sounds over and over again. The paint will carry the energy of overwhelm where it can be witnessed on the canvas or paper. Your experience of the process and the resulting painting will hold gifts of wisdom and insight. This is the power of paint.

I would highly recommend using an art journal (a sketch book) to process your emotions - it can be stored easily and provides a private safe space to express your truth. However raw expression is a great way to begin a piece of art and working on a large scale is so freeing so if you feel called you may wish to use a large canvas.

STAGE 1 - Painting Overwhelm

Step 1: Notice The Feeling Of Overwhelm

The aim of this step is to notice what is present for you in your body sensations when you are in or recall overwhelm.

Take a few breaths and ask yourself:

Q. What does it feel like?

Q. Where in your body does it reside?

Don't worry if you don't know the answer, just be curious. Then move to Step 2.

Step 2: Paint Overwhelm

i. Allow your body to choose one or two paint colours that seem to represent how you feel in *this moment*. **Do not overthink this!** Just go to the first colours that your eye is drawn to. You cannot get this wrong!

ii. Approach the surface you are working on (journal, canvas). You may wish to play some music to help reflect your feelings or you may find silence beneficial. Trust that you know what is right for you.

iii. Painting Prompts

- Using your fingers, brush or palette knife, write words that describe how you feel (swear words are allowed!) and/or make marks that describe or represent the feelings in your body. Allow the energy to flow, be spontaneous, keep moving, work quickly and allow the energy of the emotion to move out of your body through the paint.
- If you feel the impulse, select a few more colours to represent the different aspects of the emotion you have felt into and begin to blend and spread the paints in any way that feels good to your body using your hands (on any part of your body!), brushes, sponges, rollers, rags or stamps. Experiment with making different noises with the tools on the paper/canvas. Notice if the sounds seem to reflect how you're feeling. Do more of

those that do. Add your own sound to the symphony.

- Keep the conversation going between your body sensations and the paint. Do not pay attention to thoughts. What does the emotion want to say? How does it want to move through you? Allow your whole body to move as you work with the paint. Closing your eyes may help you to be in your body and locate sensations. You can also try painting with a blindfold on if it feels good to you.
- You may feel inspired to scribble and scratch marks or words into the paint. I thoroughly recommend the cathartic practice of spraying the paint with a water sprayer and watching it run down a canvas and drip onto the floor (Note: this can get very messy!) and wipe areas away, adding more paint and repeat.
- If you get 'stuck' with what to do next, turn your canvas 90 degrees and allow the paint to run in different directions.
- The only rule is: **Do not question how or what to paint or your ability to do so, just paint!** Even if that is simply to try using the prompts I have suggested. Your mind is of no value here. This is all about your emotions and body sensations. The

result is equally irrelevant even if you are left with an ugly murky mess!

iv. There are no mistakes. You cannot get this wrong! This is a freeing and liberating exercise. Tears may flow. Other emotions may arise. You may need to scream, dance, punch a pillow. Or you may simply enjoy being with the process. All is welcome. Keep focusing on the paint and let everything move as you begin to be guided to by your body.

v. When you feel a sense of completion with this part of the process, stop and allow your painting to dry. I recommend watching the paint dry for a time to let the experience integrate into the body.

vi. You may decide that you wish to add more to the painting and repeat the process before moving on to the next stage.

Step 3: Commune With Your Painting

i. Take some time straight away to contemplate how the painting process felt for you. Did you receive any new awareness? Did you feel a sense of release? Does it feel complete or is there more to express? Stage 1 can be repeated as often as necessary. You may choose to move onto Stage 2 now.

ii. Alternatively you may like to live with your painting for a time. Have it in your physical space and spend time in its presence daily if possible. Allow it to breathe; to take up space; to speak to you. This will enhance the effects of the experience and allow it to reveal its wisdom to you. You may wish to make notes in your journal or speak out loud to your painting. Whatever feels right to you, trust that, it is key to the process.

STAGE 2 - Transmute Overwhelm

Step 1: Contemplate Your Overwhelm Painting

i. As you contemplate your painting how do you feel? What has been revealed to you through the expression? Do you feel expansive, have more clarity, and feel reconnected with who you really are?

ii. Where in your body to feel this? What are the sensations? What emotions do they evoke? Do they have a colour, a texture, a shape?

Just use your imagination without overthinking and move onto Step 2.

Step 2: Paint The Energy Revealed To You

i. You are now going to offer this energy to your overwhelm painting. Allow these feelings and images to arise inside of you and guide you in making your colour choices for this layer.

[TIP: I recommend selecting colours in either the warm (reds, oranges and yellows) or cool range (blues, greens, purples) at this point so that you don't muddy your colours unintentionally].

ii. Again you may wish to choose some music that reflects the feelings but silence may be equally compelling.

iii. Begin to work your selected paints onto your painting. You do not have to cover the entire canvas or first layer completely if you don't want to. You may wish to allow some of it to show through to add contrast and depth and in honour of your emotions and your healing process. Again, do what feels right to you at this moment.

iv. Remember you can move your body, make a noise, sing or close your eyes as you paint. Allow the feelings to flow through you and the paint. In fact you can set this as an intention for this stage. Use any of the painting prompts used in Stage 1 to keep the paint moving.

Do not question your impulses! Do not judge what's happening! It still doesn't matter what it looks like. This is all about how the process of moving the paint feels to you. This is the power of paint. Be intentional about channeling your truth through the paint onto your canvas. Allow your painting to be your medicine and it will be.

v. Stop when you feel a sense of completion.

Step 3 : Contemplate Your Painting

As you contemplate your finished painting, write down any emotions and insights that may have come to you through this painting process. You may decide to add more layers to it immediately, when it's dry or months later.

Step 4: Honour Your Painting

Your painting is magic! It will reveal its deeper wisdom to you over time by reminding you that your emotions are to be honoured through expression and in doing so you come back to your truth and inner peace. Continue to commune with your painting, meditate on it or ask it questions in your journal to glean its wisdom. Your painting is your guide. You may continue to add more paint in layers as you evolve.

The Power Of Paint To Heal And Transform

It is my highest intention that my painting process serves to empower you to honour all parts of yourself; to express and heal your overwhelm by bringing it into the light in a safe, healthy and fun way. This will help you to step into your personal power.

Paint is an incredibly powerful tool. I believe it is the language of our soul and that you were born with the ability to paint this way. I'm so grateful I have this honouring practice to express and process all my emotions and love myself in the process. It has changed my life completely. I invite you to try it.

About Kellie Ahl

Kellie Ahl is an Energy Artist & Creative Guide. She specialises in teaching her painting process to anyone who is curious by facilitating 1:1s, workshops and leading transformational Creative Women's Circles. In addition to her personal artwork, she paints live at events and co-creates powerful personal pieces of commissioned art with people to put the stamp of their soul in their space. Please visit her website www.kellieahl.com for details of her offerings. To learn more about Kellie's process, project and current artwork for sale please follow her on instagram @kellieahl1 and Art by Kellie Ahl on Facebook.

A Hero's Overwhelm

By Martin Seville

Definitions

"You're depressed and have high anxiety." That's what the doctor said.

Anxiety didn't sound right, although that turned out to be the right description. That's a story for Anxiety & Us. Depressed did sound right. Depressed, sad, low; all those things. That's a story for Sadness & Us.

My doctor, however, didn't say "You're overwhelmed." If she had though, she'd have been right. I was totally and utterly overwhelmed. Before we delve into that though, let's look at a definition of overwhelm:

Overwhelm *verb*

If you are overwhelmed by a feeling or event, it affects you very strongly, and you do not know how to deal with it.

Collins Dictionary

What a great description. Overwhelm can certainly affect us very strongly, as many things can, but not knowing how to deal with it … that's the real challenge isn't it? No matter what our knowledge, skills and experience are, we just don't know how to deal with it; and that can feel so disempowering. It opens the floodgates to doubt, worry, anxiety, not feeling good enough and more. For me, work and failing health had overwhelmed me. That's why I was sitting in my doctor's office.

So, let's explore this further, because there are things we can do to avoid and deal with overwhelm. It took me travelling to the edges of life and back to discover them, but they are there and now it's my privilege to share them with you. My words are particularly relevant if you regularly get overwhelmed by the amount of work you have. Unfortunately, this is far too common an occurrence, but the four steps I'm about to explore with you have the power to shift everything. Collectively I call them my "Work Leadership" model and they are designed to move you out of trying to manage everything and into making clear and focused decisions as a leader. This isn't about job titles and hierarchy though; this is about being the leader of your professional and personal life. Ready? Let's go!

Step One: How We look At work

As a conscientious worker, I wanted to do a good job and not let anyone down. If I did this, I'd get rewarded fairly, provide for my family, and live a good life. That sounds reasonable, doesn't it? Maybe you share a similar view. So, how could that possibly lead to overwhelm?

Well, I guess the question is how far are you willing to go to provide for your family? In a corporate world of performance management and regular restructures the pressure to do a good job intensifies, as does not letting anyone down. Doing a good job often isn't enough to secure a good rating. You're encouraged to go above and beyond; to take on more responsibility. You're driven to stack the evidence in your favour, so you get a good review and aren't the first one out in the next restructure. If there's even an inkling of letting someone down or making a mistake, that could count against you.

So, how do we respond? How did I respond? By working harder and longer. Let's be honest here too, working harder just means working longer hours. We get caught in a trap of taking on everything asked of us, without question, and seeking additional things to add to our to-do-list. All to ensure we do more than a good job, don't let anyone down, so we can keep the job and income we have, to provide for our family.

Getting fairly rewarded becomes a contentious topic because it's subjective and, if you don't get paid overtime, you significantly cut your hourly rate by working longer hours.

Just think, if you're paid to work 8 hours a day, but you work 12 hours, you're reducing your hourly rate by 33% … and giving your company nearly 1,000 hours of free work each year! We don't see this though because we're too busy focusing on getting everything done and not letting other people down. The irony here being that aren't we letting ourselves down? Working late. Exhausted. Not spending quality time with our family. Stressed. Unhappy in the relentless pursuit of getting it all done and not letting people down. We lose perspective. We lose ourselves. We get overwhelmed. So, what can we do?

It All Comes Down To Mindset

When we believe we must do everything that's being asked of us - and more - we're on a one-way ticket to overwhelm and worse. The truth is there is always more that can be done. That's how businesses grow. There's always something new that can be created, improved, reviewed, analysed, resolved.

In the relentless quest to do more, however, we make it personal. We believe that it's our capability that's in question. If we can't do everything, by last Friday, we're a failure, not good enough and will suffer the consequences. In reality however, it's likely that you do have the capability to do everything being asked of you … you just don't have the capacity to do everything being asked of you at the same time or by last Friday. In my experience our capability is rarely in question. Even if we haven't done something before, we can be resourceful and learn how to do it. What it really comes down to is how much you're trying to get done in a limited time frame. Think of it like this: our capability is limitless, but our capacity is limited. There are only so many hours in a day. It's also important to remember that, with few exceptions, an organisation or manager rarely has a complete handle of everything on your to-do-list. There isn't a filter that stops when you're at full capacity. You need to be that filter.

So, it really is all in how we look at work, and there's a simple shift in mindset that can help us, from thinking I'm at work to do everything to …

I'm here to make the biggest difference.

This simple shift has the power to change everything, in fact this lays the foundation for the next steps. Consider this, are you really employed to run around trying to do everything, or are you employed to advance the company, department, or division goals as far as possible. Sure, these goals are achieved by completing actions but are you spending your precious time and energy on the ones that will make the biggest difference? It's so easy when we're overwhelmed to go for quantity over quality. Lots of small wins may feel like progress is being made but are they making the biggest difference?

When we shift our mindset to making the biggest difference it changes what we do. We automatically aren't interested in a relentless, exhausting, overwhelming race to get everything done. We're not going to take on more without question. In fact, questions, as we'll discover in the next step, become our best friend ... because now we're interested in *understanding* everything in front of us, so we can make empowering decisions. So, how do we make those decisions?

Step Two: How We Look At Our Workload

With our new way of looking at work and our role in it, it's a natural next step to look at our workload. At its height my perfectly organised Excel spreadsheet, that housed all my workload, consisted of an eye watering 800 actions. It was beautifully organised into tabs, dates, people, and details, but this was not a to-do-list. This was a heart attack in a spreadsheet! It didn't matter how many actions I ticked off in a day, a week, a month. There were so many actions left, that there was no satisfaction, no sense of achievement or progress. It was a full-time job to keep track of everything, let alone complete actions ... and let's not forget the list was always growing, as is the nature of business. When we get into the trap of thinking we need to do it all, this is what happens.

Maybe your list isn't 800 actions long - I truly hope not. Maybe you don't use an Excel spreadsheet. Being honest though, how long is your to-do-list? How many things are you getting overwhelmed about? Do you have them written down or typed up? Or are they just floating around making your head spin? Do you really have an actionable to-do-list or just a long list like I had? Most overwhelm, in my experience, is created from a long list of things we think we need to do and little time to do them, and it's becoming clear how that can happen. So, what can we do?

It All Comes Down To Questions

With our newfound mindset of making the biggest difference, we need to start asking questions of our to-do-list. As a top tip, if it's not written down or typed up, start with that. It's so much easier to organise and ask questions when you can see the actions in front of you. Also, a long list is likely to bring on overwhelm, so look to categorise the actions. For example, group those to do with a particular project or those that all contribute to a common result. Whilst we haven't asked our questions yet, we will have reduced our overwhelm, because it's feels less overwhelming to visually deal with three to five categories of work, than a long list of 50 actions.

Our mission now is to reduce our list down to the three actions that are going to make the biggest difference; and we'll do that by asking three simple but powerful questions. I know that sounds ridiculous when we start with such a long list but trust the process. These aren't the only three things we'll ever do, these are just the three that we will focus on next. They will be our actionable to-do-list for tomorrow. Instead of getting overwhelmed by 50 actions, we're going to get focused, confident, and certain about three actions that will make the biggest difference, and in doing so fulfil our role to the company and give us a sense of achievement. Sound good?

Now, the precursor to asking questions is ensuring you know what the objectives and goals are of the company, project, department, or division you're working for. Without this, you'll never be able to focus and get a clarity of actions that are aligned. So, ensure you know these. Then, ask these three questions of the actions in front of you:

1. Why is the action required?

2. What are the consequences if this action isn't done now or ever?

3. Which actions will make the biggest difference?

In a world where everything seems urgent and important, these powerful questions soon reveal what you should really be focusing on. Let's bring them to life.

Why?

There's a big difference between a report being needed for a team meeting where it might be discussed next Friday, and a report required for the CEO of the company who is flying in specially from Switzerland on Monday morning at 9am to make some business-critical decisions about your division. You'd think it would be obvious, but there can be so much false urgency and importance in business that it can be difficult to distinguish … until you ask Why?

Consequences

Using the example above, there's a big difference in consequences if the report isn't ready for the CEO's business-critical meeting compared to not being ready for the team meeting. This isn't to say the team meeting isn't important, but with a greater understanding we're able to see what piece of work has greater business driven priority.

Biggest Difference

The previous two questions will give you a greater understanding and help narrow your list down. Now it's time to ultimately decide where you focus your time and energy. On the shorter list you now have, what's going to make the biggest difference? In the example we've been using, it's clear what we need to focus on - the report for the CEO. Sometimes though it's not quite as obvious, which is why a greater understanding helps.

As a heads up, sometimes as a leader, we just need to decide. If you have three actions in front of you that seem equally as impactful, with powerful whys and clear consequences, that's great. You have your to-do-list. Now just pick one to start with; or get a second opinion if you need to. The most important thing is we're now looking at a clear, impactful three actions, not 50.

It's amazing how these first two steps can increase your sense of control and confidence - something that's often missing when we're overwhelmed. You are also far better prepared, with solid business rationale, to manage the expectations of others and negotiate when non-priority pieces of work are scheduled. So, what next?

Step Three: How We Look At Our Time

Now that we know what we need to do and why, it's time to focus on getting it done. The challenge we often have here, however, is that we can easily get distracted, interrupted, or tempted to take on more. In fact, when we've been overwhelmed for so long, we're in a pattern of attempting to do multiple things at the same time. I remember it vividly. I had so much to do and was so worried I'd miss something. I'd have multiple tabs open on my computer, flicking between different pieces of work, piles of paper documents on my desk, emails constantly popping up, my mobile phone and landline primed to interrupt me with some urgent message. This doesn't even account for the walk-by interruptions. I felt like I had to be prepared to react to anything and everything, whilst also keeping as many things as possible moving forward. This juggling act significantly contributed to my overwhelm, and maybe you can relate. So, if we're going to focus on those three actions with the biggest why, consequences and difference, we're going to have to approach things differently. But how?

Stop Multitasking

This is it. My top tip on how to focus your time: stop multitasking. There are so many myths surrounding multitasking and it's time to bust them. The simple truth is human beings cannot multitask. Now, I'm not talking about patting your head and rubbing your stomach or walking and listening to a podcast. I'm talking about activity that requires our focus and concentration ... like those purposeful and impactful actions we've identified. It's physically impossible for us to focus on more than one thing at a time. What self-confessed multitaskers are actually doing is switching between tasks, but in doing so they open themselves up to making more mistakes, not completing tasks, being more overwhelmed, and taking longer to complete tasks. Far from increasing effectiveness and productivity, multitasking decreases it. This isn't just my experience; it's backed up by science. Two studies come to mind, and I highly recommend reading The ONE Thing by Gary Keller with Jay Papasan, who delve into these and much more.

Firstly, a study by Stanford University Professor Clifford Nass. He set out to discover what the secret was behind effective multitaskers. In his study he set the same task for 262 people, split between high and low multitaskers. To his surprise the low multitaskers - in other words those who focused on one task at a time and got it done before moving onto the next - outperformed the high multitaskers on every metric. Every metric!

A second study by researcher Dr. David Meyer discovered that multitasking on simple tasks can increase the time it takes to get the tasks done by up to 25%. For more complicated tasks the time increased by over 100%!

Just think of all the long hours you've been working and how much of that time could potentially have been reduced if you had focused on one thing at a time. Time is our most precious resource, and we often say we don't have enough of it, so getting a handle on this can be life changing.

Our recipe for reducing overwhelm - and your working hours - is really starting to come together, don't you think? So, how can we give our most purposeful and impactful actions our undivided attention? Try these top tips:

1. Schedule a block of time and stick to it.
2. Turn off your phone or put it on silent (mobile and landline if you're still using one).
3. Only have tabs open on your computer for the one action you're taking.
4. Silence your email notifications.

5. If you work in a busy office, to avoid walk-by interruptions or distracting noise, book out a meeting room to complete the task, wear noise cancelling headphones if you're allowed or work from home.

6. Let people know you're unavailable for a period of time.

This is how you focus, take back control of your time, make a bigger difference and even reduce your work hours. Suddenly, you're turning into a confident leader, role modelling how to distil the unmanageable into focused, results driven action. This has all been about taking control, and we've done this by knowing what to focus on, why it's a must and how to get it done. This approach alone has made a radical difference in my professional and personal life. So, job done, right? Well, nearly. Let's explore the fourth step.

Step Four: How We Look At Our Habits

Consider this: our lives are made up of the sum of our days, our days made up of the sum of our daily actions and our daily actions are the result of our daily habits. So, it all comes down to habits. We're not talking about biting fingernails here, we're talking about what you choose to do and how you choose to live each day.

If we're to reduce overwhelm, not just now but into the future, we need to be consistent with the things that are going to keep our overwhelm in check. It's not enough to think about making a difference, asking questions, or focusing our time occasionally.

I can certainly see that back in my corporate career my consistent approach to mindset, workload and time had become a habit and the result it produced was overwhelm. So, our mission here is to use, on a consistent basis, what we've now learnt about shifting our thinking and actions to produce a sense of control and confidence, as well as making a bigger difference and reducing work hours.

Now there are many things we can talk about when it comes to habits, but let's keep this simple and focused on putting into place what we've already learnt.

The Benefits Of Change Outweigh The Benefits Of Staying The Same

Change can be tricky. It will make us feel uncomfortable, we may doubt whether it will be worth it, we may worry about the consequences. I spent 20 years fearing change, which compounded my overwhelm and stress because the world is always changing. I had to learn how to embrace change and see it differently. What I discovered was that, yes change can be uncomfortable and create worry, but on the other side of change is learning, growth and a better version of ourselves. We must be patient, focused and kind to ourselves when we have moments of self-doubt, but it is worth it. Even when things haven't quite worked out as I had planned, I still felt I'd moved forward positively.

So, let's anchor in these new habits with three simple steps:

1. If you don't change your mindset, workload and time habits what will happen?
2. If you do change your mindset, workload and time habits what will happen?
3. Schedule in daily reminders.

Let's explore these in a little more detail.

If You Don't Change

Naturally we don't like pain or suffering, in fact our brain is always on the look out to avoid it. Interestingly though, sometimes the pain and suffering we're in can feel more comfortable than the potential risk of change. There are plenty of examples of this in history, but I know this to be true from my own experience. I was overwhelmed, stressed, depressed and anxious for years. I privately complained like a broken record about how I felt, and yet I didn't do anything to change it. I was afraid. I hoped and wished something external would change to somehow make things feel better. It turns out, it wasn't just me. Millions of conscientious, hard-working people around the world do this too.

So how did I change? My overwhelm, stress, depression and anxiety got so bad it forced me to make new decisions. Now, in my case, my mind and body literally started shutting down on me and a new chapter of burnout, self-harm and wanting to end my life started, before one conversation saved my life and I travelled a new path to be better, do better and help others with what I learnt. For you, I don't want you to reach that point, and who's to say you would. But you do know that if you continue your current path of overwhelm, life will get worse. So, write it out.

What are all the things you're going to feel and miss out on if you continue as you are? What relationships are you going to damage or lose? What's the impact on your health going to be? What shadow of the life you're capable of will you live? If this feels uncomfortable, good. If this feels emotional, good. I'm not being unkind here; you need to see that a path of overwhelm will bring you pain and suffering that you are just not willing to accept. This is the kick start you need to say enough is enough.

If You Do Change

With your newfound motivation to change, let's ensure you have a compelling vision of your future that will further inspire you. When I had my moment of "enough is enough", I was in an art room in therapy. We were working on my self-esteem which was rock bottom, but suddenly, I stood up and it became clear who I was, what I stood for and how I wanted to live. I didn't have all the details figured out, but I could see a better life for me and my family, whilst serving and supporting people all over the world. Even with a tremendous amount of uncertainty about how I was going to do it, I had enough clarity of what and why to make the decision to leave my corporate job and pursue a life in coaching. For 20 years this had been unimaginable, but this compelling vision for the future, coupled with saying enough to the pain and suffering, was exactly what I needed.

Now your story and this moment defining your compelling future doesn't have to be as theatrical or career changing as mine. But it can be just as profound. Even staying in your current role, if that's what you decide, you can come up with a vision of how you want to feel and act at work, the sense of achievement and control, the confidence, the quality of life you'll enjoy outside of work. The impact on your health and what that enables you to do, the improvement and joy you'll get from your relationships with your partner, children, family, or friends. Take some time to explore a world in which you're not controlled by overwhelm. Describe it and feel it. Make it so realistically compelling that you're drawn to it and know you'll do whatever it takes to make it a reality.

Schedule It

Tapping into your motivation and inspiration, now it's time to follow through. This is simply approaching your workdays with the mindset of making the biggest difference, of focusing only on up to three actions with the biggest why, consequence and difference and getting those things done. They are unlikely to be the only things you do in a day, but they are the most important and anything else will be a bonus. Habits and results are formed by consistency, so using scheduling can really help. But what could you schedule?

1. At the start of each day, when you drive to work, walk through the doors at work, or open your laptop, deliberately,

intentionally, and powerfully remind yourself that you are here to make the biggest difference. Ideally say it out loud to really anchor it in. Make it your mantra.

2. At the end of each day and / or the beginning of each day decide on your top three things that must get done. Write them down. This gives you clarity, control, and certainty.
3. Block out time in your diary for focused action. Make this time non-negotiable.
4. Set yourself daily reminders in your phone of your new mindset, workload, and time principles; and even details of your compelling future.

Give yourself every chance to tap into your what, why and how of living a life without overwhelm. Be kind to yourself though as well. You won't get it right all the time. You'll slip and stumble. It's so easy to give yourself a hard time when you don't do something you set out to do, but it's okay, you're human. When we slip, our brain has a habit of saying, "see I told you it wouldn't work" and before we know it, we give up. 90% of new year resolutions end up like this, if indeed they ever get started. So, flip the story. Instead of focusing on perfection and getting it right ten times out of ten, consider where you're starting from - zero out of ten. So, every day you use your new approach to mindset, workload, and time, recognise it as a great step forward. Maybe you get up to five out of ten. Fantastic! That's five days out of ten that are better. If you're routinely hitting eight out of ten, then you're making incredible progress. Keep this up, you will feel the immediate and longer-term benefits.

Reflection

What a whistle stop journey we've been on. We've tackled overwhelm head on and I hope you'll start using what we've explored. Our approach to mindset, workload, time, and habits has the power to create overwhelm and stress. It also has the power to release us from overwhelm and stress. The beauty of this four step Work Leadership model is that one step naturally leads into the next and the compound effect of shifting each of these things adds up. Individually they make a difference, but collectively they can transform the quality of your professional and personal lives. I wish you an incredible journey into your compelling future, without reaching the point of sitting in a doctor's office overwhelmed without knowing how to deal with it. You now have four powerful steps that can help. Trust the process, have patience, be kind to yourself and remember … you are the hero of your journey.

About Martin Seville

With a successful 20-year corporate career, life seemed good. Behind the smile and the sunglasses, however, there was a battle with life-threatening mental illness. From this trauma, however, Martin discovered his life purpose.

He now coaches, mentors and inspires from the stage as many people as he can, to improve their quality of life and avoid the dark paths he travelled. He shares his story in support of and to raise awareness of the millions of hard-working, conscientious people around the globe suffering in silence, and who desperately need to know there is another way.

Martin describes his mission as becoming the hero of your life story. www.martinseville.com

Martin dedicates this chapter to his Guardian Angel wife, Emma, his wonderful boys, Mum, Dad, family, friends, mentors, coaches and health professionals who helped him overcome overwhelm. This is for all those ready to regain confidence and control.

Three Steps to Avoid Work-Related Burnout

Jonny Cooper

1. Work monomaniacally on a singular, coherent project or goal that makes sense to you right now
2. Say "NO" to temptation, offers and distractions from anything and everything else
3. Reach out for help from people who are already successful doing what you want to achieve

Burnout steals hope and destroys motivation. It, quite literally, sucks the life out of you over time. *Thomas Oppong*

I don't want that to happen to you, and I'm betting you don't either!

From Overwhelm To In-Powerment

By Annemarie Wilson

Before we embark on this journey from overwhelm to *in-powerment,* I ask one thing of you; do not 'believe' anything I say. Our beliefs form the box of limitations that we try to 'think outside of' and it is paramount that you honour your own journey and choices along the way. Just for this moment though I encourage you to step outside that box altogether, and maybe suspend the habit of giving power to your beliefs. The mind is like a parachute that only works when it is open. Please allow the following words to move through your open mind like a gentle breeze, notice what resonates with you and let the rest go on their way.

You may notice I have used the term *in-powerment* and not empowerment. In the Oxford dictionary the meaning for empower is this: "to make someone stronger and more confident, especially in controlling their life and claiming their rights". The implication here is that the power is given from one person to another. My aim is for you to locate that power within and *in-power* yourself.

Our Current Times

As technology and industry grows and evolves at ever increasing rates, our time and attention is relentlessly grabbed and distracted in numerous ways. With a constant stream of images, voices, values and opinions affecting our consciousness through multiple forms of media, it is easy to become confused and distracted. Our ability to acquire and sustain clarity is often compromised. It's no wonder that making even a simple choice or decision can send us spiralling down into a place where we would rather just be left alone.

Then 2020-21 brought a whole new level of overwhelm across the globe, on a scale that most had not experienced before. This has had a devastating effect on many, with overwhelm becoming an unwelcome and almost expected part of everyday life. It is an undeniable truth that overwhelm diminishes our quality of life, disconnects us from our innate self and reduces our capacity to know what we are feeling and consequently what we want.

The uncertainty, restrictions, feelings of disempowerment and helplessness has been felt by everyone through the field of collective consciousness. Even if we have been able to keep ourselves out of fear we are in sympathetic resonance with the stress and anxiety of all of humankind. We are all affected.

This is compounded by the fact that now, more than ever, what happens worldwide is brought into our awareness daily. We can no longer ignore the corruption, poverty and suffering of our fellow man. Alongside this the constant cacophony of noise from the social, cultural and familial principles and dictates, saying 'this is what you should be doing, thinking and believing', it is no wonder we feel bewildered and discombobulated. There is a sense that we can no longer sit on the fence, like some deep inner part of us is urging us to think about where we stand and what we stand for. Most of us want a different and better world, we just don't know where to start.

It is fortunate that amidst this seeming chaos and noise, exists the seeds of potential and possibility that create positive transformation. You can change the world with your own unique contribution; but it must begin with you.

The biggest change you can affect is within you. As within, so without. Your thoughts, words and actions impact the collective consciousness. Rippling out and changing the field in which all matter and all that matters, exists. This is true magic.

So, who am I? My name is Annemarie. I am a magnificent human being, I am special, I am unique, and I am infinitely powerful! And so are you!

I am honoured to have this opportunity to share some insights with you. My intention is to increase your awareness and understanding of power. This is the unlimited personal power that exists within you. It is the connection to your soul and its vibrational frequency of love. I hope to offer you the possibility of remembering your true magnificence and to experience a more meaningful life. When you live your life from this place of power there is no room for overwhelm.

Let's Talk About Power

So, what do I mean when I say power? Firstly, I will address what it is not. It is not a hierarchical position, it is not bestowed on you, it is not a title or a sense of supremacy over others. It is not accessed or acquired outside of you. It does not rely on anyone or anything. It does not dominate or involve force.

This power I speak of is a naturally confident state of being, a fullness of presence, an awareness of your true nature and origin. It is self-sustaining and unlimited. It is the true expression of your innate humanity. When centred in your power you have access to your inherent wisdom, you think, speak and act in alignment with your most authentic self. As there are consequences to your every thought, word and action, this personal power requires responsibility, self-respect and integrity.

It is a popular misconception that money is at the root of the actions and behaviour of the general population, but the truth is that it is always power that is sought. Money creates an illusion of power. We are encouraged to value ourselves by what we own, our status and position, and the opinion of others. The more disempowered a person is the more they seek to acquire these external concepts of power. While it is true that we come in with nothing and we leave with nothing, the power-full Soul is immutable.

Equilibrium

In the Merriam-Webster dictionary it states that equilibrium means "a state in which opposing forces or actions are balanced so that one is not stronger or greater than the other" and "a state of emotional balance or calmness". In French the word libre means free so I like to imagine that equilibrium could also mean "equal freedom".

A bully is generally perceived as a person, whether child or adult, who enjoys tormenting or degrading someone who is vulnerable. This act of putting another down is their attempt to place themself above them in a position of power; to be power full. Although this is a clear example of an imbalance in the power dynamic it is something we can all be guilty of through more subtle and pervasive ways. Something as simple as the need to be right in a discussion amongst friends is still an attempt to 'be on top'. We are mostly unaware of how the disconnection from our own power impacts so many aspects of our life and the relationships we create.

There are a multitude of ways that we create disequilibrium and not just by taking power from others, we also give it away. You are clearly giving your power away when you allow others to make decisions for you or that involve you, without your input or permission. We give our power to those we believe have authority over us or have more knowledge about something than we do. From early childhood we are told to respect our elders, respect and trust authority; but when are we encouraged to respect ourselves and respect and trust our own authority? Everyone deserves respect but that doesn't mean we give them our power too. Of course, if someone disrespects us then we must look at what we are allowing. As adults we always have the choice of who we choose to spend our time with and how we let them treat us.

It is with good reason that so many of us feel the necessity to explore inner child work. Most of our adult issues stem from childhood when we felt helpless and hopeless, because of our inability to affect a change in our environment or situation. There is no finger pointing here as it is a generational pattern of learned behaviour repeating itself through our parents or carers. There is also difficulty in finding balance between wanting to protect a child and encouraging them to stand on their own two feet when appropriate.

With disempowerment beginning in childhood this disequilibrium is accepted as 'the way things are'. We don't even notice that we are allowing it.

Health And Wellbeing

Let me give you an example that highlights this. For many of us, when we were children, if we got sick, we were taken to the doctor. We grew up thinking this is what you do. No-one ever told us that we are responsible for our own health and wellbeing.

The main methodology of allopathic medicine is to label symptoms and offer medicines to eliminate them. Often a rather hopeless prognosis is given that can have a detrimental effect on the patient's psyche. Before you know it, you are giving your power to a diagnosis without realising that the power to heal resides within you.

Because each person is a unique individual with their own set of circumstances underlying their symptoms, it is impossible for a doctor to observe the patient in a holistic way and uncover the root cause of their dis-ease. Respect the knowledge your doctor has but also respect your own wisdom too. Your body gives you symptoms to inform you that something is amiss. If you sit quietly and ask your body what it is trying to tell you, it will respond. It may not be immediate but if you pay attention, you will get an answer. Another way is working with Emergent Knowledge. (See later reference.)

We are not educated in school about how to take care of ourselves, to listen to our bodies and question our symptoms to see what we could learn. To eat real food, get plenty of fresh air and sunlight, spend time with loved ones. In today's world we are told the air is polluted, the sun is harmful while food is becoming less real and more processed and our connection with loved ones happens through a screen more often than in real life.

It is interesting to witness how people are so personally affected when a celebrity dies. There is often an outpouring of grief and reflection equivalent to losing a close loved one. We are hardwired to be a part of close-knit communities, sharing our joys and sorrows, each supporting the other. This has been replaced by watching the made-up exploits of fictional characters on a screen and has become more socially acceptable than forming real-world relationships with other humans, even our closest neighbours. These celebrities have shared more of our time than our families and friends, so it is understandable that their loss can be felt so deeply.

There are steps you can take to change this, and they are easy to implement. It is likely you know them already but in our busy distracted lives it's all too easy to put them off for another day, so I feel it is worth being gently reminded. Discover the fresh real foods that energise you and make you feel good. Spend more time outdoors getting in touch with the elements and nature. Spend time with friends and family whose company you enjoy. Get enough quality sleep. Do more of the things that inspire you and make you happy. Sing, dance and laugh often.

These simple things are the best medicine and are fundamental to your overall health and wellbeing.

So, how do we restore equilibrium? Although we have spent our lifetime giving our power away, fortunately there is no need to take that power back. This implies that our power is finite; or those that we have given it to own it and can hold it over us. As you will discover this assumption is incorrect.

Your personal power is an unlimited resource that comes from the soul. I have intentionally used the word re-source because the prefix re means 'go back to' and the origin of your power is the One Soul, the source that created this world and all that exists beyond it. Each human being's unique soul is intimately connected to the One Soul expressing the infinite possibilities and potentials within creation.

I invite you to explore the following three ways that have proven to be effective in developing and nurturing the connection to your innate power.

Being Centred

I would like to begin with a simple process that you can do right now. It is borrowed from the brilliant teachings of Silvia Hartmann with a few embellishments from me. Before you start it is essential to set your intention in the present tense. Intention gives structure and meaning to the aspirations of the will. It also gives direction and clarity of purpose to the bodymind system.

- State your intention aloud or inside your head e.g. "I am connected to my centre", "I am centred within" or whatever works for you.
- Rub your hands together vigorously for about 20 seconds.
- Say the words "This is me!" and point to the place on your chest where this 'me' is located.
- Place the centre of your dominant hand over this point and place the other hand on top.
- Breathe steadily, deep into your belly and release with an audible "Haahhh" (like a gentle sigh)

Most people find their 'me' spot is located on or just above their heart. This is your Heart Centre and by placing your hands there you are making the connection to your inner essence, your most *power-full* self. This position is centring and grounding and places you in the here and now. The Heart Centre is also an entrance to your soul.

Now the soul does not have a physical location, and no-one can say for certain where it resides but in my own experience and that of many others, you can access it through your Heart Centre. All energy holds information, and the soul is a field of energy that contains the blueprint that defines you as the unique being that you are. It exists beyond the physical, material realm yet it infuses your physical vessel with energy, information and the life force that animates you. It is said that we embody only a small fraction of our soul as its vastness is impossible to contain within the confines of a dense human body. We are only given what we can handle, but there is always more we can access when we are ready to evolve.

An interesting thing to note is that the Heart Centre is also the location of the thymus gland which is the seat of the immune system. Studies have shown that lab animals unsurprisingly experience a sense of helplessness, which causes them to develop weaker immune systems and an increase in tumour growth. Our immune system is our sense of self and when we are centred in our power our immunity is strong and robust.

When we are not centred, we cannot access our power effectively which affects the exchange of power between ourselves and others. If this is not rectified, then we end up feeling drained and fatigue ensues. When we are given support, sympathy and empathy this can become a secondary gain, and dis-eases such as chronic fatigue syndrome can often have this underlying pattern. Secondary gain, in this instance, is a rather inaccurate term as it implies the person chooses to be ill because it benefits them; what is really happening here is that by receiving this attention from others, there is the sense that the power that was unwittingly given away, is in some way being restored. This dynamic does not benefit anyone in the long term as everyone has responsibility for sourcing their own power from within.

This leads me to the second step of this centring process that follows on from locating your heart centre.

- State your intention e.g. "I am connected to my soul".
- Using both hands tap the tips of your fingers firmly in the same location as your Heart Centre.
- Say out loud or in your head "Me, Myself and I" 3 times or more as you tap.
- Return your hands to your Heart Centre.

This part of the process has many benefits. It stimulates the thymus gland and awakens our sense of self. It amplifies the sense of being centred within. The words "Me, Myself and I" are what I call the wholly (holy) trinity, because saying them focuses our attention on the 3 ways we describe and experience ourselves, especially when we say them with meaning and affection. This forges a stronger connection between our ego self and our soul – in other words it enables more wholeness. It is worth mentioning that the word holy originates from an old English word hālig meaning 'wholeness'.

Connecting To The Love Within

We are often told "you need to love yourself!" but what does that actually mean? More importantly, how do we do it?

Often the word love is used so flippantly it can lose its meaning and relevance. We say things like "Ooh, I love that fabulous dress", "I love this song" or "I love chocolate". We can also see here how easy it is to confuse real love with treating ourselves with the things we 'think' we love. We fill ourselves up with food, our wardrobes with clothes that may never be worn, or our homes with all manner of unnecessary items. We think these things make us happy, but they never fill that empty place inside where love is absent.

This is not the love spoken of in a 'Hallmark' sentiment, it is a fuller, more encompassing energy that is almost impossible to describe with words, but I will endeavour to try. This love is expressed as compassion, kindness, acceptance, courage, gentleness, peacefulness, humour and even anger! One thing is certain, to really experience love it must come from within. It's not something we take from others or something we do. Love is a state of being.

So how do we cultivate this state of being that we call self-love? We can begin by observing the way we treat our loved ones, including the animals that are part of our lives. Notice what we are happy and willing to do for them without question. How we care, support and nurture them. Can we honestly say we treat ourselves the same? Do we think we are less deserving? Does that make any sense?

If we look at our relationship with children, we can understand this better (insert 'pets' here if that is your preference). As they explore and discover their world we accept their mistakes, accidents and behaviour as part of their learning curve. We do our best to be patient, forgiving and understanding of their actions even though they can make us angry and frustrated. We do this because we love them.

This process of learning, discovery and exploration in childhood does not stop as we 'grow up'. It is a necessary part of our life journey and experience. Where does it say that on our 18th birthday, we suddenly have all the answers and mistakes are no longer acceptable? Does that mean if we make mistakes we are not loving, loved or lovable? So why then do we criticize and judge our so-called mistakes as wrong or bad and chastise ourselves for being so stupid?

Firstly, there are no mistakes - only lessons. Secondly, whilst learning and evolving from these lessons our capacity to love and be loved remains unchanged. The very fact that we are participating in this challenging and sometimes difficult existence means we are absolutely deserving of love. There will always be challenges, for they are the catalyst for our metamorphosis and evolution.

So now for the final step in the centring process, except it's now a centring, self-loving and soul connecting process. Each of these steps can be done separately but there are greater benefits to doing them all together. I like to do the sequence 3 times – you do what feels good for you. There is a video of a longer version including other steps that can be found on my website.

- State your intention. If you are doing all 3 in sequence, then just state your intention once at the beginning e.g. "I am centred within and connected to my heart and soul - I am loving, loved and lovable" or your own choice of words.
- With your hands on your Heart Centre as before, focus your attention on a space within your chest and behind your hands.
- Imagine this space within your chest is the place where the energy of your soul enters your physical body. You will know where that is. Feel into it with your senses.
- As you breathe in through your nose, imagine you are breathing the energy of your soul and filling every space in your body with it, and as you breathe out from your mouth with an audible but gentle "Haahhh", allow it to expand outwards into your entire energy field surrounding you. Feel the love growing and expanding.
- You can give this energy a colour of your choosing if you so desire.

Note: If you find it difficult to feel the love, then think of someone you love and notice what that feels like. Let that feeling grow and place your hands where you feel it and move it up to the Heart Centre.

It is time to accept and love yourself exactly as you are. Remind yourself you are a remarkable 'work in progress'. Take the time to notice when you berate and criticise yourself and ask, "Would I say that to my best friend / partner / child?"

Begin to show yourself the same patience, forgiveness, acceptance and understanding you give to others. Nurture and encourage yourself like your life depends on it – because it does!

Know Thyself. "For also knowledge itself is power" – ***Francis Bacon***

The words 'can' and 'know' have the same root as an Old English verb 'cnawan' which combines the meaning of both. 'To know is to be able' or 'if you know then you can'. The word knowledge-able demonstrates this connection too.

In 1958 science philosopher Michael Polanyi demonstrated that knowledge is personal, constructed of patterns of neural activity within individual brains. This neural activity is informed by our nervous system delivering the data from our cells, organs, glands and senses.

The human brain can process 11 million bits of information every second.

Our energy fields exist in more dimensions than we can see with our eyes and potentially hold even more information than our brains. These energy fields along with the electromagnetic toroidal field of the heart, expand many metres beyond the physical body. They are constantly tuning into and sensing the energy around us.

The brain and energy fields are not the only repositories of knowledge. We also have the superconscious mind that is the innate wisdom of the soul. When the superconscious, brain and energy fields are working as one it creates our inner knowing, our intuition.

To better connect with our intuition, we first need to accept that we have this vast reservoir of knowledge available; and then know we have the ability to access it. Our intuitive responses are the very first thought or feeling we receive in response to a question or situation we are experiencing; either internally or externally. We can often miss it or even dismiss it, as our ego thinking jumps in at lightning speed with its opinions and beliefs. This ego thinking is fuelled by the conscious and subconscious mind, and we are so used to our thoughts coming from this place that our intuition can easily be drowned out.

When we are accessing our intuition there is a sense of knowing it is right. It feels like truth. Our head and our heart are aligned. The more you listen and pay attention to your first thought or reaction, the better you get at tuning in to your inner knowing. It does take practice but once that inner knowing becomes your source of wisdom, your life will flow with much more ease. You gain clarity around choices and eventually there are less choices to make as you begin to know what is right and what serves you best.

The Shadow

Knowing thyself is loving and accepting all parts of yourself - this leads to freedom in its truest sense. An important aspect that must be addressed is uncovering the bits we have hidden; the parts we deny. Denial underlies many of our less pleasant behaviours and causes us to project what we deny onto others. Our external world mirrors all our aspects back to us, including what we try to hide. Often we see evil as something that is 'not us' and we point our finger accusingly at the 'bad' people over there.

To become whole, we must accept that within each of us exists the potential of evil. We have the miraculous ability to create life and we also have the ability to end it too. Would you protect yourself or your child from a violent assault – even if you had to use violence yourself? Would you choose to end the life of an injured or suffering animal when nothing more can be done to help them? I suspect that yes, you would. Does this make you evil? When a long suffering battered woman or man turns on their abuser and kills them, does that make them evil?

Accepting our potential to do the things we have labelled as evil in others frees up more of our power. If we were unable to defend and protect ourselves and our loved ones, humanity would never have survived. There is of course a caveat; this power over life and death must be tempered with love and wisdom. We are all aware that there are some people who do unacceptable things to others, and I hope by now you have an insight into why this happens. It's all about power, love and wisdom. The more disconnected a human being is from their soul, (their innate source of power, love and wisdom), the more despicable their actions are. This disconnection is always a consequence of abuse in its varying forms and is often perpetrated by a loved one, or someone in a position of power. When we understand this, we can clearly see why such 'evil' behaviour exists.

There are many great courses around shadow work and if you have the time, they can be an excellent option. You can also help yourself by paying attention to your emotions, feelings and reactions as they happen. They are vitally important communications from both your inner self and your ego self. If it is possible in the moment, do any or all 3 of the exercises I shared previously to get yourself centred again. The next step involves asking yourself some questions, so it may have to wait until you have a moment to yourself. If this is the case, then write a note with just enough information to remind you of the issue and your reaction to it.

The best and most effective method I have found for this questioning process is called Emergent Knowledge/The Power of Six. If you register on the website http//:www.ekology.co.uk you can access a process called 'The Iterator 1'. This involves asking yourself 6 questions that allow you to access your own knowledge. Doing this process once will give you insights but if you repeat the process 5 more times you will likely achieve complete transformation. It doesn't have to be finished in one sitting. This brilliant method can be used for absolutely anything you want to understand or resolve, including health issues.

A Final Note

There are some terms that are given a negative interpretation, such as self-centred, self-important and selfish. Being self-centred is exactly where you need to be. Why would you want to be anywhere other than centred in the core of your being? Self-importance is the awareness of your own significance, the relevance of you. Being selfish is putting yourself first.

There is the well-known instruction when travelling on an aeroplane with a child, that in an emergency you must put the oxygen mask on yourself first, before your child. This is the perfect analogy of how attending to your needs first is beneficial to yourself and others. Focusing on self does not mean 'to the exclusion of all others'. It means being your most effective self and being able to offer more in service to others. It also benefits others by setting an excellent example.

Another thing that has a negative interpretation is the ego. Your ego is not something to deny or overcome. Your ego exists because the human being exists in duality. This is something that cannot be changed. The ego has served us well by creating our unique personality. That personality is our soul expressing itself as a human being. Although the ego is often running a program that is based on outdated beliefs, it always tries to protect us and keep us safe. Let your ego be guided by the love and wisdom of your heart and soul, and the program will be updated.

A final word on power. An interesting thing happens when you become more *in-powered*. You become more responsible, more respectful of yourself and others. Your inner knowing tells you that everyone has the same power, everyone has a soul and there is no need to dominate another to procure their power - or give yours away. That's a wonderful place to be.

Ralph Waldo Emerson said, "To be yourself in a world that is constantly trying to make you something else is the greatest accomplishment".

Becoming *in-powered* is a fundamental step that lays the foundations for your journey through life. Sometimes we have issues that we struggle to deal with on our own. There are many excellent therapies and therapists that can assist you to overcome them.

Over the years I have researched and trained in many varied techniques and modalities, and I would like to share 3 books I highly recommend. I have chosen them because they are *in-powering*, simple and enjoyable to do, and ultimately assist you to 'Know Thyself'.

Star Matrix **by Silvia Hartmann**

Silvia is the original founder and creator of Modern Energy and Star Matrix is her most recent endeavour. It is a culmination of her vast knowledge and experience working with energy and love. Star Matrix is the definitive journey to explore all the wonder and potential of your many positive life experiences, that have been forgotten or lay dormant in the hidden recesses of your mind. With great ease, you will find yourself remembering and reliving many joyous, funny and poignant moments of your life. These revelations and memories are life changing and almost magical in the way they open you up to your highest potential.

Coming to Wholeness **by Connirae Andreas**

Another simple and effective method that can be done by yourself or with a practitioner. Connirae has four decades of experience in the field of transformation, and this is her most recent work. Awaken yourself to a deeper sense of wellbeing.

The Power of Six **by Philip Harland**

Philip Harland has written this excellent guide explaining how 6 simple questions can transform any issue you desire to resolve. It is based on the understanding that all the knowledge and power to resolve these issues lies within.

About Annemarie Wilson

Annemarie Wilson is the creator of a new and unique method called The Soul In-Powerment Method that enables you to access the innate wisdom, creativity and infinite love of your unique soul to bring more joy and meaning to your life.

Annemarie has spent the past 35 years studying and researching many topics from physics to metaphysics and everything in between, to understand what creates optimal functioning of mind, body and spirit. This, plus her own life experience, inspired her to create this method that allows the focus to be on what can be achieved in the here and now, without the need to revisit the pain and heartache of the past.

It is of particular benefit to women who prioritise everyone else's needs and happiness before their own, who can end up feeling tired, disheartened and unappreciated. If you would like to know more, her website is www.annemariewilson.co.uk

Chasing My Tail, Dropping Balls, Managing It All

By Parul Banka

I almost didn't make it to this book. I was busy chasing my tail. There was upheaval going on in my personal life. Work was at a crucial point as I had decided to pivot significantly. Poor health. Compromised energy. Chronic fatigue. Too many doctor's appointments before the Christmas break. New varifocal glasses were ordered. The new glasses arrived. Migraines and eye distress; turned out that the prescription was wrong! Prescription and glasses had to be redone.

Visa renewal in progress, restricting travel outside the country. There was no opportunity to see my parents back in India. An unwell Dad. A small abscess escalated into an emergency surgery. A nightmare that continued for the next 9 weeks. Concern that Mum might get sick playing the full-time carer. Sadness and remorse because you should be with your family because they need you but you aren't. I was juggling too many balls. Soon, overwhelm began having a gala time in my life.

Overwhelm, The Lurker

While it is possible to experience positive overwhelm, the word 'overwhelm' tends to evoke negative pictures in our minds. The images that we conjure up are:

- Struggling to cope.
- More needs to be done than available time and energy permit.
- The unfinished to-do list keeps getting longer.
- A persistent 'all over the place' feeling.
- Our prioritisation and time management skills prove inadequate.
- We get into our default mode: freeze, flight or fight.
- We feel unsafe and sensitive about everything.
- We are stressed.
- There is no pause. Constant action. But nothing gets done.
- We fail to be present in our present, thereby missing out on the joys of life completely.

When we start experiencing these symptoms, it is an indication that overwhelm is lurking somewhere close.

Is Overwhelm Only Negative?

That's an awful lot of ugly stuff about overwhelm. Didn't I fleetingly mention a positive side to it? Yes, I did.

We can feel overwhelmed because there is too much goodness in our life. I experience it every year on my birthday. I receive at least 500-600 messages on social media and I acknowledge every single one of them. The personal and bespoke messages receive a personal and bespoke response. All of it takes time and energy. This is in addition to phone and video calls with friends and family.

I feel inundated with gratitude and love because so many people have paused to wish me happy birthday instead of just scrolling by. They took time out of their busy day to call me and made me feel special on my birthday. It is beautiful.

It is also overwhelming but in a good way. There is no element of people-pleasing in choosing to respond to everyone individually; it is something I love to do even though it feels a bit much in the moment.

Overwhelm, A Tornado

Overwhelm can be like a violent tornado threatening to swallow everything it touches. It is important to heed the warning signs that announce its arrival. It is wise to not get sucked into it. How? Let me share a few ideas.

Overwhelm Approach 1: Being Aware That The Overwhelm-Tornado Is Approaching

We can only deal with what we know is happening. To be able to deal with overwhelm, we need to identify that we are overwhelmed. We cannot tweak, reset, improve, or get rid of what we do not know exists. Being open to the idea that you may be experiencing overwhelm is a good start.

Overwhelm Approach 2: Be Mindful Of Your Symptom(s) Of Overwhelm

There is no one symptom of overwhelm. It shows up differently for different people. Through mindful observation, I know that overwhelm knocks on my door in the following forms:

- When I feel that I am chasing my tail.
- When I am busy but little or nothing is getting done.
- When I am tempted to drop some of the 'balls' I have been juggling.
- There is an accompanying feeling of not being present; a lack of joy because I keep missing important moments.

The visual images or symptoms I shared earlier are not comprehensive but they will give you an idea of what to look for. Once I notice the symptom(s), it is time to look at the next step: to identify the cause or the seed.

Overwhelm Approach 3: Identify The Seed

Everyone's seed of overwhelm is different. What comes easy to one person may send another human in a whirlwind of overwhelm. A few questions to clarify how it impacts you are:

- Do you get overwhelmed in the face of a crisis?
- Is it the everyday aspects of life that overwhelm you?
- Maybe it is a combination of both?

I have noticed that I get overwhelmed with day-to-day tasks more than a big crisis. Or it is the everyday tasks within a crisis that overwhelm me. I know that it may sound strange but there is a logic to it.

A crisis is akin to a fire breaking out. When a fire breaks out, extinguishing it takes precedence over everything else. A crisis is urgent and important. All resources must be directed in managing it. Nothing else matters. When I find myself at the epicentre of a crisis, I prioritise it over everything else. I direct all my energy and resources in dealing with it.

One of my strengths is that I am able to think clearly, objectively and practically during a crisis, which makes me an excellent crisis-manager. The biggest crisis I have faced in my life is cancer. Getting through cancer needed all of my focus. However, there was something interesting I noticed during cancer. The very act of undergoing treatment did not overwhelm me as much as dealing with the sub-components of it.

I remember that the cancer diagnosis was followed by a roller-coaster ride of medical appointments. I had to attend several appointments every week. I was spending a lot of time at the hospitals. Every appointment meant that I had to reach out to my insurance company and get it pre-approved.

I did it a few times and realised that taking care of admin (claim authorisation and pre-approvals, the bits and bobs related to insurance) were stressing me out and overwhelming me. It felt like a distraction or inconvenience as I wanted to focus all my energy on my treatment.

Overwhelm Approach 4: Feed The Seed What It Needs

The insight that the admin related to insurance approvals was overwhelming me pinpointed how I could help myself. I reached out to Debbie, my point of contact at BUPA, my insurance company, and shared with her that I was feeling overwhelmed with the admin.

I was worried that I might miss some pre-approvals and end up incurring huge bills. All the consultations were with specialists and all scans were specialised, which meant they were all expensive, and hence my fear of incurring huge bills.

She understood and said that she would take care of it. She sent me a blanket approval email that pre-approved every consultation, scan or treatment I may have to undergo over the next several months. She also said that she would liaise with the contact person at the hospital on my behalf, if required. Such a relief!

Hundreds of subsequent admin steps were made redundant with that one conversation. Situation resolved! If I had not figured out what the seed was, I would not have asked for Debbie's help.

If my seed of overwhelm wasn't the admin, reaching out to Debbie would have helped but wouldn't have resolved the situation. If what I needed was emotional support whilst going through an aggressive treatment, being accompanied by my husband would have tackled overwhelm and not the admin. Get the point?

During a crisis, we have limited awareness of what is available to us. It is important to be resourceful and get a grip of all your options.

Abraham Lincoln captured the lack of resourcefulness beautifully when he said, "I have been driven many times upon my knees by the overwhelming conviction that I had nowhere else to go. My own wisdom and that of all about me seemed insufficient for that day."

Overwhelm Approach 5: Getting Priorities Right

When feeling overwhelmed, it is important to ascertain our priorities for two reasons:

- As we navigate life, our priorities change. What was important before may no longer be valuable to us. Focusing on our top most priority will bring our focus back to what is valuable and relevant, thus alleviating overwhelm.
- Overwhelm usually indicates that we think we need to do more than we are able to. Taking a stock of our priorities

helps us focus only on what is important to us. Rest can be delegated or dropped.

Overwhelm Approach 6: Do, Delegate, Drop

Knowing our priorities brings our options to the fore.

Here is a powerful way to look at the Do, Delegate, Drop concept. It factors in our competence and skill as well as interests.

We **do** the tasks that are highest in priority, where we have the skills, or when we need to do them ourselves.

While undergoing cancer treatment, no matter how difficult it was, I was the only person who could do it for me. My loved ones could support me but they could not do it for me.

Delegate what can be delegated. Our level of competence and interest determines what belongs in this category.

Can I do the accounts for my business myself? Yes, I can. Do I want to do them? No, I don't. Can I delegate them to someone? Absolutely, yes. Accounting does not interest me and I know that a qualified accountant would do a quicker and a higher quality job than I ever could. My brilliant accountant takes care of everything related to accounting and taxes for me.

Drop: Are there any tasks that can be dropped altogether?

In what feels like aeons ago, I would cook lunch every morning. I would start my day with lunch preparation - we are talking full, cooked Indian meals here; think freshly cooked flatbreads and a main curry - get ready for work, commute for over an hour to reach the office for a 9 am start. I do not do that anymore.

I am no longer attached to the story that food must be prepared as close to the time of consumption as possible. Most days, I prepare it on the previous evening and it tastes delicious the following afternoon too. It is a bonus that I now work for myself and do not have to commute to an office at all. But lunches aren't cooked at 6 am anymore in my home.

My story about 'dropping the balls' has also changed over the years. There was a time I associated it with inability to cope and saw it as a weakness. That's not the case anymore. I now understand that dropping balls doesn't make someone incapable or weak, nor does it mean that this was the only choice they had. I appreciate that this could be the choice they made based on their priorities.

With the help of my new story, I love 'drop' as much as 'do' and 'delegate'. In fact, when I feel that I am chasing my tail, I choose drop over the other two.

We get into knots thinking that everything we need to do is indispensable. We behave as if the weight of the entire world is on our shoulders. We feel encumbered with the story that we are responsible for the life and well-being of fellow humans. But the truth is that none of us shoulders the weight of the entire world and most of us aren't responsible for the lives of other people. When we get that, we find out that a majority of tasks that overwhelm us can wait, and we find a way out of overwhelm.

Are there any stories you can drop that would, in turn, help you drop a few things off your to-do list?

Overwhelm Approach 7: Accept That Overwhelm Is Normal

Resisting overwhelm is unproductive. On the contrary, acknowledging that overwhelm is normal brings our focus to 'How can I deal with it from 'This is so stressful!'

The former can help us deal with overwhelm; the latter can only stress us more, potentially making things worse. It is a powerful shift from focusing on the problem to focusing on the solution.

Overwhelm Approach 8: Ask For Help And Get It

Asking for help does wonders during overwhelm. I know that organising things at home regularly overwhelms me. I do not enjoy organising stuff and tend to procrastinate. But it is also true that my threshold for an unkempt house isn't particularly high. When stuff has been left out for a while, it starts getting on my nerves. Reaching out to the other human who lives with me and saying, "I need help with organising xyz", helps.

We can suffer alone with tasks that feel hard or drudgery or we can ask for help from people who are willing to help us. Debbie, my point of contact at the insurance company, was willing to help. But I had to ask for her help.

We must make crystal clear what xyz is. Expecting the other person to mindread is a recipe for disaster. At times, it is possible to ask for help for free and at other times, it may require an investment. Asking for help from friends or family falls in the former category whereas hiring a coach falls in the latter. While the thought of making a financial and energetic investment can be intimidating for many people, it is always substantially lower than the cost of staying overwhelmed.

Overwhelm Approach 9: Develop Self-Care Practices

Knowing our boundaries, learning when to stop, stress management, and being kind to ourselves when our reality looks different from how we want life to look, all form part of self-care.

Setting stretch goals is important but if we keep stretching, without taking time to recuperate and reset, we invariably deplete ourselves. Overwhelm often shows up when we are trying to do too much. Knowing our boundaries gives us the space to recuperate before overwhelm or burnout can set in.

When we pursue a big goal, taking breaks helps disrupt the cycle of constant stress and overwhelm. Looking after ourselves is important for our own sanity, effectiveness, efficiency and managing overwhelm.

Overwhelm approach 10: Control, Influence And Acceptance

We, human beings, love predictability and certainty. We love setting goals, planning, acting, and knowing how our actions will pan out eventually. We love doing what we can to influence or control our desired outcome.

Control gives us a feeling of safety. It also feeds our ego because it builds the illusion that we are driving our life as we want it.

However, the truth is that while we may want to control most circumstances in life, there is little we can control. Every situation has several variables. Except for our choices, we cannot control how other variables will respond to us or the choices they will make.

Knowing the difference between what we can influence or control and what we can't, is a game-changer for improving the quality of our life.

Whenever I find myself in a difficult spot, including overwhelm, I ask myself the Do, Delegate and Drop questions.

"What can I do about any of this? Is there someone I can easily and efficiently delegate it to? If not, do I drop it for now?"

If there is anything I can do about it, I get busy doing what needs to be done.

When I cannot do anything about it, I change my focus to accepting that the situation is out of my control. I further explore if delegate is feasible. If not, I drop it.

Overwhelm is inevitable when we try to control or influence something we can't.

When I was unwell, I did everything I could to give myself the best chance against cancer. Attending all appointments diligently, learning as much as possible about cancer, eating well, staying active, exploring complementary therapies to aid recovery and support my mental health; I did them all.

But was the prognosis, surviving cancer, in my control? Is preventing recurrence of cancer in my control? No. What is in my control is eating healthy, exercising, managing stress and reporting anything amiss or alarming to my doctors. Knowing that I can be an active participant in my health journey, and taking action to support my health, will tackle overwhelm. On the other hand, if I try to control my prognosis, it will only lead to disappointment.

When I knew I could not travel due to visa processing, I focused on staying in touch with my parents on video and phone calls, instead of beating myself up for not being with them.

"God, grant me the serenity to accept the things I cannot change, courage to change the things I can, and wisdom to know the difference." *Reinhold Niebuhr*

Overwhelm Approach 11: Consider If Overwhelm Is Such A Bad Thing

As I inch towards the conclusion of this chapter, in an ironic, almost bitter-sweet way, I consider if overwhelm is such a bad thing. I know that the admin tasks related to insurance bogged me down. But they did so, because I had access to insurance, the best treatment available in the world and a chance at putting up a fight against cancer. Not everyone has these resources.

I know that there are moments when living beyond cancer overwhelms me because life feels hard. But it happens only because I am still here. Not everyone touched by cancer survives to experience these difficulties.

I know I delegate accounting for my business because I do not enjoy it. But I need to deal with accounting because I have a business. Not everyone has the opportunity to build a business.

I know that when I am chasing my tail, I drop balls. But dropping those balls means that I have the freedom to make that choice. Not everyone has the freedom of choice.

Life is full of paradoxes (life-death, day-night, yin-yang), which makes it interesting.

Therefore, for each of these 'causes of overwhelm' I am eternally grateful.

Overwhelm Approach 12: Enjoy The Ride While It Lasts

My final invitation to you is to enjoy the ride while it lasts.

One of the major factors that lead to overwhelm is when people don't get the results they desire. I used to be the person who would soldier on and push through and do more when results weren't up to my expectations. However, doing more didn't help, because not doing enough was not the problem to begin with.

A friend recently reminded me, "Meet life where it is, not where you want it to be" during a conversation. Wise words, indeed.

We can be so focused on the destination that we forget to enjoy the ride. I can easily fall into this trap if I am not careful. When I shift my focus from destination to the ride I am on, life gets easier and happier. There is less overwhelm as the pressure to get somewhere is lifted.

It is crucial to remember that our ride, be it for a specific situation or life, wouldn't last forever. It is, therefore, important to enjoy it while it lasts, happily, as best as we can.

Why? **Because life is too short and too uncertain to make a different choice.**

About Parul Banka

Parul is a career coach based in London, UK. She helps high-achieving ambitious mid-senior level managers in Consulting climb up the corporate ladder through personal development, building visibility and personal brand through storytelling and speaking. She helps them succeed on their own terms, without getting sucked in a rat race and freeing up time for family, health, and life. With *Overwhelm And Us,* she has become a published author for the 6th time.

Parul loves travelling. It fills up her soul with delight. Writing poetry is her closest idea of being in a trance. When she finishes a poem, she often needs to go back to it to discover and appreciate what she has written.

She truly believes that we can change the world through our story. Write to her at parulbanka@caramelcoaching.com if you'd like to develop a powerful story that will enable you to connect with, inform and inspire your audience.

Breathwork

By Faizah Jamal

Breathwork Facilitator

Mental wellness starts with HOW you BREATHE,

Breathwork is fundamentally two things - the Power of the Breath, and the Power of Thought.

Otherwise known as Conscious Connected Breathing, it is a breathing technique that is simple to learn, yet very powerful in supporting you as you navigate your way through day-to-day challenges.

Breathwork allows your body to release tension and stress naturally, teaches you to let go of suppressed emotions, It makes you more self-aware and be in charge of your life.

Your thoughts create your reality. Breathwork reminds you to be mindful of your thoughts and words. Through Conscious Intent, Breathwork provides you with the life skills to create a more embodied way of living.

In early April 2022 a DJ of a major Singaporean radio station was taken ill and admitted to hospital due to overwhelm and burnout. I am not familiar with him as I do not listen to that radio channel.

What I do know is how alarming, and how prevalent, is the sentiment like his "I've been stressed out with some rather large issues at work for the last few months" yet he didn't listen to his body until it decided to yell louder and give him this huge health scare, to the point that he now realised "it's time to slow down and gather my senses..."

His remark "For now, I'm excited to try this thing people call sleep or something" is flippant, but this is no laughing matter,

This whole "I-must-be-DOING-things-and-be-busy-ALL-THE-TIME to-be-worthy" is a very limiting belief.

Too often in Breathwork I see people who think that setting boundaries, learning to say 'No", and giving themselves time to pause, feel and just BE, is weak. And when they do come for sessions, they have such chaotic thoughts in their heads that they find it so difficult to simply lie down and Breathe.

At the end of the day, no company or organisation is going to be there for you when your health is all wrecked. Only you can take the responsibility - and the consequences - for your own lifestyle choices.

In Breathwork we say "Do you want to be knocked down by a feather, or do you want a ten ton truck hurtling down towards you?"

Always listen to your body; it's constantly giving you messages if only you would pause.

Illness is only inevitable if you don't stop to really listen, and be aware of how your disempowering thoughts and beliefs affect your health - physically, emotionally, mentally and spiritually.

Most importantly, learn to Breathe - fully, consciously and intentionally.

Because Conscious Breathing literally keeps you alive.

A Posy Of Resources

by Carolyn Street

This compilation is predominantly tailored for the neurodivergents among us. The 'Ode To Grandpa' doesn't discriminate (tongue in cheek). Go with the ones that feel right to you.

- If you read the amazing books that are super bestsellers like 'Eat That Frog' by Bryan Tracy (I loved Bob Proctor RIP) or any of the motivational books or try approaches expertly and at times scientifically created such as 'The Pomodoro Technique' which is one of the methods that can work - read them with self-compassion.
- Have patience with others who cannot understand that no, writing it down is not failsafe. Neither are timers and schedules. The one book that turned it all around for me was 'You Mean I'm Not Lazy, Stupid, Lazy or Crazy' by Kate Kelly and Peggy Ramundo.
- Access Consciousness is a super goldmine of helpfulness. My first experience was with Monisha Ashok who is the doyenne of Access in Singapore. We had finished a project and met for dinner. I was beyond overwhelmed by a dayful of nothing

going right. I had spent half an hour looking for my car in the wrong car park. My previous client had gone way overtime. I had had nasty feedback at work (as usual an admin fail). I had lost my inner smile; the Core of me had been rocked. My then fiancé had left. Somehow I didn't ask for a rain check. I made it to Little India where the hustle and bustle are an overwhelming thing at the best of times. Monisha told me to repeat after her a phrase and I was so done-in I just complied and went along with it: 'Who does this belong to? Return to sender with all consciousness attached'. The fog and overwhelm shifted then lifted. We had a lovely dinner.

- There are plenty more phrases like 'What else is possible?' and I share them liberally with clients and friends. Access has some great body-processes and I recommend them heartily. I didn't go as far with Access as I could have as I have what works. Best phrase of all in my experience is 'What's right about this that I'm not getting?' Truth be told I have had an avalanche of overwhelming things happen over the last six months. I already have stress and overwhelm-induced serious symptoms (that led to my ADHD diagnosis). Access and the practices that follow and precede this chapter all rock.

- What rocks the most is this book project and the team which have been indispensable along with (special mention) 'The Blue House'. None of which would exist without our El Edwards. Truth.
- All the sharings in this book. Use with discretion of course; we don't know your triggers nor can we ensure that no misunderstandings cause mishaps. If in doubt, clarify with the author. Seek a professional you can trust.
- Cry. Yes, for real. Tears unload the spine, said Mary Burmeister (JSJ) and 'tears unshed cause other organs to weep', as is frequently quoted by Marisa Peer. If you need structure or a format look for a meditation session that features 'The Mystic Rose'. My teacher Maitreya does them beautifully.
- Sign up for a Jin Shin Jyutsu self-help class. An in-person one if you can. You can never love yourself too much (says Wayne Hackett who fixed my back in my first JSJ seminar and thus spared me major surgery in my cervical and lumbar

spine). This book, the sixth one, has a purply-red cover for a reason. The other five are the same. The covers and subjects relate to the 'Depths' of Jin Shin Jyutsu®.

- Find something that isn't overwhelming. Treat yourself. Another of my favourite Access-isms is: 'Just for me just for fun don't tell [nor harm] anyone'. Find and do an act of service; what you sow you reap.
- Old school and out of fashion but high on my list is the 12-step suite of programmes. Codependency Anonymous was a saviour when I had a major breakup and ensuing breakdown.
- The 7th Path by Cal Banyan. Brilliant for clients who are averse or resistant to hypnotism. Speaking of which, Rapid Transformational Therapy is the only hypnotic 'technique' that has ever worked on or for me. My brilliant mind loves to communicate and participate in processes and takes offence at being sidelined. RTT works with the mind's 'critical factor' to upgrade and update the data it works with.
- Get a diagnosis. I was serendipitously diagnosed with Attention Deficit Disorder with some Hyperactivity at age 50 and a half. Many of us neurodivergents are

prone to overwhelm having 'tried' to step up to other people's standards and plates for years,. I went and had my heart checked twice due to debilitatingly noisy, painful palpitations. They found nothing but the Cardiologist had a suspicion that ADHD-induced stress (having to work extra hard to meet others' expectations and standards) might feature. He was right and the symptoms go away when I remember to take a tablet ad hoc (Propanalol in my case; get checked out please).

- Finally you are invited to our 'And Us' Facebook group where many of us and a hundred or more friends of the series are there for you. I show up most days with a live video and cover all manner of tools, techniques, remedies and sharings to alleviate the overwhelm, anxiety, sadness, anger, fear or frustrations folks are facing. Membership is free especially if you have this book or one of the others.

An Ode To Grandpa Stan, My First and FabBest Life Coach

TL;DR only cos this has turned into a monster while trying to morph into a decent piece on overwhelm.

1. Enjoy your Grandfather and yep your Grandmother - or their ersatzes - from either or both sides. Mum's mum gets an Ode of her own soon.
2. Love your own company.
3. Have loving nicknames for people that lift them up.
4. Allow people to lift you up. But you keep yourself up.
5. Collect your thoughts - this may mean 'meditate' or 'just chill' to you but to me it means 'let your mind find the good and let go to let come'. No fiddly lists required if you don't fancy them.
6. Have a sense of humour. Quirky is the new dressed-for-success.
7. Play little games with loved ones. You never know how significant the memories of those special interactions will be.
8. Buy people sweets and treats but avoid diabetes. Seriously, seeing Grandpa suffer with dietary cannot-haves and close-up and personal encounters with others faced with the truly horrid consequences of the inordinate hideousness diabetes can cause .. just no. Besides, no-one needs to live on an underwhelming diet. Of course if Rich Teas are your thing - you do you.

9. Prepare to enjoy your grandchildren or ersatz grandchildren.
10. Hug trees even if you need to pretend not to.
11. Above all: protect your energy.
12. Eat breakfast.
13. Coin new words and make new ones. Portmanteaux are the new [fill in the blank]. See 5 and 6 above.
14. Let people talk as fast as they like. Speed up your hearing. They are super afraid of forgetting and of boring or overwhelming you. Also life is short.
15. Pay attention or you'll miss vital lessons that might help you pass exams - half LOL.
16. It will pay dividends in the end. As 'they' say: if it isn't okay then it isn't the end.
17. Oh and make sure you have enough word count for your content - Help! - half LOL.
18. Add yours here :)
19. And another for luck.
20. Go on, one more for the road and a nice round twenty.

I would love it if you could share them with the group in Life Issues Transformed And Us, this community's Facebook group. And now onwards to the real sharing from my heart to yours.

'It'll pay dividends in the end, T - mind the bones and keep your wits about you - careful how you go sweetie and see you tomorrow!' was my grandpa Stan's way of reminding me that life is worth living, to take care and to protect myself from the unforeseeable shocks and challenges of life. 'Mind the bones' still bemuses me to this day. That was his goodbye phrase each time I left after a week or so's stay with him over half-term. Our joke was that every day is a tomorrow.

T? It was short for 'Twinkle-toes', his nickname for me. He had another nickname for me - Buttercup. As life would have it my now-husband Rennie randomly started calling me Buttercup soon after we met. 'They' say a girl marries her dad (I am sure 'they' mean his Doppelgänger); I married my Grandpa's avatar.

Stan taught me the value of 'collecting one's thoughts'; his term for regrouping and re-centring himself in his threadbare armchair after making his way down the narrow staircase each morning. Nowadays people make their mark and money out of teaching others to quieten the mind. I had a headstart thanks to Grandpa. His cue for the two of us to get the Cornflakes and silver-top milk and breakfasty things on the table was him thumping his hand rhythmically on the arm rest before he'd start quasi beatboxing to a Big Band tune. He'd get the respective record out, I would put it on and our day would start. He took time to elicit stories and hear me out - all the stories of school, the good, the bad and the ickypoo I was desperate to get off my chest but feared overwhelming him with. Everyone else said - and many boringly still say - I talk too fast. He would say 'let me rev up my hearing engine so I can keep up'.

He was an extraordinarily tall, slim man with the bluest of eyes who had been medically boarded out from work and put on an early pension due to a couple of heart attacks amounting to heart failure that was attributed to post-traumatic stress disorder from his years serving in the war. My mum, a medical doctor, knew these things. As he aged he took to coming down the stairs on all fours, backwards. The sequence changed as he would have to do his thought-collecting ritual at the top of the stairs or sometimes midway. Then the quasi-beatboxing would start and so would the little games. At nighttime he would say 'night-nights Twinks expect me when you see me. Shall I run you a bath?'

On reflection I was probably a source of overwhelm for him; being a widower providing refuge for an eleven-year-old granddaughter -

who tended to rock up every time half-term rolled around - isn't the most ordinary of situations for an introverted soul like him to be in in their twilight years.

'I'm a loner you see' was another utterance I would hear on occasion. It seemed to be a non-sequitur each time, apropos of nothing. It sounded to me like an apology of sorts though I was happy to fit in with him and his foibles. I felt sorry because I had the perfect time every time. All I wanted was to sit in my special spot at the other side of the fire - which was always burning no matter the season - and read. I needed no entertainment nor interaction, bookworm that I was and always have been. At times I would practice my flute for him or try to remember what we had done in ballet class (hence the 'Twinkle-toes' moniker). The highlights of each day involved taking a turn around his once-splendid garden and fetching his copies of the daily tabloids from 'Jenkins'; the tiny shop a few doors down Ringwood Road. Just a few paces from the shop was a small clump of trees which was my favourite place in the world to sit and just be. We had our little games that seem bizarre to those I describe them to. One I still play is counting the syllables in words I encounter. Constantinople was his must-have trump.

We'd spend quality time with the trees, birds and fresh air and just be. Grandpa had one special tree he would lean against, eyes shut for a few moments before he'd signal to me to head back 'in case the chilblains come along'. Can anyone else say they had a tree-hugging Granddad? Another headstart for me.

As an older teenager I would go alone as he acquired what he called 'sea legs'. 'The Star, The Mail, and The Sun please. And a packet of Benson and Hedges. What'll it be today? Refreshers or hula hoops?' We would play 'eenie meenie minie mo', he'd pass me some cash, kiss my cheek and off I'd go. It was the mid-1980s and the area was as safe as the proverbial houses. I was always careful not to tarry too long lest he remind me 'I'm a worrier, you see - just like your mum' (his beloved daughter in law) on my return.

Another reason why I felt like an agent of overwhelm to Grandpa was because the proximity of his place to my boarding school meant that not only was it the most simple choice as my go-to place for half-term but a storage spot for my belongings. I know deep down he loved to have me stay for those few days at a time. Friends would invite me to spend the breaks with them but I picked Grandpa most times. Hand on heart I loved the adventures at my friends' houses and accepted all invites for weekends away at their beautiful country homes. The ease and just being myself at Stan's was what I yearned for. I had all the best opportunities and I am ultra grateful for them. Besties remain to this day. That said, school could be overwhelming at times. So much competition and complication over who 'went around' with whom, who had the most horses, who had started her period with all the gory deets and who had 'gotten off with' their boyfriend in the woods - more gory deets yada yada.

Pfft! The catchphrase from my chapter in 'Authenticity And Us'.

All of my things were stored in Grandpa's front room over the holidays (we were not encouraged to leave our belongings in the dormitories at school - most inconvenient for us overseas pupils). Instead of irritably demanding to know when my stuff would be out of his face (not that he ever went in that room as it reminded him of Grandma) he would obtusely say to me 'when are you decamping your goods and chattels?'. As much as I wanted to soothe his angst - as camouflaged as it was - I could not satisfy his need to know because I had no idea myself.

Grandpa was my first wise person, as you may have gathered by now. And a contender for the most wonderful ever.

Prior to my coming to boarding school in Dorset about an hour's drive away from Grandpa and Grandma's we would spend the Summer holidays visiting them from Singapore where mum and I live now. I first met my dad and his parents at six months of age; the first of a series of biannual then annual visits. Grandpa had the most magnificent garden. My brother and I then my sister would marvel at it. Here in population-dense Singapore one rarely sees a garden that isn't a park. Apple and pear trees, rhubarb and runner beans, strawberries and potatoes and lavender and blackberry bushes. Stan would help me collect ladybirds and explain how the aphids attacked the tomatoes while my attention strayed to how silky though scanty his silver hair was and the pinkies of his scalp. And how he always smelled of bubble baths, specifically Mr Matey. No wonder I got a 'U' for my Biology 'O'Level - half LOL.

As an ambiverted empath and highly sensitive person I was always slightly bemused and a little disconcerted every time we went on a drive or outing be it to Bournemouth for shopping or to the stony, blustery beach at Hengistbury Head or to Swanage or to London for dad's week-long business trips to the Head Office. Grandma (who passed away when I was barely nine) would come along and always joined in. But Stan would stay in the car even as we spent a couple of hours out and about and he always stayed at home when we went on short trips, usually to Aberystwyth in Wales where my dad went to University.

On the first day of my first term (September 1981) - the start of a thirteen or so week period before I would fly home to Singapore and family for the Christmas holidays I had my very first French lesson. From Grandpa, who had seen my timetable. I would be joining a class which had started French at age seven. This made my parents a little concerned. Grandpa quipped 'eety kweety make nokka' and he and dad had a good laugh (a private joke leaving me and mum looking blur). 'My Twinks will be spouting Flaubert at us in no time - more laughs. For the first time I felt like 'I got this'. Which I did; thanks to remedial lessons with a Mr Odell and other gifts I thank my other Grandma for, I came top in class at the end of term and have been a French teacher for the last 26 years. Flaubert's Trois Contes were on the reading list for 'A' level French literature as life would have it.

But I digress. It came time to set off. Dad drove Grandpa's Triumph Herald the hour or so's journey to Motcombe Park, arguably the most beautiful estate in the region. We were invited to tour the school after dropping my 'goods and chattels' off in the dormitory. Everything the dining hall the rooms, the grounds were overwhelming in size and a unique vibe I cannot adequately describe. We then took a tour of the magnificent estate. Yes, Stan stayed in the car.

When it came time for them to leave he said his five-phrase goodbye for the first time. I was too busy smiling and unpacking his words to feel any separation anxiety as the Herald turned the corner and disappeared into the actual sunset leaving me with Catherine Jeffery who had been assigned the role of my 'shadow'; tasked with helping me settle in. Being a 'day pupil' she went home shortly after and I went to face the madding crowd of girls unpacking and sobbing because they were homesick. It never failed to amuse me how they could be homesick when they would be going home a few hours away at most in a couple of weeks.

I followed Stan's example and learned to love my own company even as the Mean Girls did what mean girls do. I was different and that entailed overwhelming episodes I don't care to recount. They all help me be the person I am today.

My rationale was 'no biggie - I would go see Grandpa in a few short weeks and all would be well'. Which it was.

There came a time when visiting Grandpa became a pop-in-pop-out affair with a cup of tea with two Sweetex saccharin tablets and two or three of the Rich Tea biscuits I would bring him. Type Two Diabetes had set in and he was super disciplined, following his doctor's orders to the letter. The conversation invariably centred around portions and allowances. There was always beatboxing even when the sound and energy became more delicate then frail then just the barest shadow of itself.

'Stay the weekend next time like the old days and we'll play cribbage' became the ersatz farewell. I would laugh as my (then undiagnosed) ADHD aka brilliant mind was as attracted to the prospect of cribbage as the idea of having only Rich Teas for a daily snack.

My mediocre A level results and a fascination for the Cheviots and camping took me up North to Newcastle to study for a single Honours degree in German (German had usurped French for a spell) and the visits petered out. One weekend in my third year a friend Andy, who had met Stan at his new residence, a nice-ish nursing home a few days prior, was visiting and decided to teach me cribbage so I could finally share that experience with Stan during a visit we were planning for a fortnight's time. Andy lived near Stan and was my proxy of sorts. My bestie Fatima heard the phone ring. It was mum with news of Stan's passing. Collapsed lungs no surprise he had only had the fags for kicks. Diabetic complications. [That is what made me vow to turn the tide on my own genetic patterns with 3 diabetic grandparents and two diabetic parents. And so far so good.] He had a postcard I had sent via Andy beside him.

That was my first ever dose of true-blue overwhelm. I sat quiet.

‘Collecting our thoughts, yes?’ said Andy.

I realised I was thumping Fatima's arm rhythmically.

'Strangely comforting?' She stated the obvious, necessarily.

We sat in silence then had tea with two saccharin tablets and a few Rich Teas each.

Frederick Stanley Street of Ringwood Road, St Ives (not the pretty one) certainly had a knack for preventing and preempting overwhelm. My efforts in the making of this book are dedicated to him for those reasons and more. I still feel that Twinkle-toes is my higher self of sorts even though in reality I have inherited Englishwoman's calf from Grandma Grace and am anatomically and temperamentally just like her, with a fishwife-esque physique and - to the outside world - extroverted, adventurous and sarky, mouthy but deeply loving, educator and empathic tendencies. And a touch of her coolness; she knew all the words on Top of The Pops. And she taught me to knit, albeit left-handed. She gave what she had and it was always better than she thought. An Ode to her will appear in an upcoming instalment no doubt.

About Carolyn Street

Carolyn is a type 7 with a lot of 2 Enneagram. Her MBTI is 'advocate' except she doesn't like to be labelled 'introverted'. She advocates for extroverts who have misplaced guilt and fear of offending voyeurs - oops - introverts as well as for introverts who get overwhelmed and offended and (seriously) cannot get a word or look in edgeways. Seriously, she helps extroverts, introverts and ambiverts like herself to be the public speakers and sharers they know they can be. Combined with that is her drive and desire to get people on the path of finding their audience and sharing their messages. This book is part of that purpose.

This series is her most major work to date.

Carolyn's 'niche' is anxiety-related projects (in JSJ we say projects not problems) and she believes that healing comes with self-expression and the ability to know and trust oneself. She offers a bouquet of healing and empowering modalities. Clients call her 'happy pill-ar' because she brings an attentive, deep listening awareness, lightness and spaciousness to her work. Clients see her as a stabilising and grounding influence and appreciate her joy and appropriate, interestingly fun vibe.

Recent clients have had breakthroughs in public speaking, being published authors, leadership, AD(H)D, hyperhidrosis and getting pregnant naturally. She attracts gay singles and couples and misfits and kids who have been bullied whether by other kids or their teachers and -sadly- parents.

Carolyn has had an awareness of energy emitting from her hands similar to reiki since she was a child. While on her own search for answers to various questions and existential queries she discovered she had the double whammy of polycystic ovarian syndrome (PCOS) and hypothyroidism.

In 2003 she discovered JSJ, short for Jin Shin Jyutsu. While experimenting with JSJ self-help she went for a routine ultrasound which showed that the cysts had cleared from her ovaries. JSJ also cured severe back issues and averted serious surgery. JSJ is invariably part of her work with clients. NLP usually also features Perceptual Positions and the 'Swish' technique.

In 2017 Marisa Peer who developed Rapid Transformational Therapy (RTT) caught her attention and Carolyn used RTT to initiate some significant weight loss and improvements in her vision. She became an Advanced RTT therapist and was cured of the hypothyroidism (hormone levels normalised and remain normal) and had significant improvement in many aspects of her life.

The bouquet also includes Tapping, Access Bars body processes and clearings. Carolyn is currently enjoying working with the Compassion Keys by Edward Mannix and will soon add that to her bouquet of offerings of which this is a small posy.

Carolyn's hobbies are keeping the LITandUs facebook group going, reading, travelling (virtually these days). Not to mention public speaking and making books like this one. She is an active and selective Toastmaster enroute to her third Distinguished Toastmaster award (all that admin - who'd have it? smile). She lives in the east of Singapore with her mum Shanta, Steven Rennie, her SpouseGrouse, and recently adopted cats Cue and Hugo.

Carolyn is contactable at carolyn@litconsultings.com or via Facebook messenger @ https://www.facebook.com/carolyn.street

Create A New Beginning!

By Authentic Deb, Debbie George

Why Chapter 8?

I picked chapter 8 because 8 is the number of new beginnings from a biblical perspective. While the physical and mental stress of experiencing overwhelms genuinely sucks, it is an opportunity for a fresh start. If you are anything like me, then you know the joy of living in a state of flow, peace, and high vibes, and yet you also know that stinking feeling of being overwhelmed. You have three choices. Ok, there are more than three, but you catch my drift.

- Run and Hide
- Rest and Recharge
- Create A New Beginning

Create A New Beginning

I want to preface that these bullet points are areas that I have seen play out in my own life and journey of growing and healing as a person. This is my story, and it may or may not resonate with you. My hope is that you will connect with all or part of my own sharing about navigating these seasons of overwhelm . It has not always been pretty. There are years that I sulked in the "run and hide" category, because I had yet to learn how to love myself and give myself the space to evaluate and heal. And that brings me to a point I want to make before we dig in. The greatest lesson I have been learning is to love myself. That is a packed statement and can mean different things for different people.

You may say, "Deb, I love myself!"

We all love ourselves to a degree, but that does not always translate to loving our true essence unconditionally. I believe part of what causes an overwhelm cycle in our life is not so much the external circumstances in our lives, but the internal dialogue that we are experiencing that is often guilty of measuring ourselves against our perception of other people's lives, success, etc. We pile expectations on ourselves, often unconsciously at a soul level. Then we experience overwhelm when we don't measure up to our own expectations. Since this is happening subconsciously, we just "feel" overwhelmed, and can't seem to put the finger on where this feeling is coming from. We feel it in general, which can manifest in tiredness, withdrawal anxiety, depression, hopelessness, etc. Sound familiar?

How many times in our lives have we stopped ourselves just short of greatness, because we felt the physical effects of being overwhelmed at a soul level? When I refer to the soul, I speak from a viewpoint ofBody, Soul, and Spirit.

I believe that we are spirits (eternal) living in a body (flesh) and have a soul in which our mind, will, and emotions reside. You may have heard the phrase "soul tired" or even "bone tired" and, last but not least, "I have no energy." We use these antidotes to explain what is happening, at both an unconscious and a conscious level.

For me, I know that the moment I start to feel physically overwhelmed is a sign that it has been cooking for a while. My soul can be like a slow cooker, that just sits there on low heat for hours until finally, you open the lid, and there is a beautiful, hot, delicious-smelling dinner ready for you to consume. Slow-cooking of the soul itself, though, is an entirely different matter.

Overwhelm is the effect of slow-cooking on the inside, without any measures in place to let off some steam or turn down the heat. If you have ever removed a lid from something scorching or boiling, then you know that you were probably blasted in your face with hot air.

If our emotions or way of processing the environment around us go unchecked, then it is inevitable that when all that slow-cooked turmoil finally comes to the surface, we end up in the vicious overwhelm cycle.

This, my friends, has been an ongoing learning lesson in my life. My goal is not to never feel the effects of Overwhelm, but instead to be a good chef of my emotional kitchen, if you will, by making sure that I am processing and making corrections to my recipe as I go.

What Is An Emotional Kitchen?

As I am writing this, I love the just-coined phrase "Emotional Kitchen". It sounds like a title to a book I am being called to write (stay tuned!) Remember when I said earlier to " Love Yourself". Since I am rolling with the cooking theme, think about it this way.

"Love yourself, like a gourmet chef loves his food!"

If you are cooking a souffle, you have to tend it just right, or the whole dessert will flop. The same with our emotional state. Love yourself like an award-winning chef watches over his food! Listen to the verbal and non-verbal clues that your subconscious sends out. These are telling you that what's cooking in your emotional kitchen needs tending. Notice, I did not say. Tending your kitchen is not about yelling, shaming, guilt-tripping, or second-guessing.

We don't yell at our food to cook perfectly. (Ok, maybe some of you have yelled at your food.) The point is that in the kitchen, a chef assesses, tastes, and makes minuscule adjustments to the ingredients. A pinch of salt might be necessary, but not a whole shaker.

When experiencing overwhelm, we often tend to over-evaluate, over-criticize, and overcorrect, which does nothing but make things bigger and more soul-sucking. So while you may say, "Debbie, I face my stuff," you may also be tackling it head-on and making it worse.

Run and Hide

There are those of us who are of the Run and Hide variety.

You put your hands over your eyes and tell yourself nothing is wrong. If I can't see it, it does not exist, so I am going to either try to ignore all the warning signs and keep overextending myself physically and emotionally to keep up this ruse of "All is well," or I am going to sit on the couch and watch life go by, wondering why I can't be successful like all these people I see on Facebook that I have actually never met. Still, surely their life is amazing compared to mine. I will just sit here and listen to all the crap in my head that tells me I am not enough.

Sound Familiar? Come on now, we have all been there at some point in our life. I mean, just look at this "And Us" series of books, specifically Sadness, Anger, Fear, Anxiety, Authenticity, and Overwhelm. That is some shit right there. Life happens, and we are going to experience all of these emotions or states of being at some point every dang day.

Can I get an amen from the person who comes in late to church, sits in the back row, and leaves early. You know who you are, and let me digress for a moment. You sit in that back row and take care of yourself! Some days that is all you got, and that is ok. I hope we are all on a path of learning from life constantly, and one of the ways we do that is to LOVE YOURSELF.

There, I repeated it. Here is my take, and I say this entirely from the point of walking the exact same road we call life. Life is hard, and lessons learned in life do not usually come easy. However, once we learn a lesson and put it in our emotional cookbook (see what I did there?), then we have one more ingredient to use in our emotional kitchen to cook up a whole lotta love and acceptance for ourselves. I mean, come on, what would you rather have in your kitchen? Guilt, shame, imposter syndrome, and unbelief, or would you rather have Joy, acceptance, fun, faith, and all other sorts of magical goodness that you store in your soul cookbook?

It's All In The Sauce!

Hmmm, I am hungry now. I do love me a good sauce to put on my food. Sauce, gravy, you name it. I love to smother my food in tasty things that tend to make my thighs slap and cuss at each other when I walk, but I digress! We each have a choice of what we feed ourselves.

I am not saying that when we learn to love ourselves, we will never feel overwhelmed. But there is a big difference between feeling momentarily overwhelmed and functioning in a season of overwhelm.

Rest And Recharge

Rest and recharge, two of my favorite words and activities, filled with endless ways of accomplishing a soul reset. This is when the food you cooked up, i.e. (Overwhelm), is burned and smells terrible. No pinch of salt will fix it, and you would make yourself sick to continue to try to eat it. We would not do this with actual food, so why should you allow this to happen in your soul kitchen? You have cooked up a mess; now what? Throw the food away and sit down and allow yourself to rest in whatever form it looks like for you. Your way of resting may be different from others, which is more than ok.

Part of breaking the Overwhelm cycle is to break the cycle of measuring your life against what you see or perceive others to be doing. We could and perhaps we should write another book entirely devoted to the subject of Comparison. Frankly, comparison kills your soul and dampens your spirit, and when your soul is tired, and your spirit is dim, then I guarantee that your physical body will find a way to manifest all that crappy food in your soul kitchen.

So many aches, pains, and diseases in our bodies are attributed to internalized stress in its many forms.

You my friend are a unique individual, and not a single person now or ever will be exactly like you. And that in and of itself makes you the reader 100% amazeballs! Yes, I said it. Amazeballs! Seriously one of my favorite words to use. Anyhoo, what was I saying?

Or yea. Rest.

When we take the time to rest, we naturally recharge; however, I believe both are worthy of mentioning together and separately. Oftentimes rest is needed before recharge can happen.

For me, rest is a lot of sleep. It gives me the opportunity to quiet my mind, and let my physical body relax.

It's like knowing that there are things to do or experience that will get you excited and ready to face a new challenge; however, you are so burnt out that you have got to sleep or find other ways to quiet your mind and body before you can take the next step.

Sleep allows me to quiet my mind and relax my physical body. I am a vivid dreamer, and it is not unusual for me to receive healing messages while my body and soul rest and my spirit receives revelation from heaven.

Giving my soul time to rest and breathe in turns gives my body the energy to

get up off the couch. Much of what I have gone through has started in my mind first and then manifested in my body. I have experienced both ends of the spectrum regarding running and hiding versus resting and recharging. Give this girl some deep sleep over several days and let the recharge begin!

Recharge

Now that we are rested, body, soul, and spirit, we can begin to finish the rest and recharge cycle by doing something that motivates you and puts a smile on your face.

Recharging for me looks different depending on where I am emotionally. The beach is my absolute go-to place to recharge. I will sit on the edge of the water and listen to the waves for hours. This may look like rest for some, but it is a recharge for me. The water speaks to me; the waves show me endless possibilities and invite me into the deep waters of my own brilliance and show me that I am indeed limitless. I walk away fully recharged and have restocked my emotional kitchen with fresh, new ingredients to empower me to live my best life, full of joy. Once that is accomplished, once I am rested and recharged, I am ready to face my obstacles and create a new masterpiece, which brings me right back to the title of this chapter.

Create A New Beginning

Earlier in this chapter, I discussed throwing out the mess we have made in our emotional kitchen when it becomes inedible.

One of the most amazing things I love about my life's journey is that I am the chef, and I can start over anytime I want. As long as I am still breathing, I have every opportunity for a "do-over." Remember that I mentioned the number 8 and the start of this chapter, and its meaning is a new beginning?

This biblical view of the number 8 resonates with me profoundly. The number 8 symbolizes everything that can be wonderful; new beginnings are available to me every moment of the day when I reach for them.

New Beginnings

To create a new beginning is to value yourself over all the harmful noise that assaults us, both internally and from the outside world. Make no mistake, you are facing a barrage of negative or limiting voices all around you. We see it in ads that show only the thinnest of bodies to high-profile humans that seem to have everything going from them. Watch enough tv, tik tok, Instagram, Facebook, or other social media platforms, and you will see that we are inundated with thoughts, visuals, and opinions that subtly pressure us to live up to or perform at some invisible standard that we can feel but not touch.

I Have Good News!

You are not obligated to let anything into your soul kitchen that does not serve you or taste good! You, my friend, are never stuck, and I sense that many who read this need to hear this, and I will repeat it.

"You Are Not Stuck!"

While it may feel like it, and there may be circumstances in your life that may hinder you or disrupt the timeline you had placed on yourself, the reality is that you can Create a New Beginning. In my opinion, it is not about starting over. That phrase is so stone age and brings me the mental image of failing and sucking it up to try again. That is not the image I let run around in my soul kitchen. That is not how I have designed my kitchen surroundings. I mean, think about it. Would you decorate your favorite spot with sad, dull colors and with signs on the wall that imply that you suck? That means that you are not enough? That implies that you did not reach the mark, so you're going to suck it up and " start over?". The short answer is NO! Why on earth would we design our kitchen or house, for that matter, in a way that belies the persona of "not enough," I failed, etc. Not me, not this kid (ok full-grown adult-sigh).

I believe in new creations, new beginnings, brand new! I am not settling for re-heating up some old stinky meal that I did not like the taste of the first time around, just because my mindset has not caught up to my reality. The reality is that I am limitless in my ability to recreate myself repeatedly while learning more about myself along the way. I can do anything that I set my mind to if I want it enough. I create what is important to me, and I continue to take stock in my soul kitchen and replace and revise as needed.

The joy of knowing deep in my being that nothing is impossible for me brings me deep peace. In times of Overwhelm, I pull from my cookbook and create something new. I give myself permission to rest, recharge, and then, when ready, cook up something delicious for my soul and move on with my life.

So my fellow Soul Chefs, I leave you with this thought.

You are more than enough! You are a unique, brilliant masterpiece crafted by a creator that finds you fabulous and worthy of every ounce of love and acceptance in this vast universe we find ourselves in. Nothing that you can do, say, or experience makes you any less of a human being, any less worthy of love, and any less of well… Anything!

"You Can Recreate Yourself"

You can recreate yourself. You have the power and the ability to create new beginnings for yourself, moment by moment, day by day.

I encourage you to not let any negative thing into your emotional kitchen that would tell you otherwise or limit what you believe about yourself. If no one has said it to you or if you need a reminder, here it is. You are loved. You have value. You are amazing, and you will not change my mind or your creator's mind about that. Thank you for reading this chapter, and I pray that it blesses and encourages you to keep moving forward!

About Authentic Deb

Authentic Deb is a prophetic minister, author, speaker, teacher, and mindset coach, bringing encouragement, humor, and wisdom through practical and spiritual life teaching.

A gifted speaker and mindset coach, one of Debbie's greatest joys is helping others see how amazing and unique they are by encouraging them to live their most authentic life. The freedom to accept who you are and live in that freedom that is authentically you is crucial in creating the life you want to work for yourself and not against you.

No matter where you are in your journey, Debbie has a beautiful ability to speak your language and encourage you on your journey. You can find links to her books, cd, or book a prophetic coaching session on her website AuthenticDeb.com. You can also reach @AuthenticDeb through Facebook, YouTube, and Instagram.

Letting The Darkness Out

By Gali Rosas

The art that comes out of overwhelm
can be quite dark,
and not at all representative of our day to day
selves.
The art that comes out of overwhelm
can be beautiful,
and haunting,
and resonate deep into the trauma
That we bury way down deep.
The art that comes out of overwhelm
Demands to escape
From the places where it's been locked up
tight.

This poem was born of overwhelm,
and it does NOT represent
who I want to be,
Or who I am,
(most days)...
But uncomfortable as this "hard truth" might
be,
This poem DOES shed light
on this bit of shadow.

This poem serves
as a reminder

that rescue or not,
my beacon survives,
And darkness itself
Cannot exist
Without light.

And that makes all the difference.

Free

By Gali Rosas

Today I'm flying free
The overwhelm is gone
Weight of the world has been lifted
Light as a feather
My spirit soars

Remembering Our Past

By Gali Rosas

I miss you.
I miss the way things used to be,
when we didn't even realize that we were
so free.
I miss the happy times, and the sad,
because at least we had each other,
and that made things not so bad.

It may sound pathetic,
and childish,
and more.
This is me being vulnerable,
gazing through memory's door.
I miss you.
I miss all that we once shared.
When I look back and remember,
there is no doubt you cared.

As I remember, I believe with all my heart,
That you cared as deeply I did,
As deeply as I still do,
my half-smile hinting at the familiar ache,
of the past that lives within us,
as we live each present day,
forever changed

The Voices in My Head

By Gali Rosas

The figures on each shoulder, these ever-present voices in my head, are not an angel and a devil, as Hollywood has made them out to be. They are not all evil, or all pure. In fact, like so many of our thought creations, they don't exist at all, except as actors in our imaginations.

The angel and devil on each shoulder aren't really opposites at all. They are a made-up movie construct. A metaphor to help us name and so disarm, the constant tug-of-war within ourselves. They are not yin and yang, not id and superego either. Both crave structure… and freedom. Both yearn to do what feels right, also understanding without accepting the time-test proven truth, that too much of a good thing, can quickly become very very bad.

My mind tells me to do do do, while my heart tells me to rest. Even the time spent pouring out these words is a sacrifice that I shouldn't be making, over and over again. This time so lovingly devoted to creation, is time NOT spent in sleep, and the guilt is… overwhelming.

"Stop saying should! I can't, I can't. I can't!", the not-devil insists on repeat. Then "Yes. You can. Just do it.", the not-angel insists just as adamantly. The seesaw within teeters to and fro, sometimes one side drives the other down, other times they balance, fairly even.

Do I have control over every up and down? Do I have control over the force, frequency, and speed of these hills and valleys? Maybe yes, and maybe no, and maybe some, not all. Maybe I'm not meant to know, and that's okay too.

It's fine. It's fine. I'm fine. I'm not broken inside… although medication does help the inner turmoil that tows me in Overwhelm, when left to its own devices. Instead, I use every device that I can find, every tactic, strategy, and skill to be the person that society insists is ideal. Okay, okay, I admit that I don't use them all. I have learned tons though, over the years of ups and downs, the Mania, Depression, the exhilarating energy and it's unbearable opposite. I've learned a lot of tactics, skills, and strategies, because I needed to find a way to survive, and I was blessed with opportunities for help, both professional and otherwise.

So my coping skill toolbox has lots of different options, and that's a start. My coping toolbox isn't perfect or full, and I honestly don't open it as often as would be wise, but it's still better than not having anything to turn to or try, when those red danger flags haven't been enough. Right? Yes. It's fine. I'm fine. I'm not broken inside. These thoughts that tug me, to and fro, that tell me "DO" then tell me "NO", they are not angel, devil, or individual entities at all. They are something else entirely.

So what are they? They are arteries and veins, two integral parts of one essential whole. Just like our physical arteries and veins, they are controlled by heart and brain alike, and neither is effective at its purpose without its counterpart. It's been said that the heart is the most powerful muscle of all, and that the brain has potential untapped. For now, I don't strive to be all powerful, or to unlock any imagined superpowers. For now I write, rest, and live. I work and play, and strive for balance each day, living and learning, and sometimes taking deep breaths, to remind myself that it's okay to choose one pursuit over another, with no guilt or shame required.

In this moment, I choose write and left. In the next, I may choose right and rest.

I'm allowed to be both creative and logical, structured AND free, and whether you agree or not, this is the story of me.

The Last Straw That Breaks Us, And The One After That

By Gali Ahuva Rosas

What is "The Last Straw"?

The theme of this chapter is "The Last Straw", which is one way to describe the tipping point from whelm to Overwhelm. The idea behind the term is that if a camel is carrying a load of straw, each individual stalk is light, barely weighing an ounce, and yet as the quantity that we carry grows, so does the weight. One inconsequential addition at a time, our burden grows until… Oh no! That last skinny straw, one that by itself might weigh almost nothing, suddenly tips the balance, and the proverbial camel collapses under the weight. So too does Overwhelm manifest in our lives. Each unmatched sock, each speck of dust or dog hair, each activity on our to-do list, is an addition to our mental load. On its own, each "should" is manageable. Together? Well eventually, we all find our breaking point, and if you've read this far, then you've probably felt, or seen loved ones feel, the pain of an Overwhelm breakdown. This chapter is about our last straws, our broken backs, and how we get back up, and continue on after that.

So Why Bother Even Talking About "The Last Straw"?

While I can't speak for everyone, I can tell you why I chose to contribute. Why bother sharing? Why brave criticism and consequences? Partly, it's to pour out my heart, my past, my secret trauma, and let the very process of putting this out there heal some of the pain. True, my sharing is partly selfish; however even more important, the purpose and passion behind this chapter is to help YOU heal. If reading about my experience with rock-bottom Overwhelm will help you to cope with your own, or that of your loved ones, then it will be well worth any imagined negative consequences. And isn't that why we're all here? All the writers and all the readers… Aren't we all here to share our versions of this universal experience, to give and receive support, and to feel a little less uncomfortable with capital "O" Overwhelm, with Anxiety, Sadness, Fear, Anger, and the constant struggle to show up with Authenticity? Maybe yes, maybe no, but just in case it's so, buckle up reader, away we go!*

Note - This chapter is addressed to YOU, dear reader, and it's written a bit like a conversation, because you're not alone. This chapter is addressed to you because its mission is to give support, in ways that I have often craved, but didn't know how to seek. This chapter's goal is to validate our pain, to ease it, and to help guide us all on this journey of making Overwhelm recede. This chapter and its neighbors in the entire "And Us" series are self-paced, so please, just say "No" to the unspoken expectation that books must be read in a timely, beginning to end manner. Please. Put it down and pick it up as needed, and receive its gifts in God / The Universe / Nature's perfect timing. Whether you go in order, or flip to a random page, the power in these writings will help you feel less strained.

Where Were We? Ah Yes, The Beginning.

For me, the crushing collapse of Overwhelm can be triggered by all sorts of straws, some that I see coming a mile away, and some that sneak up quietly, each and every day. These incidents are almost always followed by the other "And Us" book topics, Anxiety, Anger, Sadness, Fear, and lack of Authenticity, which shows up as hiding my truth. All of the above are physically and emotionally exhausting, and I tend to need a good long sleep to fully recover. Ever had a hangover? (That's okay, you don't have to answer.) Those dreaded symptoms of a headache biding its time, ready to roar at the slightest trigger, of feeling all around tired, can't concentrate, brain dragging like it's under a thousand pound weight? That's what the aftermath of an Overwhelm episode is like… for me. Your Overwhelm could be different from mine, with its own personality, appearance, and outward response. Just like people, who are "all the same, yet all different", we can empathize with each other's experience, and we can imagine how WE would act in the same situation. Are you waiting for me to get the point already, spill the juicy details, and list the strategies that have and do continue to save me? Read on… I promise I'll get there.

The Point (Part 1)

Just like so many other universal struggles featured in this series, Overwhelm is both inevitable and manageable. If you're human, there's a 99% chance that you'll see or feel capital "O" Overwhelm. *Shout out to any future robot readers!* But I digress. Please don't fact-check the above, because 88% of statistics are made up on the spot, and you can take THAT to the bank. Throughout this chapter, I will capitalize the word "Overwhelm", because this is a serious, real, and larger than life state of being. This is different from a little bit of stress that can be fixed by putting on a brave face and just doing what needs to be done. This is a Category 5 hurricane that can't help but make itself known when it passes through. The metaphor of Overwhelm as a dangerous and devastating storm isn't as crazy as it might sound. We can actually prepare ourselves for Overwhelm episodes, like we can prepare for a hurricane, when we allow ourselves to see it coming, and when we allow ourselves to take it seriously, and take action to minimize the impact. How? Read on…

Management Tactic #1 - Check for HALT - H. A. L. T.

This chapter's first, and possibly most essential strategy in managing Overwhelm, is to recognize that awareness is everything. And yes, all of those "V"s are absolutely necessary, you can stop underlining me spell check! These extra "V"s are in here because this is important. If you're distracted or drowsy, that's totally fine, but this is the time to PAY ATTENTION!

Red flags, early warning signs, and blaring alarm bells, they always exist. Yes, ALWAYS. They exist in every Overwhelm storm, and learning how to spot them makes a huge difference. One trick to look for red flags is using the H.A.LT acronym to practice checking-in with yourself, with any kids in your life, and with any adults that act like kids. (It's okay to admit that you've thought it, maybe best to keep it quiet though). H.A.L.T stands for Hungry, Angry, Lonely, Tired. You might also put H on double duty and include Hot, because for real dude, environmental triggers like temperature are a pretty dang big contributor too. These H.A.L.T needs are just like oxygen, they're some of our very basic needs that demand to be met before we can focus on anything else (shout out Maslow for your hierarchy of needs! Google that later). These needs must be met at our very foundation, or watch out world, crazypants is coming out to play. We all have a crazypants side, even me. (Hahaha okay, okay, ESPECIALLY me.)

Before you speak, or act, or spiral into stinkin' thinkin', ask yourself if these needs have been met. Hanger, that hungry + angry beast of an emotion, is real y'all, and if you don't believe me, then just hang out with a hungry baby or toddler. Young kids are a window into the very core of our human needs, with no filter, and it doesn't take a Child Development textbook to know that naps and snacks are a kid-wrangler's saving grace. Also patience, because infants, toddlers, preschoolers, teenagers, young adults, old adults, and really old adults… heck even our non-human companions tend to be extra irritable and aggressive if they're hungry or tired!

Management Tactic #1 is to HALT. Stop. Check the scene for safety, then proceed with caution. Seriously. It's not a coincidence that "check the scene" is also the first step to do before giving first aid. Awareness of what's going on around you makes a huge difference in any situation, so HALT. HALT. HALT.

HALT. Check yourself. Then step outside yourself and check around you. If you find Hunger, Anger, Loneliness, Tiredness, (or seriously uncomfortable temperature) choose wisely what you say or do next. Note: In case you forgot to give H double duty, try T for Temperature, (or P for pain) because any kind of physical discomfort can have a huge impact on our emotions, so it might be best to add whichever extra letter to our acronym, and check for feelings of too hot, too cold, or too injured. These uncomfortable environmental red alerts can overshadow every other, and are definitely a major obstacle to every other management tactic. Heck, I can't even recognize hunger if I'm hurting!

Now that you've explored the importance of H.A.L.T, it might be a good time, if you have a mental wellness action plan, to pull it out and try some coping skills. My action plan is a list of triggers, consequences, and coping strategies, itemized for each of the major areas of life. It answers the questions, "What does my physical body look like when I'm unwell?" "And my relationships?" "How about finances?" Etc etc. Then it talks about how I can turn illness into wellness in each area, and ends with going through the list again with the opposite question, "What does it look like when I'm well?"

My action plan was born from a particularly terrible incident of Overwhelm, one that I would never wish on any person or family, but that taught me so many lessons that I really needed to learn. I won't share the details here, out of respect for its potential to trigger others, and yes, maybe a little bit out of fear, shame, and regret. Note: If you want details, they're later in this chapter. If you prefer to avoid that particular stew of intense emotions… that's okay. Skip the subsection titled "Spilling My Secrets Part 3". Don't worry, there will be a trigger warning to remind you, because even though I'm not a doctor, I very much resonate with the motto of "First, do no harm."

For our current purposes, suffice it to say that I very adamantly ignored quite a few red flags, crashed really hard into a brick wall of Overwhelm, and landed myself in a 6 week

Intensive Outpatient Program of daily therapy. My IOP experience started with rock-bottom, but then helped me find the tools that I needed to climb to the top of the emotional mountain... and open my eyes with confidence to the other peaks behind and ahead. Each of us has an emotional mountain range, yes I said range, and each of us is well on our way to becoming an experienced climber, maybe even an expert. In this metaphor of navigating life's challenges, some of us are sherpas, some of us are novices, and all of us are in this expedition of the human experience together.

Spilling My Secrets - (Part 1) [This isn't the trigger one]

Want a peek into a real-life Overwhelm episode? I'll share a few. The first actually comes from my elementary school years, and 20+ years later, it's still an inside joke with my parents and siblings. For context, I'm stubborn. Like really stubborn. Like really really REALLY stubborn. And I probably get a good bit of that from my parents. This first Overwhelm anecdote is about a time that my parents and I went head-to-head, and you can imagine how fun that was for everyone. So we were in the family car, on a long trip - mom, dad, older sister, older brother, and me (no dog yet). I was in my usual back row middle seat, because to this day, the smallest person gets the smallest seat. Sorry short people, that's just practical. So as I sat, and we drove, something happened. I don't remember exactly what it was, and it doesn't really matter, but probably some sort of standard sibling squabble. Anyway, I ended up crying, which was very typical for me at that age (and it still is to this day). Long story short, I needed a tissue. So I asked for one, in the standard kid-fashion one-word way. No, "Can I have", no "Please", just the very irritating demand-ask, TISSUE. Naturally, my parents tried to raise me right, and demand-asked that I say "Please". Cue stubborn side. The rebel in me refused. Guess what happened next… The "do-not-negotiate-with-terrorists" parenting style refused right back. And here we are, 20+ years later, talking about how I cried the word "tiss-ue" for 3 hours, all because I refused to say please. That's actually not an exaggeration. It was bad. I dug my heels in, my parents stood their ground, and my poor siblings went from whining to laughing at how I just wouldn't quit. This was in the days of cassette tapes, and I clearly remember them recording my ridiculousness and trying to show me how irrational I was acting. If any one of us had checked the scene with HALT, we would've pretty quickly figured out that I was very probably hungry, angry, and tired. This trifecta of "do not go head-to-head", practically guaranteed the stand-off would be stressful. My mom clearly learned her lesson, because when I recently called her, overwhelmed and stressed to the max by one of MY daughter's temper tantrums, she gently advised that I pick my battles, and never EVER go head-to-head with a toddler. They say that kids get many traits from their parents. Well my kids definitely inherited quite a lot of stubborn dig-in-your-heels determination… and fighting fire with proverbial fire leaves us all burned and burnt out. As a coworker and friend (who's actually a fellow author - Chapter 8) once asked, "Is this really the hill you want to die on"? In most cases, the answer is "No. Not really", and it's best to put aside our stubborn pride and find a way to compromise, or else be prepared for tired eyes and an Overwhelm hangover. Still reading? Good. There are a few more important points, more management tactics, and more real-life stories in the pages to come.

The Point (Part 2)

For those needing soundbites that can be shared with loved ones and clients who don't want to read the book themselves, no, we can't avoid Overwhelm forever. Yes, you're going to be overwhelmed at some point, as I have been, and as every member of my family and friend-group has been. Yes, you're going to experience Overwhelm, but that doesn't mean you're powerless. The cliche statement, "happiness is a choice," isn't just fancy words from an out of touch therapist. It's actually a real thing. In any situation, we can choose to turn the other cheek. We can choose to keep the peace. We can choose to stop the cycle and turn the tide. If someone is yelling at you, believe it or not, you're not required to yell back. (This is a reminder for myself as much as for anyone else.) Yelling back is aggressive. That in itself isn't bad, but it is fighting fire with fire, and it's rarely, if ever, going to de-escalate the situation. Whether you're dealing with a crying kid, a screaming adult, a teeth-baring dog, or a hackles-raised tiger, getting into a shouting match generally doesn't fix the problem. So make a different choice. True, this is much easier said than done. True, our thoughts, emotions, and behaviors can be contagious, and it takes a lot of practice to reign in the instinct to "give as good as you get". Also true, it is absolutely life-changing to empower yourself to change your response. Say this to yourself if needed, because as much as we really, really, really want to change others, we only ever truly have control over ourselves.

Moral of this story, YOU have power. Use it wisely.

Management Tactic # 2 (There are 3, so don't quit on me!) - Disengaging

Another strategy for preventing and managing Overwhelm is to recognize that disengaging makes a huge difference. If you're distracted or drowsy, that's totally fine, I am too, but this is another key time to PAY ATTENTION!

Tactic number one talked about awareness. Okay, good start. The alarm bells are ringing loudly. I hear them. I see the red flags. Now what? No beating around the bush the answer is disengage. This tactic looks different for everyone, and could even be totally different from one situation to another. If you're on the phone, you might need to use that magic mute button and take a deep breath. In with the good, out with the bad. Big breath in, 2, 3, 4, hold it, hold it, out, 2, 3, 4, 5, then back to normal. This isn't some complicated meditation. It's just one deep breath, maybe followed by another, or as many as you need, and it helps. (Note: There are lots of other breathing techniques that other authors might cover in this book, like square breathing, but for now, just try this one.) If you're in-person, you might need to clench and unclench your fists, (or your toes if you're trying to be subtle), and make a conscious effort to keep yourself (and your face) neutral. You don't have to fake a smile, as that’s not always helpful. However, letting anger or disappointment show on your face is going to impact the other person. It’s going to, whether you admit it or not. Don't have a good poker face? Me neither. Sometimes it's more helpful to walk away. Storming off isn't always ideal, or possible, so maybe start by taking one (or a few) steps back, or finding a way to ask for a pause. In my house, we use the words “pause”, and "reset", and even if one or the other person isn't ready to pause, we really try to do it anyway. We disengage anyway, because it gives us space to stop escalating and take much-needed time. It gives us a quiet way to respect the other person’s Overwhelm alarms, even if we aren’t there ourselves. One interesting idea that has helped in my life, is to tell the other person where you're going, and why. If it's an adult, you can say that you're going to take a walk "to calm down". For a kid, you can tell them that you're putting yourself in time-out, until you're ready to make good choices. I've done both, and oh my gosh storming off to put MYSELF in time-out instead of my kids, was so amazing. I had a rare few minutes to myself, there was no more Overwhelm trigger of trying to force a frustrated kid to be quiet, still, or understanding, and the kids got to monkey see monkey do some healthy emotional regulation. Plus, they're kind of obsessed with me, so walking away was a huge negative reinforcement for them. If you've ever tried a failing time-out, you know what I mean. It's hard. Disengaging helps.

Now time-out can be a condescending phrase to use with grown-ups, so tough conversations often have me choosing a different coping skill. These moments don't happen all that often, but when they do, it's a huge help to communicate that I need to walk away in order to reset, that I can't always estimate a time frame, and that I do intend to come back… (yeah that was a fear I didn't know was happening) and finding out about it was a game changer too. FYI, the "explain where you're going instead of just taking off" idea came from a therapy session, and professional help is really… helpful. Shout out Dr. E!

In both the kid and the adult scenario, I made the choice to disengage, to use my power over my self to manage my emotional tornado, and in a little while it was gone…. at least until the next storm. Whether you choose to go on mute, take a breath, tense and relax different muscle groups (look up progressive relaxation)... or if you try to pause, reset, storm off, walk away... or even if you find your own altogether different tactic, YOU also have power. YOU can manage overwhelm, before it turns destructive, by empowering your self to disengage.

Spilling My Secrets - (Part 2)

This next real-life story comes from my teen years. I must've been about 17 years old, mature enough to think that I knew everything, naive enough to be absolutely wrong. If memory serves me well, which it often does not, it was college application season, and my mom had granted my older sister not just permission, but the responsibility of making sure my submissions were completed. Looking back, I can't blame my mom for delegating this monumental task. Putting aside the stress and frustration of nagging a stubborn procrastinator (that's me), my mom wasn't born in this country, and my older sister had not just applied to, but also recently graduated from a top-tier university. That's the goal right? Plus, did I already mention that I'm stubborn? As a teenager, this must have frustrated my parents to the edges of their own Overwhelm cliffs. I mean, think about it. When my parents honored my wishes, and did not remind me to write the essays, I'd procrastinate for waaaay longer than was wise. On the flip side, when they taught discipline with either a gentle or firm nudge, cue the stubborn side. I reacted with hostility, and refused to make progress out of sheer spite. My internal dialogue went something like, "THEY'RE not the boss of me! These are my applications. This is my future on the line, and I'll write those essays when I'm good and ready!" A lose-lose situation for all involved. Throw sibling drama into the mix and…. You guessed it, the situation was a powder-keg ready to explode. In a moment of Overwhelm that manifested as boiling rage, I shouted at my sister. She was only trying to help, but had pushed in a way that was less "let me share my wisdom", and more "kick in the pants, just get the job done". She warned me to back off, to walk away before I said something that I'd regret; but of course, it was too late to hold back. All these years later, the regret is still so strong that I refuse to even write the words that left my mouth that day. Suffice it to say that I had wished her terrible pain, and am really really REALLY glad that the universe ignored my request. The craziest part of this whole story is that I brought it up to my sister recently, still afraid to acknowledge but finally brave enough to apologize… and she didn't even remember the incident! This memory that had haunted me with years of shame and regret was not even a blip on her radar. Crazy… but actually, not uncommon at all. We build things up so much in our minds, holding on to these toxic feelings that become Overwhelm straws, and a lot of times, our worst fears don't match reality at all.

The Point (Part 3) [Still not the trigger part]

So we've covered awareness, and that's a great beginning. We've covered prevention, and that helps a ton. This third management tactic is equally, if not more important than either of those that came before. Even if you've taken all the steps, made all the "right" choices, and managed situational triggers… incidents of Overwhelm can still happen, and that's okay. The key to surviving, and thriving, through these experiences is to give yourself grace. Disarm the shame and guilt that often follow incidents of destructive dysregulation. Observe and let go of these troublesome thoughts. Watch them disappear, as tiny bubbles floating off into the distance, or as scraps of paper consumed by a campfire. Give your rescued-from-drowning self permission to wash up on the beach, to rest from the ordeal, to process, and to move on with your life. Maybe you'll be changed by each Overwhelm incident, as I have been in ways big and small. Maybe you won't, and that's okay too. There is no right or wrong way to survive

Overwhelm. The important thing is to survive, to get back up after your proverbial back has broken, and to keep finding ways to find peace, and carry on.

Management Tactic # 3 - Recover

The third and final strategy that we'll explore in this chapter is recovery. There will be moments when, try as we might, we cannot or did not avoid Overwhelm. We found our way through, somehow survived, and are left to deal with the aftermath. The straw that broke our proverbial camel's back is not the end, and so we must also look to the one after that. We must find a way to recover. So what does recovery look like? Well, it's not one-size-fits-all. Recovery can be physical - drinking some water, taking a nap, getting medical attention for bruised fists that may or may not be the cause of that hole in the wall....(I'm not judging, promise.) Recovery can be emotional - coming to terms with the facts of the situation, letting the tears flow, confiding your worst thoughts to a trusted friend. Recovery can be relational - explaining, apologizing, and/or making amends to those who may have been hurt, whether it was on-purpose, by accident, or a bit of both. Recovery might look like distancing yourself from the experience, packing up the lessons learned, and focusing attention on the present moments. Recovery might also look like reliving the experience in a safe space, inspecting the events, and understanding the facts and perceptions with the wisdom of hindsight. Recovery could even look like planning for the future, making your own mental wellness action plan, to have or give your loved ones to keep, just in case. The best part of all these angles and options is that they're not mutually exclusive. You have the power to pick and choose one, or all, or none of these recovery tactics. You have the power to forge your own path, with all that this would entail. You have the power to unlock the prison door of Overwhelm, and to never again be trapped in its cage. You have the power to recover. You are not alone. This season is not forever. You've got this.

Spilling My Secrets - (Part 3) [TRIGGER WARNING]

This last real-life story is actually from just a few years ago, and it's the one that feels the most raw and risky to share. (Stop reading here if you feel that you're on your own emotional cliff right now.) When my daughter was 11 months old, yeah, just a month away from her very first birthday, I was Overwhelmed by postpartum depression, and I didn't even know it. My family saw me spiralling, and offered options, but I refused to get help, and they couldn't force me because... well, see the earlier story about my strong stubborn streak. I was in major denial, so the emotions and stress, the loneliness and exhaustion kept on building, until the flood started to drown me. Rather than fight for survival, I gave in to the formerly passive, now active and constant suicidal thoughts. In that moment of complete Overwhelm, where the stress-straws felt like they were too many and too heavy to carry, I took a bunch of pills. Thankfully, my medication bottle was only half-full at the time. Thankfully, my family was home, and acted on the instinct to check on me, instead of giving me space. Thankfully, it was a mood stabilizer and not something stronger in that bottle. Thankfully, I didn't really want to die. In my half-asleep state of being about 90% ready to just succumb, a small but fierce part of my soul found the courage to mumble what I'd done. My hope for each of us is that we nurture that guardian angel piece of ourselves, so that when our conscious mind is exhausted and done, our spirit will have the strength to bring us back to life, and to all the amazing things yet to come. (There are always amazing things yet to come, even if you absolutely don't believe it right now.)

Physically, there was no damage, thank God. Emotionally, well there's definitely some trauma from that event. All who were impacted by my actions carry some trauma deep inside. This is my burden to bear, but also my burden to lay down. Just as we can allow experiences to add straw after straw to our emotional load… we also have the power to remove straw after straw. Through faith, through family, through forgiveness, and also through some other F words that I won't name, we can lighten the load. Metaphor aside, we aren't actually camels, and we have a lot more control over our baggage than we might realize.

This first and only suicide attempt was a wake-up call that could not be ignored. I ended up completing IOP, an intensive outpatient program that took me away from my day-to-day routine, and into a much needed healing space. During those 6 weeks of Monday thru Friday, 9am - 12pm therapy, I sat with others in similar battles, and "did the work" of healing. I gave myself permission to accept my Bipolar diagnosis, and to accept the hard truth that going off my medication contributed a ton, and medication compliance actually makes a big difference. In that space, my cohort and I shared tough truths, and accepted feedback. We were supported through our individual Overwhelm journeys, with medication management, coping skills training, meditation, and more. Even though we each fought our own battles… we fought them side by side, and that made all the difference.

Thankfully, my country has a medical leave job protection law, and I qualified, and my family was able to keep the bills paid while I worked through the issues that had landed me in IOP. Not everyone is so lucky, and that's why this book is so important. At the end of the 6 weeks, it was time to "graduate", and I felt ready. Well, scared definitely, but also ready. The Intensive Outpatient Program had given me the unique combination of space, time, support, and skills that I needed to be able to go back to "normal", and all that "normal" entails. I was forever changed by the experience, and still remember the way that I didn't take care of my illness, and it almost took care of me. I still find myself slipping back into those old unhealthy habits of job and perfectionism over all else, but I have the skills from IOP. The program did not release me from the 6 weeks, or from graduation day empty-handed. I took with me a binder full of helpful handouts, including strategies from both CBT and DBT (that's Cognitive Behavioral Therapy and Dialectical Behavior Therapy, each different, each valuable). The handouts covered topics like affirmation statements, laddering to identify unhealthy core beliefs, distress tolerance tactics, assertive communication, and more. This binder included phone numbers, apps, and websites where I could seek support. This binder included messages of encouragement, appreciation, and hope from peers in the program, some of whom I still keep in my thoughts and text message circles. This binder included my wellness plan, a new and treasured personal resource explained earlier in this chapter. The plan included triggers, favorite coping skills, and next steps if I started to slide back down the slippery slope of Overwhelm-fueled Depression. This binder included all of those resources, and still does, because it is too precious to ever discard. (Shut up - I'm not a hoarder! Lol) Overwhelm looks different for everyone, and my experience with a local intensive outpatient program gave me an opportunity to build much needed awareness, to build up much needed self-defense tools like disengaging, and to leave with a written record and plan for recovery that my loved ones can access if needed.

The Point - Again

Overwhelm is universal, and unpleasant… and temporary. There are strategies to prevent, and to manage, and to move forward from Overwhelm incidents. If the last straw has come and gone, and you see or feel the relentless weight of Overwhelm creating chaos in yourself or others, please know that each of us has the power to take straws off the camel's back. Each of us has the power to grow and learn from the experience of being burdened with more than the last straw. You are not alone. This is not forever. You've got this.

Closing Message

Over and over again, through Overwhelm and other experiences, I have learned that mental health matters. Let me repeat for those in the back, MENTAL HEALTH MATTERS. Please keep in mind that although I have years and years of personal experience with both therapy and medication, I am not a doctor. PLEASE empower yourself, as I seek to empower you. Give yourself permission to seek professional help. Only you can decide if you're ready to accept options, and there are always options. If you're not ready, at least consider this…. If everyone around you is suggesting that you need intervention, well that's not coming from nowhere. I'll repeat another encouraging message, because it's absolutely worth receiving often, YOU ARE NOT ALONE. THIS SEASON IS NOT FOREVER. YOU'VE GOT THIS.

Postscript

It might seem like I've got it all together, ha, as if. Can you believe that this chapter was born and raised during not one, but multiple episodes of Overwhelm? Even as I write this sentence I have tears drying on my face. Overwhelm isn't going to disappear, and that may be hard to hear, but you can survive. I am surviving... and sometimes that's enough. Thriving will come next. That's all for now. Thanks for reading, and good luck.

About Gali Ahuva Rosas

Gali is a chronic overachiever, overthinker, oversharer, and oversensitive individual who struggles with low self-esteem, high functioning anxiety, Crohn's Disease, and more. She has recently been growing in her confidence as a writer of poetry and prose, all the while working a "day-job" as a full-time Customer Service Representative, full-time Mom and full-time people-pleaser. Overwhelm is not new for Gali, and neither is the desire to help others through sharing her stories. For a peek at her poems, visit Instagram.com/GaliGaliGumdrop, or http://getbook.at/LoveLouder. (With the capital "L"s) Want to get in touch? Please do! You are encouraged to start a conversation at http://MidnightMommyMoments.blogspot.com. Truly, follow that nudge, you might be surprised to see how one little message, like a butterfly's wing, brings exactly what you need. I promise to be a safe space, and I don't make promises lightly. Take care friends. You've got this.

What is Overwhelm?

According to Zachary Shiloh

The verb is defined as 'to bury or drown beneath a huge mass'. That's what a dictionary would classify it as. *breathes*. I've been alive 35 years. I have experienced overwhelm repeatedly as I grew up. What's my earliest memory? It goes back to me being in Pre-Kindergarten. A man threatened me to cooperate with him. It wasn't sexual. I am happy and grateful for that…I did the activity. I didn't know why but I knew my parents would be upset with me. I wanted to make them proud. I didn't want there to be trouble.

Being someone who stopped having parties at age 10. Growing up to not like parties as you change. Seeing them mainly as family gatherings then wither away.

Living in a body you were ashamed of. Not being able to have milk, cheese, or other dairy products. Crying because your loved ones were able to eat things like pizza-with-everything (whereas you had to get all the toppings taken off). Hurting because you couldn't experience the whole range of your second fiancée's cooking (knowing that you are lactose intolerant).

Having foods you loved then abusing them. Not eating because you were legitimately hungry. You hid yourself from the world. You didn't really love yourself. You hated how you looked.

You were discouraged about the vessel that contained your soul. You were made fun of when you tried to be comfortable half naked, let alone in your birthday suit.

Told to put on a shirt because you made your sister, mother, and other females uncomfortable.

Seeing the country you live in as a divisive place. Experiencing brothers (living in different states) be separated by political allegiances. People in one state booing another over sports teams, gun laws or whatever reason.

Working for the biggest retailer in the world. Slaving away nearly 12 hours a day. Do so by mandatory extra time up to 5 days. Regular time is a day less.

Staying employed where the rules are disregarded daily. Where you can lose your job based on how much time you have off. Being around slouches who cry, whine, piss, and moan all day (on their phones nonstop especially during the busiest working hours).

Surviving nearly 18 months of madness. Being in a place that conflicts with your beliefs. Staying in the same location because you need an income. Knowing if you left (with a snap of your finger) that you'd have no income.

Working with someone who burned you. A man who is in 3 writing families you are in. An individual who paved way for a best selling book series. Someone you considered like an older brother.

Being aware that said person was in a forthcoming book with a respected friend. Knowing that you have to go through him to make history. You wanted no part of being anywhere near his name featured; yet you want something for your first solo book.

Try using something that is supposed to be a uniter. Feeling as if you're alienated. Being jealous of people who are living your dreams. Watching folks hee haw at work with it on their mobile device.

Using something which played into losing who you felt was your soulmate. Questioning how successful you can be without it completely. Having the fear of missing out when big things happen (which you absolutely care about).

Feeling as if you're trapped in your own skin. You feel sexually awkward. You question your identity at times. Being what you are goes against the religion you were raised in.

Knowing some people are discriminative towards others who love dual or same sex.

Possibly be killed over your sexual orientation. Can't enjoy anything sexual fully because of who raised you. Being chastised for loving to hear people moan pleasingly.

Having to do things based on your gender. Being blasted when you do the opposite.

Wanting to be to yourself. Biting your tongue when you know you want to speak up. Being called anti-social. Being told to be more outgoing.

Not taking chances out of fear. Living in regret negatively. Not accepting things as they are. Letting naysayers project themselves onto you.

Be a published author in less than a year. Become a best-selling author. Receive an invitation to collaborate with someone who respects you as a writer. Feel as if you have nothing to offer said person (or group of people).

Gain another writing best sellership. Feel as if you are going nowhere. Continue building your network in the writing industry. Gain more collaborations. Repeatedly ask yourself "what can I offer to this wonderful person who wants to work with me?".

Look at all of the best selling books. Let your jaw drop. Really take in what you have accomplished. Realize that your next best seller comes 2 days before the original co authoring is exactly one full year old.

Try becoming a Holistic Health Coach. You want to help people (especially women) improve their mental, physical, and spiritual health. Gain a few clients. Believe in their potential then watch them drop off and drop out.

Know that you let them work with you for free. Notice the same recurring pattern occur. Kick yourself in the ass when you lose another client. Be clientless by what was supposed to be your one full year anniversary.

Question your value in the coaching world. Try rebooting yourself multiple times. Feeling as if what you been taught (by some awesome people) is absolute bullshit. You don't want to enroll in anymore self-help whatever.

Hear a voice in your head justify working a job that doesn't suit you. Let that same talk spit out further details. Try to hold back your tears (as you fight back timed again). Cry yourself to sleep or during your full awakened day.

Dust yourself off. You won't let your pride as a general person die. Do you fight or take flight?

If that isn't overwhelm? What is overwhelm to you, my beloved reader?

How do I fight my overwhelm?

I start my day with non negotiable silence. There is no excuse. I go my first 2 to 4 hours with no audio.

I make time to journal. If not with pen to paper then mobile device memo (or notes). Give myself 25 to 60 mins straight (or points through my day).

I meditate throughout my day.

When audio is finally on, I don't expose myself to the news. I stay away from what I feel is negative. I got no time to hear how the world sucks, governments are dividing us and what else is killing us off.

I have a person to talk to. Someone who will let me be myself. Vice versa.

I am aware of what I eat and drink. Little to no sugar in my food. There is absolutely no sugar in drinks.

No alcohol or smoking.

Before I shower, I say to my naked self "I love me some me. This is non-negotiable". I hug myself. Take a hot then cold shower.

I work on my breathing throughout the day.

How Overwhelm Affects The Chakras

By Zeeba Khan

There is a way of breathing
that's a shame and a suffocation.
And there's another way of expiring,
a love breath,
that lets you open infinitely.
- Rumi

Ayurveda

More than 5,000 years ago, Indian sages developed Ayurveda, which continues to be one of the world's most powerful mind-body health systems. Ayurveda is a science of life ("Ayur" meaning life and "Veda" meaning science). The two main guiding principles of Ayurveda are 1) the mind and the body are interconnected, and 2) the mind is the most powerful tool to transform the body. There is no separation of the consequences of each one on the other. Ayurveda is holistic healing.

This ancient Indian system of medicine is based on the idea of balance in bodily systems and uses herbal treatments, yoga therapy, exercise, meditation, breathing exercises (pranayama), diet, and nutritional supplements to help people stay vibrant and healthy while realizing their full human potential.

Ayurveda teaches us that health is not merely the absence of disease, but rather that our natural state is one of health, happiness, and an inner sense of well-being. This is achieved when our body is clear of toxins, our mind is at peace, our emotions are calm and happy, our wastes are efficiently eliminated, and our organs are functioning normally. Ayurvedic healing is about balance, and the more we are balanced, the more we will be healthy.

Ayurveda is a personalized approach to health, and knowing our mind-body-spirit constitution allows us to make optimal choices about diet, exercise, nutritional supplements and all other aspects of our lifestyle. It teaches the art of mindful and conscious eating and how to incorporate it into our life by showing us that food not only tastes good, but is good for us. What we put into our body dictates the quality of our life. If we use food as medicine, we will be delightfully surprised at how much better we feel and how much more clearly we think.

Some Ayurvedic suggestions include:

- Eat a colorful, delicious diet to balance our doshas
- Get plenty of sleep

- Follow the rhythm of nature
- Move our body
- Stoke our digestive fire
- Relax

Will Practicing Ayurveda Make Me Hindu?

Some people are reluctant to practice Ayurveda because they are misguided by the belief that Ayurveda is affiliated with a particular religion, namely Hinduism. But Ayurveda is not inherently the property of any religion.

While Ayurveda definitely encourages a connection to the Divine, it never outlines what this relationship should look like or by what name we should address this Higher Power. Simply put, the manifestation of the Divine will be different for different people based on their beliefs.

Many studies of resilience find that survivors of any tragedy or trauma who do well adhere to strong philosophies or spiritual traditions. Many faith traditions – including Hinduism, Buddhism, Judaism, Christianity, and Islam – incorporate all of the ingredients for resilience. They offer guidance for parenting and moral conduct; provide role models, mentors, and community support; teach and invite practice in self-regulation; and place a value on the greater good.

A connection to the Divine, a spiritual practice, cultural beliefs, or a sense of purpose help us to make sense of our experiences, and in the process help us to keep calm.

The takeaway is this: A connection to something greater than ourselves – whether it is a spiritual practice, cultural beliefs, or a sense of purpose – allows us to rise above the present crisis with the wisdom of eternity. The connection can be purely spiritual and not religious in any way.

Basic Principles of Ayurveda

The basic principles of Ayurveda are that there are five great elements (or panch mahabhuta), three mind-body-spirit constitutions (or doshas), and seven body tissues (or dhatu). The five elements are earth (prithvi), water (jal), fire (agni), air (vayu), and space (akaash).

These five elements create three doshas.

- Prithvi + Jal = Kapha
- Jal + Agni = Pitta
- Vayu + Akaash = Vata

The Vedic scriptures say that there is an inextricable link between humans and the Universe: "Yat Pinde, tat Brahmande." As is the

Universe (macrocosm), so is within the human body (microcosm). The entire cosmos or Universe is part of one singular absolute. Everything that exists in the vast external Universe (macrocosm) also appears in the internal cosmos of the human body (microcosm).

Tridosha Theory

Based on our dosha, we exhibit different kinds of emotions, reactions, and character traits. The dosha we are born with never changes.

Characteristics of Vata Dosha

Vata is movement both inside and outside the body. Those with too much Vata experience heart palpitations, loose motion, are fidgety, have rapid eye movement, move very quickly and are mentally spacey. Their goals, emotions, and physical movements change quickly. Those with too little Vata experience laziness and are idle.

Vata characteristics include:

- Creative, quick to learn and grasp new knowledge
- Slender, tall, fast walker
- Tendency toward cold hands and feet, discomfort in cold climates

- Excitable, lively, fun personality; changeable moods
- High energy in short bursts
- Tendency to tire easily and to overexert
- Full of joy and enthusiasm when in balance
- Responds to stress with fear, worry, and anxiety, especially when out of balance
- Tendency to act on impulse
- Often have racing, disjointed thoughts
- Generally have dry skin and dry hair and do not perspire much

Characteristics of Pitta Dosha

Pitta is transformation, conversion, fire, heat, and intelligence. Those with too much Pitta experience difficulty in interacting with non-Pittas (because they perceive them to be slow thinkers and dumb), get angry quickly, have bad tempers, and become aggressive very fast. They do not instruct; they demand. They are problem-solvers and execute plans, Type A personalities: they generate work, love to lead, tend to be the boss, face consequences, are very stressed, and are addicted to work. They are prone to diabetes, arthritis, dementia, and have too much gastric acid which can lead to gastrointestinal problems. Those with too little Pitta experience food poisoning.

Pitta characteristics include:

- Medium physique, strong, well-built
- Sharp mind, good concentration powers, orderly, focused
- Assertive, self-confident, and entrepreneurial at their best
- Aggressive, demanding, pushy when out of balance
- Competitive, enjoy challenges
- Passionate and romantic
- Strong digestion, strong appetite, get irritated if they have to miss or wait for a meal
- When under stress, Pittas become irritated and angry
- Uncomfortable in sun or hot weather, heat makes them very tired, perspire a lot
- Good public speakers, generally good management and leadership ability, but can become authoritarian
- Subject to temper tantrums, impatience, and anger
- Typical physical problems include rashes or inflammations of the skin, acne, boils, skin cancer, ulcers, heartburn, acid stomach, insomnia, dry or burning eyes

Characteristics of Kapha Dosha

Kapha is the end product. Those with too much Kapha experience laziness, sluggishness, are heavy, overweight/obese, get stuck in life easily, and have a sedentary life in all aspects – job, diet, and lifestyle. They are prone to eye problems. Those with too little Kapha experience diabetes and allergies.

Kapha characteristics include:

- Easy-going, relaxed, slow-paced
- Affectionate and loving, forgiving, compassionate, non-judgmental nature, stable and reliable, faithful
- Physically strong and with a sturdy, heavier build
- Slow speech, reflecting a deliberate thought process
- Slower to learn, but outstanding long-term memory
- Soft hair and skin, tendency to have large eyes and a low, soft voice
- Tendency toward being overweight, may also suffer from sluggish digestion, prone to depression
- Gentle and essentially undemanding approach to life, very calm, strive to maintain harmony and peace in their

surroundings, not easily upset and can be a point of stability for others
- Tendency to be possessive and hold on to things, do not like cold, damp weather
- Physical problems include colds and congestion, sinus headaches, respiratory problems including asthma, allergies, and atherosclerosis (hardening of the arteries)

Pancha Kosha

Ayurveda treats illnesses via diet, herbal supplements, therapy, exercise (yoga therapy), and meditation. It is a holistic approach to healing the human body by improving health on all five levels of being, from the grossest sheath to the subtlest, respectively.

Annamaya Kosha

Annamaya kosha refers to the physical sheath, or the human body, and is the grossest level of the five levels of being. The body is a system comprising of genes, DNA/RNA, cells, tissues, and organs. Food and diet nourish the annamaya kosha.

Toxins occur in the body at the annamaya kosha level. Physical pain of any kind, such as a torn ligament, is an example of toxin at the annamaya kosha level.

Pranamaya Kosha

Pranamaya kosha refers to the energy sheath and is the movement of life energy in the body. Prana imbalance is the bridge between the stressed mind and the sick body. With each breath, the endocrine system, sympathetic nervous system, and parasympathetic nervous system all send nutrition to every part of the body. With slow breathing, the transmission to the brain is reduced, thereby slowing down and calming the mind. Reducing the speed of breathing at the pranamaya kosha level conserves precious life energy. By controlling the breath, the patient uses only the required amount of energy and does so in the most utilitarian fashion.

The toxins that occur at this level in the body are hypersensitivity and aggravation of the mind, which leads to weaker reflexes. Deep inhalation helps to release these toxins.

Manomaya Kosha

Manomaya kosha refers to the mental sheath and is controlled by the sense organs. Emotions are the root causes of a person's joy and distress. When emotions become powerful, they begin governing a person's actions. Regular yoga practice helps to bring the mind and emotions under control.

Examples of toxins at the manomaya kosha level are jealousy, anger, and lust.

Vijnanamaya Kosha

Vijnanamaya kosha refers to the psychological sheath. It is the conscience within that continuously guides decisions. The hypothalamus, which is the part of the brain that is the master gland of the body, is the seat of discrimination of the limbic cortex, which houses emotions. The hypothalamus is also the powerhouse of knowledge, giving meaning and purpose to life, setting life goals, and searching for truth.

An example of a toxin at the vijnanamaya kosha level is attachment.

Anandamaya Kosha

Anandamaya kosha refers to the bliss sheath. It is when the body is not diseased or when the person is full of positive energy and is satisfied — there is peace in the mind and in the soul.

Karma yoga is adopted in treatment as it is action in relaxation. It teaches complete bliss and contentment while at work and to convert all work into non-work by learning the art of "action in inaction."

An example of a toxin at the anandamaya kosha level is dissatisfaction.

What Are Chakras?

The Sanskrit word chakra translates into "wheel" and indicates movement. Chakras are energy vortices that correspond to various organs and nerves in the body. They hold the energy of your thoughts, feelings, habits, and deeds. Although there are hundreds of chakras, there are seven main chakras that run from the base of the spine all the way to the crown of the head along the central channel of the body called the sushumna nadi.

Nadis are pathways or channels of prana, or life force energy, in the system. In our energy body, there are 72,000 nadis, all of which originate from three basic nadis – the ida, the pingala, and the sushumna. In essence, there are 72,000 different ways in which the energy or prana moves throughout our physical body.

The chakras along the sushumna nadi are the power centers where the left channel (ida nadi) and the right channel (pingala nadi) intersect. Our physical body thrives when the chakras and the nadis are open and prana is able to move throughout our system with ease. When a body is balanced, energy flows freely and can be energizing, revitalizing, and peaceful.

Chakras address the many needs of being human. The three lower chakras (i.e., the root, sacral, and solar plexus chakras) relate to material and physical matters such as survival, sexuality, power, and confidence. The heart chakra is at the center of the chakra system and holds energies related to love, kindness, compassion, and empathy. It is the gateway between the material and spiritual realms. The upper chakras (i.e., the throat, third eye, and crown chakras) relate to authenticity, intuition, and Divine connection.

When we balance our chakras, we are helping to satisfy our Soul's need for safety, security, creativity, transformation, love, authenticity, and connection with the Divine.

What we think, feel, and experience in our mind and heart manifests in our physical body. There is not a thought or feeling that doesn't have a vibrational impact on our physical body. Our cells, organs, and systems process our thoughts and feelings just as much as our mind and heart do.

Any kind of disturbance or disease in the body, mind, or spirit can cause blockage and imbalance. The goal of the energy body is balance. So if you feel like your life, emotions, or body are out of sorts perhaps because you are overwhelmed, take a closer look at your chakras to discover where you can begin to restore balance.

There are unique and specific ways to balance each chakra, including practices for increasing the energy of a chakra when it is too low, and practices for calming the energy of a chakra when it is too high – especially when the cause is overwhelm.

First Chakra

When there are anxious, avoidant, or inconsistent attachment wounds from birth to 6 months of age, as an adult we will always be seeking survival and safety. The adrenal glands are the part of the body that respond to the perception that survival is threatened and this activates a sympathetic nervous system arousal pattern. Any attempt as an adult to heal will not be successful if the adrenals are unhealthy. The most important factor is to re-establish a strong sense of safety within ourselves.

To balance your first chakra, remind yourself to be more present and grounded each time you see red outside. With regard to diet, eat clean, lean proteins and organically grown red fruits and vegetables such as beets, cherries, apples, and pomegranates.

Second Chakra

The sacral chakra represents creativity, emotions, and relationships. When there is wounding between 6-18 months of age, shame and guilt can become deeply seated within the physical body. The sexual reproductive organs are the parts of the body that respond to the perception of being victimized. Over time, this feeling of victimization can lead to resistance to choosing life and this creates a destructive pattern that stifles creativity and drains us of energy and motivation. Eventually this can manifest as cancer in the physical body.

To balance your second chakra, notice the emotions you feel and how you respond to them. With regard to diet, eat healthy fats and oils such as extra-virgin olive oil, sesame oil, flaxseed oil, hempseed oil, fish oil, coconut oil, avocado oil, and wild-caught fish. Also eat orange foods like carrots, mangoes, melons, oranges, tangerines, sweet potatoes, and yams.

Third Chakra

The solar plexus chakra represents transformation and self-empowerment. When there is wounding between 18-36 months of age, feelings of blame, persecution, and rescuing can become lodged in the physical body. The liver, pancreas, and gallbladder are the parts of the body that respond to the perception of being blamed or the need to rescue another in order to feel self-worth. Over time, this feeling that others are to blame for dissatisfaction in life creates a physical disturbance that can lead to blood glucose imbalances and liver issues such as non-alcoholic fatty liver disease.

To balance your third chakra, expand your chest and let your shoulders relax. Do this pose 3 times each day. With regard to diet, eat complex carbohydrates and fiber. Also eat yellow foods like vegetables, whole grains, ginger, lemons, and legumes.

Fourth Chakra

The heart chakra represents compassion, expansion, service, and love – love that is both given and received. When there is wounding between 3-7 years of age, a pattern emerges that involves a fear of loss and a numbing out to prevent us from feeling the overwhelming sadness and grief that accompany great loss. The thymus and heart are the parts of the body that respond to the perception of loss, loneliness, and abandonment. Over time, the continual fear of loss and abandonment can lead to co-dependent relationships, where we have a tendency of staying in abusive relationships and resenting our partner.

To balance your fourth chakra, open your heart to release sadness while walking in nature or walk barefoot on the earth. Spend time in nature, especially with trees. With regard to diet, eat leafy greens.

Fifth Chakra

The throat chakra is the seat of communication, expression, and authenticity. Wounding between 7-12 years of age can result in patterns that lead to the repression of self-expression. The thyroid and esophagus are the parts of the body that respond to the perception that is communicating thoughts, feelings, dreams, and desires are dangerous. Over time, the continual repression of the voice can create a pattern of thyroid or esophageal disease.

To balance your fifth chakra, say something positive to yourself out loud today. With regard to diet, eat more iodine-rich sea vegetables to support your thyroid with minerals. Moisten and open your throat with soups, sauces, and juices, as well as fruits that contain a lot of water such as melons, grapes, tropical fruits, peaches, and plums.

Sixth Chakra

The third-eye represents intuition and seeing what cannot be seen with the physical eyes. Wounding between 12-18 years of age can result in patterns involving a perception of being invalidated and can lead to defensive patterns of projection and judgment. Projecting disowned parts of the false self can create dysfunctional relationships, unhappiness, depression, and anxiety in adulthood. An imbalanced sixth chakra can lead to bad dreams and nightmares, a lack of focus, and headaches. The pituitary gland is the part of the body that respond to the perception of not being seen.

To balance your sixth chakra, visualize your emotions being in balance right before going to bed. With regard to diet, consume high-quality herbal tea & coffee, dark chocolate, spices, and Omega-3 healthy fats. Also eat purple-red foods such as eggplant, purple cabbage, purple kale, purple cauliflower, purple potatoes, red onions, blackberries, blueberries, purple grapes, and raisins.

Seventh Chakra

The crown chakra represents purpose, self-actualization, and connection to Divine Nature, a Higher Power, Source Energy, and the true Self. Wounding in adulthood can result in patters that include doubt, grandiosity, narcissism, addiction, and a lack of self-awareness. The eyes and the pineal gland are the parts of the body that respond to the perception of being all alone in this world. The pineal gland produces the hormone melatonin (which is responsible for sleep) from the neurotransmitter serotonin (which is responsible for the felt sense of happiness).

To balance your seventh chakra, meditate, pray, or be still for 7 minutes to feel calmer and more present. With regard to diet, eat high-fiber foods such as non-starchy vegetables, berries and legumes to detox. Also eat cauliflower, garlic, peas, coconut products, pears, onions, cabbage and white beans.

The Chakras & Their Corresponding Mantras

Visit the *And Us* Facebook group to see a table with Sanskrit mantras and affirmations that can be chanted to balance specific chakras.

The Marmas

Another important doorway to the mind is found in the marmas – a set of potent energy points on the surface of the skin that are connected to deeper, more subtle energetic channels throughout the body. The marmas are also junctions where Vata, Pitta, and Kapha meet. They have great connection to a person's body, mind, and spirit.

There are 107 marma points on the body. Each marma offers a powerful access point for shifting the energy within the channel of the mind. Marmas are not so much points as they are circular bands around certain parts of the body. Working with the marmas can be an effective means of restoring balance to the mind.

Marma points are positions on the body where flesh, veins, arteries, tendons, bones, and joints meet. But at each point, one of these five elements will dominate.

Marma abhyanga, or self-massage, can rebalance the system to function healthfully. Further, abhyanga also contributes to the preventive health and longevity of the body and mind by ensuring the proper balance and flow of hormones, fluids, and immune cells.

It is beneficial to start a marma abhyanga on the side of the body that doesn't hurt. If the body doesn't hurt, then it's best for women to start the massage on the left side of the body and for men to start the massage on the right side of the body. Marma abhyanga should be avoided during pregnancy and menstruation. Each marma can be pressed and released 14-21 times. During times of sickness, treatment can be given at morning, noon, and night.

When imbalances exist in the body, the marma points become sore, but through marma abhyanga, health can be restored. To detect the marma locations, you measure points using the width of your own fingers. The major points correspond to the major chakras on the body, while the minor points are found around the torso and limbs. Thus, healing through marma abhyanga affects the chakras, physical health, and the doshas.

Balancing Your Chakras

The chakras are the energy centers which receive, assimilate, store, and express information. The seven chakras describe an architecture for your Soul and map your human experience in this physical body.

The job of the Energy Body is to help maintain the health of our physical body by taking in and sending out energetic vibrations for which the chakras act as the "conductors" that keep the energy flowing freely throughout your whole body. Our health is determined by this flow of energy from the chakras through the energy circuits and into the metabolic network of the body, as it keeps our vital organs functioning optimally. Moreover, our body uses this energy on a cellular level to maintain homeostasis of the body's systems.

In addition to protecting our physical health, each of these seven chakras represent different core aspects of our personality and patterns of behavior. On a spiritual level, our chakras relate to our sense of safety, our emotions, our personal power, giving and receiving love, the way we communicate, our intuition, and our higher spiritual Self. Identifying which of our chakras is out of balance and eating plant-based foods to strengthen those chakras can aid our overall health and well-being.

No matter how great life is going, no matter how rich or accomplished you are, there is a nagging feeling from within. And that which you're looking for cannot be attained in anything or anyone outside of you. It is the compass that you were born with that is drawing you back to your Essence because you are supposed to live this life awakened.

The drop can become One with the Ocean. Let go. Let be. Surrender. The total annihilation into rebirth, into Existence requires you die before you die, and requires Love. Manifesting our full potentiality means that we die as a separate ego; we die from all that is not Us, to become reunited with our Oneness.

Love – that Essence – makes everything possible in this life. Love invites us to connect to the invisible energy that we can really feel, that gives rise to Life and all the movements within it. That is Love.

In every encounter, in every moment, we have the opportunity to expand by getting in touch with something bigger than us which moves us to go from contraction to expansion. We delve into a Love that gets bigger and bigger and bigger.

Awakening each of your chakras allows your most genuine self to emerge. And you plant the subtle intention that you are, you create, you do, you love, you express, you see, and you understand.

We transform the world by transforming ourselves so let's stay in that space of eternal transformation and shine our light.

About Zeeba Khan

Zeeba is an internationally experienced Ayurvedic clinician, meditation teacher, energy healer and motivational speaker who uses holistic treatment to restore her patients' mental, physical, emotional, and spiritual health and to prevent disease and disorders.

She has presented month-long workshops to corporate clients, including some well-known global leaders. She has also led meditation and yoga workshops at schools internationally to incorporate wellness education into their curriculum. She has explored different types of non-religious and religion-based meditations and uses them as part of her treatments.

She is also a leading practitioner with Mindvalley's Soulvana, a global healing and meditation collective, where her meditations and podcast have helped many people around the world. In 2020, she was honored by an invitation to be part of a live interactive session hosted by His Holiness The Dalai Lama on the topic of integrated healthcare and compassion.

Zeeba was raised mainly in the United States but comes from a mixed heritage background. Her early career spanned modelling, acting, television, radio, and journalism before she entered academia and became a Professor in Communications to teach and research religious harmony across various interpersonal, organizational, and intercultural contexts.

She believes strongly that it is imperative to meditate, even in the good times, to build a silo of resilience so that when we are faced with challenges, we are not running on empty and are able to weather any storm.

Zeeba is trained and certified in the Ayurveda Sciences at Union Yoga Ayurveda, affiliated with Atreya Ayurvedic Medical College and the Indian Institute of Patanjali Yoga, associated with Swami Paramahansa Samsthana, and a registered member of the National Ayurvedic Medical Association, USA.

Learn more about Zeeba at www.zeebahealing.com and on Instagram @zeebahealing.

References

Tirtha, S. S. S. (1998). The Ayurveda Encyclopedia: Natural Secrets to Healing, Prevention, and Longevity. Bayville, NY: Ayurveda Holistic Center Press.

Out-Of-Body, Out Of Mind

By Johannah Stirzaker

A Whole Lot Of Free People Are Having A Blast Right Now! :

This verse describes my initial, spontaneous, out-of-body experience (during a bout of chronic insomnia and overwhelm in my late twenties). It aids me to evaluate a profound life experience.

Across the planet, estimates suggest as many as 10% of the population (or around 747 million) have had some form of OBE/OOBE (accepted initialisms)*. This figure has remained static since the late 1960s (suggesting a stable trend within existential experience).

If we wanted to intellectualise why OBEs happen; there are various modalities we could converse with...

Scientific Theories Include:

- Radical variance within the expected conditions of daytime consciousness (due to traumatic brain injury, epileptic seizure, near-death experience, sensory deprivation…)
- Other medical conditions (e.g. disassociation, severe dehydration, sleep disorders, trauma, severe migraine)

- Experimental/artificially-induced states (e.g. lucid dreaming, hallucinogenic/ psychedelic intoxication, theta brainwave meditation, hypnosis, electrical stimulation of the central nervous system)
- Physical exertion (e.g. response to G-forces or altitude sickness).

Scientific data has yet to definitively prove that a spiritual presence can exist outside of the physical body. It seems that the more 'complex' the science is to master (e.g. quantum physics) the more can be explained to support OBEs. In contrast; psychologists remain notably sceptical. OBE reports clash with established theories of mind. And some elements can be explained as symptoms of recognised diagnoses within the field.

Spiritual Theories about OBEs suggest that an ethereal body/soul can explore free from a physical host. Some stay within the host's environment, and some may wander as wide as the universe stretches. The main body of work here is the millions of anecdotal accounts by those with experience, the patterns of similarities between accounts, and a lack of previous forms of altered consciousness. Some people additionally speak of shifting to alternate planes of existence (via astral travel - or intentional

OBE). The theories traditionally used to address spiritual aspects originate in religious doctrine, occultism (supernatural practises outside of religion/science), ancient meditative practice, parapsychology or spiritual monism (the idea that spirit is the one true reality, nothing exists outside of it).

Whichever theories fall closest to your view; OBEs have always captured the imagination and so have been well-researched and documented.

My personal experience had an intuitive/spiritual flavour. So the challenge is to represent that subtlety; paradoxically through the solidness of language.

The setting is late night as I retire for the day.

Out-Of-Body, Out Of Mind:
As I sink heavily into familiar sheets,
With this imperfect body,
And humblest power;
I plead for a break from all humanness.
My energy is spent
My heart is knotted by a hundred dilemmas
And my mind runs hot and fast.

I feel myself drifting unusually quickly,
My thoughts start to slip;
Orphaned

Dispersing into vapour.

But now what is this?

My full form floating parallel
Gazing down upon me.
Not sickly or translucent; but clearly me
Elevated,
Soulfully-absorbing,
Indulging me in
Safe,
Solid,
Silence.

In the blink of an eye – a switch in position

I now observe my static body,
From up high.
Why am I wearing a glowing, white nightdress ?
Why is everything doused in crisp, blue-white hues ?

I have never felt so potently...
Awake
There is a white cord connected at the naval
And I look at my hands,
Wiggling my fingers tentatively;
This higher me responds naturally.

Someone is tending to me, but who ?
Do they realise that I am wandering ?

And then it occurs to me that I must be free,
Independent of my body,
Light as fluid silk,
Gently 'at one' with all creation.

And this newfound state is elegant;
Exquisitely pure.
I feel dynamic and happy;
Celebrating my body.
Vividly fresh,
Sheltered from worry,
Clear as mountain rain
Released from time.

And passionately purposeful.
Expanding through the heart,
Unconditionally loving the woman below;
Wanting to hold her secure
And let her know how magical she is.

Alas - It is just a mere taste...

As I return to my body,
So the sadness creeps ever in;
And the brain pushes to forecast,
And the body is so much heavier than before.

But now I hold sunshine in my heart,
And the knowledge of a sweet truth;
There is a me that belongs elsewhere,
Or
Everywhere.

And the love wells over,
And the tears begin to flow.

*Sources:

https://theconversation.com/youve-had-an-out-of-body-experience-but-what-kind-12765

http://news.bbc.co.uk/1/hi/health/6960612.stm

Seven Hidden Treasures Within Empath Overwhelm

By Johannah Stirzaker

Please note - This chapter contains supplementary information (on empath types, benefits of spiritual support, energy protection and empowerment techniques). These concepts were introduced in, 'A Love Letter For Empaths' (chapter eleven in 'Authenticity and Us', 2021, Youier Media).

Who This Chapter Is For

This chapter is intended as educational, supportive and uplifting. It is for anyone it resonates with - for empaths addressing overwhelm, anyone who provides empath support, or those who feel called to understand us better.

Many concepts in this piece can be flexed for use with general overwhelm. Or considerations surrounding neuro-divergence (i.e. being perceived as different from, 'the norm'). I hope there is enough inspiration here to motivate personal quests for resolution.

Introduction - Overwhelm Brings Empath Instincts To The Foreground

In this world, nothing is certain except death, taxes, and regular empath overwhelm (* see Sources section).

Empath overwhelm has two major components - what is experienced as personal, and what is absorbed from the external world. The state is much deeper (and more complex) than generic forms. Empaths can feel invalidated if its mechanics aren't discussed and accepted in public narrative.

Overwhelm (nervous energy, plus stasis) and love (healing, plus creation) are vibrationally opposite. Worries dissolve within a compassionate, soulful space. An empath's instinct is to generate healing resonance wherever suffering arises.

If overwhelm is accepted as a bi-product of human existence; there is an abundance for empaths to experience. And an even greater supply of free-flowing love for balancing purposes. Love raises empath energies - making us vibrate effervescently. We share this treasure fluidly during public service.

Recently, overwhelm has been increasing at an alarming rate. This affects all living beings; placing higher demands on empaths. But what is the actual purpose of suffering? Can we view it with ease (despite the challenges arising from such a complex experience)? How can we leave each consecutive episode fortified, shaking off any detritus that clings to us?

This chapter will reveal seven, fresh treasures within empath overwhelm. Helping us to instinctively flip our focus. We can invite light and support in (even in our darkest throes).

Suffering overwhelm need not blunt empath zestiness. We are warriors at heart. We can lean into the experience, to find the seeds by which light grows. This process fosters effective prevention against further episodes. This aligns with an empath instinct (that of converting pain to thriving).

I have been an empath for forty-six years and I'm still learning. I may help by sharing some humble musings. I already advocate for you, and all you represent. There are other supportive empaths and sentient beings here on Earth too. If you are of a transcendental persuasion; there is unlimited assistance (from spirit/the universe) to rely upon too.

Overwhelm is a 'state of being'. And no state is 'set in stone' as an empath. Keeping our minds and hearts flexible is pleasurable and prevents inertia. Testing what we perceive through our senses encourages mental suppleness. We can forge our own path out of overwhelm - by turning the 'sensory dial' down and the 'creative' one up. Empaths are experts at doing these mini-tweaks for healthier outcomes.

To demonstrate what a good 'team player' your creativity is; imagine this scene...

In the first version, light rides like a message-in-a-bottle. On an ocean of tempestuous waves, devious undercurrents and gritty splashbacks. We are set adrift in the ocean, anticipating we will drown. The clouds part. A knife of golden light breaks through, targeting a scoured bottle which has just bobbed within arm's reach. A coincidence? Or an intervention…?

Society's conditioning celebrates the dramatic stories from the sea. And the frailty of our mortality. The outlook here is always acutely-focused on the ominous. How could we ever survive against such catastrophic forces?

Take a moment to observe any sensations created internally right now?

An empath will not accept end-of-the-road scenarios. So let's flip this wholesomely.

In version two, empaths are adept wave-riders. We appreciate that fighting nature results in exhaustion and solitude. We focus on gratitude for this adventure - visualising engaged faces as we share our tales later. We feel at one with the playfulness and feisty energy of the sea. Buoyant in the belief that we weren't born to drown in wild waters. Empaths have profound instincts (as expert survivalists). That bottle has your name on it. Roll harmoniously with the waves to collect your prize. Every atom of the sea (and the planetary wisdom it holds) already flows within us. We are mighty through this oneness with nature.

The message in the bottle begins to unfurl…

'Thank you for trusting me! We were always holding you up. The storm is calming, The shore awaits you'.

How does your energy feel now? How does switching perspective improve your ability to assist yourself and others?

Now, let's become acquainted with some situations in which a fresh perspective is warranted…

Examples Of What Empath Overwhelm May Look Like - From The Outside

Please note - monitor changes that are atypical for your empath friends. Every empath is unique. There is zero will to type-cast here. All points below are felt by all seven empath types detailed in 'Authenticity And Us'. Where an example is particularly prevalent within an empath group, this is indicated.

- Avoiding human contact (e.g. changing social plans, spending time with pets at parties) – Fauna / Emotional Empath
- Becoming uncontactable
- Retreating to low-stimulation spaces for increasing periods (silence, darkness, relaxed cyber spaces) - Emotional / Physical Empath
- Blank stares mid-conversation / losing direction mid-sentence - Emotional / Intuitive Empath
- Solemnity / Loss of humour - Heyoka Empath
- Physical aches and pains - Physical / Fauna / Emotional Empath
- Disturbance / neglect in bodily routines, appetites or essential self-care
- Unable to think 'on their feet' / responsively
- Difficulty completing everyday tasks
- Loss of unique personality / responding using another's feelings or ideas -Emotional Empath
- Procrastination / lack of drive
- Atopic syndromes of immunity and skin (eczema, psoriasis, hives, new allergies etc.)

- Autoimmune disorder symptoms (swollen glands, joint pain, swelling, digestive dysfunction etc.)
- Regular forgetfulness or 'fogginess'
- Preoccupation with dream messages during waking hours/insomnia -Dream Empath
- Obsessional tendencies due to anxiety

Examples Of How Empaths May Experience Overwhelm - On The Inside

- Emotional noise - dissonant thoughts and feelings (frustration, confusion, anger etc.)
- Inability to rest mentally, trailing thoughts, rumination
- Not being in control of bodily reactions ('hypo.' or 'hyper.' states tripped subconsciously)
- Flightiness – lack of grounding
- Fragmented thought processes
- Need to distract self to feel productive
- Self-sabotaging behaviours/addictive tendencies
- Fatigue that extends between mind, body and soul
- Conflicting priorities and feeling 'pulled in all directions'
- Personal mission/objectives obscured

- Dissociation from emotions / physical sensations
- (C)PTSD symptoms or trauma responses

Empath overwhelm is not officially noted in the DSM**, but is widely-recognised on professional front-lines. It warrants separate validation, because of the level of extraneous information we absorb via our talents. We function well - even at high levels of internal overwhelm. It may not be evident externally until it reaches 'fever pitch'. Because of this, empaths must focus on emotional self-regulation, proactive care and asking for support well before saturation.

Now, let's dip into the seven hidden treasures within empath overwhelm....

1. Empath overwhelm is a natural response to how we contain and process information. Therefore, it is nothing to be ashamed of.

Overwhelm is integral to operating as an empath. We are free to express personal overwhelm - including the bits that come from our unique dispositions. We have as much right to be understood as everyone else.

There are no rules about being introverted / extroverted in our community. Outwardly, some empaths possess omniversion (or the ability to wander around the scale; dependent on situation). However, many initially process the world inwardly - so technically class as introverts.

All empath types absorb more information from the world than average. We process on a much deeper level too. We remain thirsty right up to the point of overwhelm.

Internally; the mechanics of processing mean we can complete a phenomenal workload supported by:

- heightened sensitivity / reactivity and an enhanced central nervous system (e.g. more mirror neurons in the brain)
- lightening-fast sensory feedback
- unique gating in information processing highways
- heightened sensitivity to neurotransmitters / electromagnetism
- enhanced neuroplasticity (re-routing of connections in gray matter)

Want to find out more? Info. can be found following links around 'the neuroscience of empaths' online.

The lines between what information is, 'mine', 'yours' and 'the universe's' are amalgamated as we receive. Messages come from multiple senses (including extrasensory perception). The level/frequency at which our neurological gates open demonstrate a divergent way of receiving, and lead to richly-textured oversights.

We may be less discriminating about what we consciously absorb; knowing our latter processing capacities. But this can mean we have competing information to trawl through. If we don't secure time to do this, receiving can feel progressively like bombardment. This is the way that we process naturally:

- all receivers open
- an overwhelming mess
- superb sorting
- big insights

The rewards are the level of observation, deep, meaningful input and genius we unearth by connecting the dots.

When you are talking to an empath, you are connecting with someone who is mentally vigorous. In addition to standard information elicited from conversing, we are energetically alight for every other type of communication : non-verbal cues, intuition, energetic resonance, spiritual message, environmental fluctuation etc. Sometimes we 'push the envelope' and our expendable capacity for functioning will reduce as we seek something really tasty ! At points our pot bubbles over and we shift to 'overwhelm mode'.

An empath's energetic purpose on Earth is one of transmuting the sting that comes with existential experience. We are protectors; somewhat hyper-vigilant around inconsistencies. Always seeking innovative views. We are highly responsible and immensely loyal. Due to multi-processing, we are skillful diplomats. We contain situations until the time comes for them to naturally unfurl.

For complex/multi-faceted situations there will be tension in holding space and confidentiality. Embracing this is a compassionate practice. We can either release information with immediacy (e.g. 'I've a thought coming through at the moment...') or when we have everything tied up/transmuted.

Empaths are given this huge capacity to contain because we are strong, and gifted with every type of intelligence to multitask on streams of info.

Empowered/developed empaths are those who have embraced living and working in their full empath glory. They monitor their containment levels, get selective about what they absorb, contain only as long as necessary, and release minutiae frequently.

2. Empath overwhelm is a nudge to pause... and get a prevention plan together

Personal overwhelm sobers us up to what isn't working : that we require more relaxation, that perfectionism is thwarting action, that we are stifling creative flow in our heart space, that we are over-committing with little energy... These instances are solid rationales for an overwhelm prevention plan.

To plan, we need to secure a pause for decompression - time off, delegation, stepping away from screens, or curbing that needless to-do list. The aim is to let thoughts/feelings naturally process; until creativity reinvigorates you.

Preventative action ideally would become central to our lifestyle. It can be delivered perpetually, and in sympathetic degrees (even when blissfully happy and when life is liquid gold!)

To remain healthy and empowered; empaths require daily self-care (of some description). We are susceptible to negative vibrations and need to ensure that we generate balance. This means an active search, based on knowing ourselves and what makes us feel level and nourished. To aim for equilibrium isn't just 'nice'; it is essential for anyone who exchanges energy with others.

Suggestions for preventative activities could be :

- Letting go of energy that is not ours / is destructive / is redundant
- Psychology, gratitude or dream journal routines
- Grounding visualisations / Earthing rituals
- Using social feeds to procure healthy relationships, share good news and support channels
- Activities that foster catharsis / collaborative problem-solving
- Mindfulness and taking joy in the present
- Memory, puzzles and concentration training
- Physical exercise
- Sexual (self) pleasure
- Beauty / grooming regimes
- Reconnection with nature and animal friends
- Enjoying an empath / soul-based community
- Self-development exercises
- Energy re-balancing activities (Reiki, Ta Chi, Breathwork, Yoga..)
- Time in total silence - either for silence's sake or to process

- Listening/dancing to music that matches your mood
- Development of intuitive/paranormal/caring/intellectual skills
- Fun/chillout times with friends
- Healing work on trauma (reduction of triggers, parenting the inner child, forgiveness practices, accessing professional support)
- Reducing caffeine or stimulant intake

A prevention plan can start with dedicating a regular slot daily - so that we can nurture ourselves (I secure meetings with myself in my business diary). If you are frantically busy; maybe ten minute bursts during break times would suit?

Some activities will resonate, 'clear as a bell' with you. What makes you excited and joyful? These are the adventures you are called to play with. This trying of new things is an investment in knowing ourselves and the talents we were given. It also helps counteract overwhelm inertia. The plan is to spend as much of the day as you can in re-energising states. Activities that treat yourself for being ace!

With conscious effort; an awareness of individual self returns. With energetic knowledge, we can adjust our chakra balance/

presentation so that we are more discriminating about what we absorb. And if we feel heavy-hearted; we can visualise restorative, soothing energy around that chakra. We can protect the results by switching to more mind-based/factual activities.

It is healthy to keep more to ourselves when we are depleted. We can decide how light our conversations will be, who it is best to avoid/would sap us or those to spend brief bursts with only. This skill also demands reflection around 'people-pleasing' behaviour and how we apportion our time. We need to protect our internal batteries - to be anchored to the earth, and of service to others.

Empaths are disproportionately represented in abuse recovery programmes. Many have to convert these uneasy histories. We benefit from evaluating who/what triggers our sad stories. As well as engaging in deep healing work, we can use the pain of injustice to firm boundaries up. No-one has permission to exhaust us without giving back, to use abusive tactics or monopolise our time. It's wise to observe energies from a distance before engaging. Initial intuitive feel can guide us on whether a person may disrespect our resources longer term.If we protect our sacred energies; we can increase that power to wrap it around others. We can instill safety in our presence.

3. Empath overwhelm encourages us to find healthy support systems

Being an empath is a super-demanding lifestyle. We feel most of the happiness, tension and sorrowful vibes around us. Empath overwhelm holds a mirror up to collective suffering and joy. That's a massive amount of energy for one person to reflect. Instead of persistently giving, it is healthy for empaths to request reciprocation and understanding. Let's get used to receiving with grace. The universe is there for our bidding - with friends and resources for every venture.

Now is a hot time to seek out empath support. Avenues are developing thick and fast internationally. The world is awakening to our purpose and the skills we harness. I sense a welcome blossoming - after the longest winter!

Finding support systems can be part of our self-actualisation process (the desire to rise to full potential). We can begin fostering relationships with loving people, who lift spirits. A soul family can be life-seasoned, authentic and focused on well-being. They may celebrate others; looking for opportunities to contribute positively to the world. We could contact them (from whatever level of overwhelm we are at) trusting they will donate sage wisdom.

What are the important qualities that you would want from supporters?

Candidly, asking for help is something I have had to work on. I lean towards hyper-independence. I get a major buzz from being altruistic. Like many old souls before me; I have hard-won life lessons (and served many others in crisis). Our resilience is smoking hot ! Empaths are Earth Warriors and accustomed to righting personal overwhelm multiple times per week. Learning to succeed against our overwhelm makes us (and by proxy the whole of society) more empowered. We are great at role-modeling this.

But who are our support systems for those times we receive a curveball? Or are just below ebb?

Examples could be :

- Empath authors with 'empowerment' strategies
- Digital empath summits, webinars and podcasts
- Online empowered empath and HSP (Highly Sensitive People) communities
- Social media lightworker communities (lightworkers are spiritually awakened

beings that are called to serve humanity/ the planet for higher purposes)

- Traditional counseling, occupational health and psychology services
- Spiritual communities (all denominations, or none)
- Friends, work colleagues and those who receive us authentically
- Any soul connections you create for yourself
- Hobby/leisure groups
- Nature (as the omnipresent grounding force)
- Pets and animals (who can be empaths too)

When we access help, we can communicate authentically. It is important that supporters have an understanding of how empaths operate. Strong communities have clear rules and a positive bias. We also need to monitor our networks, so that codependency (a learned behaviour where relationships are one-sided, emotionally destructive, or abusive) is avoided.

It would be remiss of me not to mention the amount of support that is available if you choose to pursue spiritual avenues/higher consciousness too. The benefits of this offering were covered in detail in, 'A Love Letter For

Empaths' in 'Authenticity and Us'. To avoid unnecessary repetition, below is a precis of what this provides :

- Respite from the norm – 'change is as good as a rest' (Old English Proverb c.1825)***
- Healing love and peace
- Total belonging and oneness
- Consciousness expansion
- Divine guidance / intervention
- Ancestral wisdom and collective consciousness (universal wisdom)
- Personal integration (important in terms of both mental health and power)
- Freedom from / expansion of time
- Synchronicity / flow states for creativity and resourcing
- Clarification in times of codependent enmeshment / conflicting priorities

I would encourage empaths to research their developmental needs; letting the universe / spirit manifest pathways to exactly what they need. The process of finding the best support is a skill in itself. It helps us to decipher our evolutionary path; putting us in alignment with soul resonance.

4. Personal experience of overwhelm awakens us to what human suffering is about. We can then offer relevant/practical wisdom to those conquering it.

Question: *'Hello overwhelm, what new insights do you have for me?'*

Pain breeds compassion. Empaths are masters at rescuing resources from 'the shadows'. We can own our overwhelm–rather than it owning us. We understand the complexities of this condition and how to unpick from its clutches. Everyday overwhelm alone (uncomfortable as it is) will never extinguish our fire.

What are you focused on in life? Because the empath's internal world is transient; we anchor to dependable notions. We understand that overwhelm may come from over-attachment to money, possessions, fake happiness and other soul-wilting devices. Overwhelm (if left untethered) breeds itself - becoming quicker, greedier, and knotted.

Self-compassion invites us to stick to 'the purest stuff'. Only weathering overwhelm for as long as it takes to rescue lessons for body, mind and soul. We have a deeper purpose for which we need to be free.

We can choose to embrace suffering wisely as a way to outsmart it. This is the nature of learning to suffer well (sifting without barriers, getting knee-deep in mud to expel the debris).If you kick a bull, it will kick you back harder. Therefore, overwhelm is often resolved patiently via a series of mini-coaxes.

There are elements within each episode which are meant to decompose and fall away without our effort. These become a fertiliser for better things to blossom. Restful insight helps us to elucidate what we need to focus on next.

Once the initial sting and shredding has gone, I encourage empaths to become their own witness; leaning into aspects of their story for concentrated periods.

When we deconstruct any dilemma, we get to play with what we thought we should avoid. We can test the material to destruction. We can pull the rug from under its ominous influence, shattering any solid core. We can pluck out elements that have become enmeshed. Or demarcate which strands are heart-based and which are extraneous thoughts. We can enquire :

- How can I change the feel of this material so that I am more comfortable spending time with it?
- How wide do the real problems spread?

- If we throw overwhelm up in the air; does it have breathing spaces within?
- What order do the pieces fall back to Earth? (relative priority / weight).

We can also deconstruct through artwork and cathartic practice. Empaths react in exceedingly deep ways. Please entertain the idea of being totally unreserved in private. Expel that energy (in fine art, the spoken word, screamed into the wind, punched through cushions...) Whatever serves your purge. Note any questions, phrases or visuals that escape during this release. No judgment, no repressing the gnarly stuff… just everything pure and honoured as it is.

Then, maybe develop these flows by flipping to find creative solutions one branch at a time. Invest time in peeling back each layer until the remnants left feel 'doable'. Things become manageable once pinned concretely. The repeated nature of ruminating makes our worries magnified. A week's worry may only fill half a page - or could be released in a few minutes of swearing with gusto!

The conclusion of session(s) could land on how you could adjust this exercise for demonstration to another. This becomes an empath resource.

When many people feel overwhelmed; they prefer to know that you understand what being overpowered feels like. They may want to get snotty, to express unsociable notions or speak seemingly 'irrationally'. You can offer a humble presence for their authentic voice of pain (to validate, to strip it back, to foster release). Because empaths have repeatedly conquered their own overwhelm (and have rapport in stacks) they are brilliant to talk to from all degrees of vulnerability.

In my experience, many people present at support services because they have been past overwhelm for some time. And have such a volume of thought that it's compromising brain function. They desire to be thoroughly heard, and to 'think out loud'. They may need encouragement to forget forecasting (an anxiety provoker). They can't change the past; but today could be an excellent step in a new direction. When clarity is compromised, they may also need assistance to prioritise an action plan. They may be surprised at the variety of suitable options they have. We can help them recognise inbuilt talents, work through barriers to progress and inspire engagement with issues through a mix of core (and fun) activities.

5. Empath overwhelm and happiness are not separate entities. Negative overwhelm can be the key to opening positive overwhelm and calmness

Question: *'How would you feel if your view of the world during overwhelm (unjust, noisy, draining...) was the only, definitive, interpretation available? How would that affect your motivation for recovery?*

Overwhelm is meant as a gateway state. At the crossroads, let's survey examples of philosophical thinking we could use. Wider study of how different cultures view human suffering is worth an empath's time/effort.

Firstly, taking the concept that there are 'good' and 'bad' states. The universe holds everything in homoeostasis (a delicate, dualist balance between creation and destruction). All 'negative' ways must therefore have an equal, 'positive' state. This could aid in 'quick switching' in sticky situations. Our minds literally turn to, 'What is the opposite of this?' or 'Where is the opportunity for love here?' After a switch we are better company to be with. We proactively change how we feel about things. It moves us into a higher vibration, and closer to positive resources/people which manifest through synchronicity (where the universe/ higher powers conspire to support us).

An alternative view is that all situations presented are neither ‘happy’ nor ‘sad’. But occur in a neutral state. We can then choose the perception we attach to them. In this concept, negative overwhelm flows amalgamated with its positive counterpart. A 'scale of happiness' does not exist. Just a fluid collection of transitory experiences. To capture the good we must be truly mindful. In a ‘present’ state, we rescue 'pockets of joy' interspersed within overwhelm. Using musical metaphor; these act as natural 'beat drops' in the drumming of life. We can breathe a sigh of relief, forget worry and re-evaluate what needs doing in the rests.

Empath states cover everything negative, positive and inbetween. We can experience supreme ecstasy in the simplest of things. We shed 'happy tears' through acts of kindness, amidst belly laughing, transcending through fantastic sex, or go blissfully silent when embraced by magnificence in nature. This ability to flex in all directions makes us highly-sophisticated, emotional characters. A key question could be, ‘Where will my pockets of joy be today?’. When they come, take a few moments to savour their flavour and offer gratitude.

If you are part of a soul-based community; the sharing of fresh joy becomes manifold. And so the sunshine meter keeps bobbing up. Ping!

6. Empath overwhelm encourages us to re-assess how and when we practice our talents

The empath community is diverse and multi-talented. Our gifts are so embedded in our core, that we may forget to pause to praise the cool selection of talents offered through us. With universal gifting, comes big responsibilities about how we foster and share them. We benefit from an oversight of our toolkit. It supports gratitude and allows us to choose whichever skill(s) will be the most effective for each situation. Conscious matching fosters higher vibrations, and lets the universe work its magic.

We can consider overwhelm thresholds before offering support. Both for the receiver and ourselves. We can meditate and observe our energy levels, so that we don't over-stretch.

When considering supporting others; we could plump for a less effort-sapping skill for lengthy projects. Or an intuitive, deep dive for time-bound transformation. If a competency does not sit well with someone (e.g. if 'clair' abilities/paranormal gifts scare them; we may choose another expertise which will not cause overwhelm). Choosing intelligently secures consent, keeps love looping between us, and offers the receiver an extra boost during transition.

There are decisions around teaming skills together. How are our aptitudes similar? How do they overlap? Is there one that stands out as being particularly unique? Complimentary skills add breadth and speed to responses.

Boundary-setting is essential for self-care. We can reserve time to dedicate to talent development. Pre-planning with others helps enable full concentration for practice, reflection and recuperation.

Deeper, intuitive activities require us to deal with personal overwhelm first. We want to come to the table clear and ready to serve. Intuitive empaths have a natural propensity for transcendental experimentation. This must be accompanied with grounding/a practical focus to stop us 'drifting away'.

The more we practice, the more exquisite the talents become. The greater the subtlety in using them. The stronger the public support for empath work.

7. Finally, discussing our overwhelm reveals subtle empath differences. It encourages community engagement with diversity

There are numerous ways that empaths react to everyday occurrences differently. As a society, there are chances to learn from this when it presents itself. This may involve asking, 'I've noticed your...reaction. What is going on for you right now?'

All people have the right to have their individual needs considered. Empaths contribute massively as advocates for others, but may feel awkward about doing that for ourselves. We can take charge of narrating our internal worlds.

Many empaths filter out less external stimulation than most people. We generate internal energy to meet demand. However, we may feel overwhelmed by experiences that the public would consider 'normal' (or even pleasurable).

For non-empaths, here are a few examples where you may find empaths subtly diverse. And for empaths, these responses are common and explainable.

Empaths are biologically, genetically, emotionally and spiritually equipped to experience more out of everyday things.

Activities, environments and advertising (designed to be sensational) may produce sensory/energetic overload. Empaths can be reactive to : loud noises, get headaches under bright lights, hide behind cushions (for horror films, hospital scenes, or acts of aggression), vomit from pungent aromas or visualising disgust, may feel suffocated in crowded corridors, or panicked in busy areas.

The power of over-stimulation can feel very jarring. As well as flushing raw emotions to the surface; it can cause 'fight, flight, freeze or fawn' survival reactions.

We may limit activities where these reactions could happen - or flinch in the presence of them (a flinch inwards increases space between the stimulus and our internal core). This protects sensibilities from being engulfed. Others may work on de-sensitisation (through exposure to stimuli) or maintaining a wide lifestyle with additional calming practices.

For emotional and intuitive empaths; parties, shopping malls, and cinemas may produce stress. There are crowds of people, differing vibrations, and complex stories. Venues tend to be extra noisy and have 'competing' sounds (how it feels with less filters) - a melee of voices, music and movement. These are often built to excite/invite chatter (which makes for a very cluttered mind space). Cognitive overload may serve as a motivator to withdraw to areas of less stimulation periodically. If you receive intuitive advice during overload (e.g. ‘'This place is not right for me'. 'Step away from the screen' or 'I need quiet') these are messages from body, spirit and brain.

Many empaths are also highly interoceptive (consciously aware of signals generated within their internal organs). We are aware of sensations that should be subconscious. And understand which feelings match which biological/physiological processes: how blood pulses in different regions, changes in temperature, when valves shut off in the body, what level of fullness their organs hold etc. Because of this, there are anecdotes of us being more sensitive to alcohol, everyday stimulants and medication. With prescriptions we may require less dosage than would be recommended for our body type/weight. We observe every change caused by medicine and provide detailed opinions when feeding back to practitioners.

With training, we are brilliant at offering advice and guidance in this area. Many empaths have healing skills in their blood. We have intimate knowledge of how recovery is optimal when mind, body and spirit are integrated.

Conclusion

Empath overwhelm is :

1. A bi-product of how we naturally process the world
2. Supported by amazing, internal physiology
3. A resource for our healing missions on Earth

All empaths utilise conscious and subconscious gifts to unravel both personal overwhelm, and states experienced by others. This process is exercised through mind, body and spirit.

Empath overwhelm is not discussed nearly enough and this affects both public understanding and support available. Too many empaths struggle privately; feeling they will be judged or shamed for experiencing overwhelm uniquely. This is a missed opportunity to support those who support us. To perform at our best, empaths require allies to ask open questions. So we can be seen as we are.

A healthy response to our overwhelm is to embrace it compassionately, observe all facets within, and release any complexities through diverse techniques. We are only ever one philosophy / perspective switch away from accessing 'pockets of joy' within.

As part of personal empowerment, empaths benefit from investigating what overwhelms us and how we can deal with that earlier/more effectively.

Every empath has a personal onus to discover what works for them. And to find complementary resources that feel fantastic!

I dedicate this chapter to every empath that has been there when needed. Every person who has trusted me with their voice of overwhelm. And every loving insight that bursts forth from stillness.

About Johannah Stirzaker

Johannah Stirzaker is a UK-based Empath Lightworker. She has over thirty years experience in serving the public. She creates bespoke services through one-to-one consultation and brokerage. She holds an honourary Bachelor of Arts with Qualified Teaching Status. Her post-graduate training is multi-disciplinary. She has had careers in Teaching, Children's Home Management, Abuse Recovery, Behavioural Modification, SEND Advocacy, Management of Information, Advice and Guidance Teams, Community Redevelopment Work (in Italy) and Holistic Therapies.

Through many years of working as a professional 'single point of contact' for those in crisis; she has experience in wellness services (e.g. Neuro-Linguistic Programming, Drug and Alcohol Counseling, Health Advocacy, Homelessness Welfare, Personal Training...) She became CPCAB Counselor-Certified in 2009. Then added Holistic Therapies a year later. She's an active Member of the Federation of Holistic Therapists. More recently, a spiritual awakening has led to an Usui Reiki Mastership and Animal Reiki Practitioner Status.

Joh runs an active Facebook page for those who value empaths or seek light-affirming connections. This is supported by an international bevy of mental health professionals, empowered empaths, life coaches, fitness and well-being experts, artists, therapists, lightworkers, fellow entrepreneurs, healers, and life-long friends.

Links:

https://www.facebook.com/johannah.stirzaker - first port of contact, to reach Joh. on Messenger, or to see if you would like to become a friend to the community.

Sources:

* Benjamin Franklin's letter to French physicist Jean-Baptiste Le Roy (13/11/1789). Quote, '...in this world, nothing is certain except death and taxes'.

** Diagnostic and Statistical Manual of Mental Disorders – a regularly updated text used by health professionals to diagnose mental health pathologies.

*** Old British Proverb from, 'Christian Gleaner and Domestic Magazine' (c.1825).

Escaping Your Personal Narcatraz

By Adriann Meyer

A place of suffocating overwhelm no one should remain in. Writing this chapter in a book about overwhelm was difficult and liberating. Difficult because, as a man, I am not supposed to be talking about feelings and emotions. Doing so is almost like breaking a sacred code that men don't feel or suffer or hurt. We keep quiet and die young. Life is supposed to be like that: "He's a man, let him suffer" are words I got to hear several times.

The exercise was also liberating. In the teaching is the healing. Liberating in the sense that I can see my thoughts on paper where they evoke less feeling and emotion rather than rattling around in my head.

Why talk about overwhelm in the context of narcissism?

Relationships are complicated things, even when life is very good. When you encounter personality pathology in such a relationship it becomes a race to the bottom. It might be a slow simmer, a marathon or it might be a sprint. But it's going to go to the bottom and that is the way that narcissistic relationships work.

One of the fastest-growing dysfunctions in the world is narcissism. Being self-centred, self-obsessed, and entitled is a growing reality stemming from the way children are brought up to the way education rewards children's behaviour.

Then there are the people, who have to deal with narcissists. who suffer in one way or another. The nature of Narcissism varies from the occasional bout to a full-blown personality disorder.

Many people are hurt in the relationship process. I've seen over the last few years studying and understanding the concept of narcissism, not just inexperienced personal relationships, but within the business context and within a small business context and how it ruins businesses because of one or two people.

There is no good news in such a relationship with a family or business.

It consumes people. People lose their way. People lose identity as they are systematically erased into nothingness. In today's parlance that is called 'canceling'. Then, when they are discarded, they must go back and reinvent themselves while trying to make sense of life while life does not make sense.

They end up with a blank page and no crayons, while the examination supervisor is standing in front of them asking. "What is wrong with you?" Can't you draw?

All this while they are often suffering from severe trauma. The world does not understand them. And those who understand it choose not to talk about it because it is just too crazy.

Deliberate Crazy Making

When you encounter a narcissist over extended periods in a personal relationship you encounter "crazy-making"

Some of the highlights of behaviours you will encounter:

Gaslighting:

This is a crazy-making technique where you begin to doubt your sanity. You are made to believe that your thinking is wrong, and you are crazy. The Narc insists that you said something that you know you didn't.

They twist events around in such a way that you come out guilty. When you speak up you will be attacked or called too sensitive. Lying is quite natural to Narcs and if you confront them about their lies, they simply never said what you are claiming they said.

Future Faking:

This is a technique to manipulate people into doing the narc's bidding by promising them a future event if they would just hang in there. This happens when the narc begins to suspect that the other person is going to leave. Promises that never materialise such as getting married, having a baby, going travelling, etc. Like getting engaged but then you realise it is fake because the only people who know about the engagement are you and her. Long afterwards you realise that you were just the entertainment department.

Apologies:

A fake (faux) apology is meant to give you a false sense of security.

Ghosting:

Ghosting happens when the partner disappears and leaves the other to struggle, sometimes cutting them off from funds and resources so that they starve.

The person will disappear for a long period and then blame you for them leaving. They might be in the house with you but you hardly see them and if you do the encounter is often quite crazy-making.

The list goes on and on but the above are the most prevalent with the people I have spoken to and in my own experience.

In the end, you end up here:

You look in the mirror, but you can't see what is there. The person looking back at you is an alien. The shadow of what you used to be, the remnants of a frazzled nervous system.

It took a while for the gentle waves to become a tsunami. It took, in the end, that Lifequake to devastate the remainder of what was your carefully crafted identity.

A Lifequake can take many forms. Sudden calamity, loss of a career, failure of a business etc, shakes the foundations of who we are because we build so much of our identity around what we do. Sometimes investing lifetimes in a relationship and then being discarded.

Now you feel like… nothing, no one.

Invisible, except to the demons taunting you as your dream evaporates.

You still wanted to… but now you can't. Doubt turns into panic and the bills keep on coming. You can't even remember where "that one" came from.

During the last two years or so everyone on earth has been touched by the shifting tectonic plates that were life before CV19.

Career and life plans went up in smoke as did so many relationships when people found themselves in lockdown together. With nothing to distract them from their busy lives, they had to sit at home with a person whom they didn't know, as they progressively found out. The person who came out when the chips went down was not the person they knew or wanted to be around for the rest of their lives.

My second rude awakening to narcissism

For many years I was aware of the concept of narcissism before it became "a thing".

I encountered the behaviour in every place I worked but I learned to dance this dance of validation and "marble polishing" (strategic sucking up) while keeping my distance and not getting sucked into the vanity vortex.

In big business, the trick is to find out what the bosses want and to make sure they get that. In business, it is all about the numbers. When we produced the numbers, the bosses looked good. This is how simple it is. I was never a "marble polisher" but it was easy to know which buttons to push. The good thing is that I could go home after a day at the corporate circus.

But this was different. I was in a long-term relationship of about 14 years. Everything was OK if my partner didn't experience any pressure.

When she did, she would change her personality into someone quite vicious. Details are not important but suffice to say, a costly mistake of making life-changing decisions while in a rage.

The dreams of a life in Austria and the relationship "until death do us part" ended with two suitcases, a train ticket and a flight home to South Africa.

I had no idea what was coming but I learned something that would later allow me to speak to and help other people begin overcoming their ordeal of being in a narcissistic relationship.

What is narcissism?

Narcissism is not a person; it is a collective state of consciousness completely taken over by the life-diminishing states of consciousness. This state is also the prevailing state in much of the business world where everything superficial gets praise and promotion. Greed is good and it is "never personal" even though it often is, most viciously so.

Your life is an expression of consciousness and the state of consciousness you are expressing determines the quality of your life experience. Fear driven consciousness is life diminishing and loves powered consciousness is life-enhancing.

80% of the world lives in fear. No wonder the world is a mess.

Of the three main categories of consciousness expression; health, wealth and relationships, relationships do not matter because they require the characteristics of respect, trust, and communication to work properly. The narcissistic expression expresses disrespect, dishonesty and demeaning and over-dramatic communication to control the partners. Thus, relationships resemble battlegrounds.

The Map of Consciousness gives one an idea. Google it, it is quite easy to find.

The map of consciousness was designed by Dr David Hawkins, a very famous psychiatrist in America. He created the map of consciousness we have today.

The map is a great tool to understand why and how human beings behave the way they do and how they think. We learn how we can move from one state of consciousness to the other, and how we can transcend and regulate our lives.

Every state of consciousness has its own stories, its thoughts, the mindstream that expresses itself through the person and if you lose control of yourself you're just along for the ride.

Recognising a narcissist.

At its most basic the collective consciousness of Narcissism (also known as NPD, Narcissistic Personality Disorder) is characterised by severe self-centeredness, possessiveness, and an inability to conduct relationships without wanting to control everything going on. This brew does not have a conscience and is a law unto itself.

The sad thing is that Narcs usually have very low self-esteem to control and dominate other people to make themselves look and feel better. To a world that only considers the appearance of things and not the substance, Narcissism is acceptable.

But this is not about Narcs. This is about those hundreds of thousands, even millions of people whose identity has been thrashed to a pulp. Those who want to find their way back to themselves.

You have been locked up in a prison in your mind. I call it Narcatraz. This is not a delightful place as many testify.

What does this have to do with Overwhelm?

Give me a minute.

People who escape, yes escape, or find themselves discarded from such a relationship suffer from many, I can only call it a trauma stew.

Severe confusion ensues because you can't believe what happened to you and nobody believes you.

Narcs are expert identity switchers. The world gets the wonderful person, and you get the "behind closed doors" monster version.

After a while, you begin to question your sanity, which is part of a Narc strategy of domination.

The cruelty and abandonment can be unbelievable in some cases.

Continuous gaslighting diminishes the partner sometimes in public.

Disappointments of future faking leaves you not trusting anyone.

The emotional abuse is real, and not all narcs are men.

When you escape or find yourself discarded, the after-departure campaign to discredit you will go on for as long as the Narc can get victim mileage out of it. But it does not go unnoticed, and the trauma bond continues to fester that energetically binds the receiver to the giver.

I do not use the word victim even though victimisation is a standard issue.

The self-judgement that you stayed in the relationship for so long is one of the biggest issues. The "why was I so stupid" can leave many with a sense of numb grief for themselves and the years they wasted.

You are isolated, and no one believes you. The isolation becomes a hermitage if you do not seek out connections with other human beings, quite often new people because you must rebuild connections with other people now. Some people struggle to make sense of how the Narc can just continue with life as if nothing happened. Sensemaking of all of this is not advisable. You will break your head.

It is best to see a psychologist who specialises in trauma, according to the experts.

The overwhelm comes when you must begin functioning in the world while simmering in this misery stew trying to patch up a punctured spirit and rebuild a shattered identity.

When more than one life quake happens at the same time, life gets challenging.

What contributes to the overwhelm?

You are not just hit with a life quake; you also must endure the tsunamis that follow. Sometimes you encounter several tsunamis; financial, finding a new home, starting over, finding a job, all while trying to find yourself again.

The children caught up in the storm suffer also. Their young minds are not always capable of understanding something you cannot explain.

In the end, people are confronted with a very difficult situation from where they must create a new way of being, often starting at the bottom rung of shame and humiliation. But it can be done even if it takes time and certainly effort.

Dealing with the overwhelm

Over time I have found several practical tools and tricks to lift the state of consciousness and encourage myself and others to take the next step in the creation of a new reality even though their senses are overloaded, and their thought world resembles the aftermath of the battle of Waterloo.

Meditation

Meditation is a great tool to settle the mind at a higher state of functioning. Brain entrainment tracks are everywhere on the internet. I used IAWAKE tracks. These tracks grow on you and as you find the ones that work for you, your meditation deepens and becomes richer and more powerful.

Activity

There is nothing like moving your body to get you out of your head and into the body. Here are some additional things you can do when you go for your walk or run.

Decide and declare that you will see the good in the world in everything and everyone you see.

Greet the people you encounter with a smile and make eye contact. This establishes a positive connection that benefits both the giver and the receiver.

Push yourself a bit to get a sense of achievement and it helps to get the system primed for some more good energy.

When you encounter a lot of head noise while walking, practice NO-Mind explained below. The results are amazing as you feel your entire system slow down. In truth, you are confusing your ego and it shuts up for a while.

If you have a tracker on your watch or phone, use it. It gives you a small sense of achievement when you reach your target step count and motivates you to keep going on those days you do not feel like it.

No Mind technique

The no-mind technique is very simple, but in simplicity is power.

When random or spam thoughts begin to surface, use the following technique, to calm your mind.

Let your awareness go down to your heart space and repeat the following phrase with as much feeling as you can muster.

"This is not real" No mind, no mind, no mind.

After a while, you will experience silence as your ego tries to decipher what you are telling it.

You will find that you can walk or run much farther, just by using these phrases, as the thinking mind becomes silent. You will have more energy to do whatever it is you are doing.

Small heart small effort

When you're hurting, your energetic Heart Space can become very small. This is not the time for massive action in any direction. What works quite often is if you ask your heart what it can do now? What can you do now with confidence? What can you finish? What can you celebrate? Find something small to celebrate and do that, even if it is washing those dishes.

Self-forgiveness and self-honour

One of the hardest things you do is self-flagellation. The proclivity to blame yourself, doubt your next word and diminish your worthiness sucks the life right out of you.

When I'm talking about self-forgiveness, I'm talking about the realisation that you are a human being and that you will make mistakes and it is and it is OK.

Honour yourself for being the person that you are. Regardless of the opinion of the other. Honour yourself for still being here even if you're battered and bruised. Every step is a step forward even if you need to take a few steps back to restart. Do not be afraid to recalibrate at a lower level so that you can pick up speed again.

Live smaller for a while, love it and begin to enjoy your own company.

It is quite OK to live smaller for a year or more as you regain your strength. If you are afraid of starting smaller then you are giving other people too much power. Don't care what others think, this is your life.

Going no contact and no exposure.

The idea is to preserve your energy and systematically take back your life. Limiting contact and exposure gives you precious time to shift your energy in a new direction.

YouTube has thousands of videos about narcissism and what it means. Very few are there to assist the people coming out of these relationships.

1. Stop watching narc videos, they all say the same things and you are ripping plasters off raw wounds when you are reminded of what happened to you.

2. Go seriously no contact. No trolling Facebook or Instagram. They know you are watching, and you can be assured there will be sting posts strategically placed to get to you, and they will.

3. Stop trying to defend yourself or explain your side of the story – it is pointless because no one will believe you. Maybe later they will, but not now.

4. Make new friends when the time comes.

5. Unfriend mutuals as far as you can.

6. Do not write soppy or accusative posts; it will fuel the fire.

Control your imagination

Ruminating is giving your imagination permission to roam free. Whatever state of consciousness you are expressing, your imagination will always be from that state, it can't be any different.

When you catch yourself ruminating, remind yourself – "ruminating again"

Directing your imagination in more constructive directions will help you come up with new ideas and speed the healing process along. A lot of healing comes as you begin to express higher states of consciousness.

Direct your mind to start looking for solutions and better ways of doing things. You will be surprised at how your ego will respond because for it to function, it needs recognition and validation. Now you have a tool to give it what it wants while your journey becomes a lot easier. Sounds woo but it works.

Bring the targets closer for some dopamine

Dopamine is a mood lifter and a part of the inner reward system. The dopamine release happens when you are exerting effort towards a goal and not when you achieved the goal. This is neuroscience* Your brain feels good when you are exerting effort towards a goal and wants to make sure that you continue doing more of that.

When you have long term goals you need to exert more effort over longer periods. Thus, the reward is postponed. When you move the goals closer your reward system kicks in faster.

Break large goals into smaller chunks and celebrate every small achievement. As you begin to celebrate more often, the anticipation of the reward starts up the reward system.

*See the work of Hubermann and Andrew Hubermann.

Reconsider stress

Stress tells you something you care about that is not going well. When you experience stress as what it is that is causing the stress and use that energy of the stress response to do something about the thing that is important to you. Do this rather than trying to get rid of the stress. It will be more rewarding.

Break the thoughts up and revise

Thoughts are expressions of consciousness from a particular state of consciousness. What does this mean?

Your thoughts are not your own. They come into your mind courtesy of the state of consciousness. Thoughts present as a thought stream. One thought following on from the other. Quite soon you will become aware of thoughts you didn't conjure up. Fear brings fearful thought streams and joy activates joyful thought streams etc.

Follow these steps in arresting and addressing the thought stream

Ask these questions:

- Is it true?
- If it is true, can you do something about it?

- Even if it is true, is there something else you can do instead?

These questions can occupy your ego nicely so that you can get some work done.

Learn to Imagineer

We are always creating our lives, every moment we are creating. This is how life works. When you learn how to use your imagination as a creative tool, you gain a great sense of power. Imagineering is stronger than what we understand as manifesting. This is creating your life from a grand vision of the future and not from the memories of the past. For this, you need to master your mind. But this is an entire book all by itself.

Simply put you must learn how to see the vision with clarity and in detail. Then you must feel it as if it is already accomplished. Lastly, you must begin to live that person first in your mind and later progressively in reality. The secret is in the feeling of your fulfilled vision. This is how you move mountains.

You are still that person

Remember you are still the person who can do life. People forget who they are when they suffer trauma. A simple exercise you can do to remind yourself is to make a panic list.

It is a list of all the things you do well, has done and your major achievements. Keep this list handy for when you begin doubting yourself or when the Narc gets you to lose faith in who you are after one of their crazy-making episodes.

Kill the little whirlwinds to stop the hurricane

You are going through a storm. Everything adds up and you are overwhelmed. Even small whirlwinds can topple you. So, it is best to deal with the whirlwinds that show up before they find a place in the storm system.

How do you do this? Make a list of known triggers and irritations. Having the list helps you identify when these "storm cells "show up and you can do something about it. The best is to avoid situations where these occur but of course, it is not always possible. Learn then when to depart the scene as fast as possible. Familiar places, invite from mutuals, meetings in places where there is a negative memory.

The Remind Game

Thoughts can drive you crazy. It is not the thing that happened but the thoughts we have about these events. Consciousness tells stories in the form of streams of thoughts presenting themselves for consideration, that is for you to add meaning and attach emotions. Emotion = energy in motion, thus feeling.

When you want to change the energy attached to a thought, access a higher state of consciousness, and bring the event back into your awareness. This is re-minding. But this time do it from a higher state of consciousness. You can use your panic list to remind you of things that brought you joy and satisfaction. Keep this energy active during the process and you might feel the emotion toward an event change. It takes some practice, but it is quite effective to dissolve energy states of fear, humiliation, and anger.

Last Notes

1. Find connections with other people who do not come from your past. Allow yourself to become a part of this new energy and for goodness' sake, don't tell your story to everyone because they will probably not understand you and will label you.
2. This one is tough but valuable. Remember the good things about the person and love that as a memory. It sets you free.
3. Take your time to heal, you have been through a hellish experience that others cannot understand. Don't rush anything and allow yourself the grace and the

peace to find your way back to you. It is also good to have someone who knows what they are doing to walk you home.

Practising the Centring Prayer

The practice of the centring prayer takes you to the place of peace where you can create a life worth living again. It works like this:

1. Download the free centring prayer app on your phone and choose the mode you want to use.
2. Choose a sacred word such as amen, thank you, presence, I receive or whatever word works for you.
3. The practice takes about 20 minutes but you can do it for longer if you wish and as you gain more control over your thoughts.
4. Find a comfortable place where you can sit in silence and relax.
5. Allow whatever thoughts to drift along and do not engage with them. Thus you do not cause a mindstream. As you learn to do this well you will notice thoughts presenting themselves for engagement but when you choose not to engage, the thought will drift along and silence will return. It is like seeing a call coming in on

your phone, seeing the caller ID and not answering the call.

6. Do this sitting in silence for 20 minutes. The app has a timer that will remind you when the time is up.
7. Sit in the silence for a few minutes afterwards
8. Journal whatever comes to your awareness.
9. Do this three times a day.

The Mindful Sighing

This is a tool to deactivate the stress response quickly. When you are in a stressful situation you can't use your mind to calm your mind. Use your body to calm your mind.

Do a full inhale through your nose and then a quick one-second inhale to fill your lungs. Then do a slow exhale through your mouth with a sigh. Do this three times and you will see how quickly you can calm down.

Many blessings.

About Adriann Meyer

Adriann is an explorer of consciousness, a transformational teacher with the gift of healing. His practical work is that of a consciousness coach and consultant helping people create a life worth living and conscious businesses.

Over the years Adriann has developed modalities and practices, workshops, and programs to assist people in the creation of exceptional life experiences of freedom, purpose, and sovereignty.

His studies include psychology, theology, quantum physics and ancient languages among other things. Adriann is also an ordained minister and an author.

What gives Adriann the right to speak about narcissism? He has lived it, all of it. As a mentor told him, now he can walk people out of their own Narcatraz and back home.

Death And Overwhelm

By Charles Sunday

Ibibo - a glimpse of life and death in a Nigerian tribe.

Losing an elderly person in some tribes comes with a whole lot of drama. Grieving ones who are left behind have also to be responsible for ensuring that cultural requisites are met. There are customs to perform with precision and exactitude, lest we offend the powers that be.

The drama is intense if the person is a man or the first son of some families.

Before I can lay my dad to rest, I have to get the recognition of his kinsmen.

Before death, he stood firm on his words that I am not his biological son and therefore have no place in his place.

And yet..

Post-death, a different story

As culture demands, I have to go to his people and show myself to them for acceptance..

This is done after fulfilling certain rights...

I have to buy a native he-goat.

I have to buy some kegs of palm wine.

I have to buy some aromatic drinks.

I have to buy some pods of the native kola and the bitter kola.

Cash is king where I live. No credit, no sir. In our currency, the Naira, the damage was around 2 million. He ain't heavy, he's Dad. Albeit a denying dad who came to me for healing and care in his last year.

When these things are done, the elders libate with the aromatic drink and a ceremony is held in my honour..

To bury him, he must not be buried in a cemetery as the first son, he must be brought back home.

A native he-goat must be presented to each family head, chiefs, youths and the obong of the community.

Drinks of various types are also to be given then cash.

There must be a funeral service which is a big ceremony in honour of the dead.

The USD 4750 hole in my pocket will mend as the overwhelm settles.

Cool At The Pool: Filtering Out The Noise So The Show Can Go On

By Wiwiek Najihah

The Overdrive

Tutoring my own children. Cooking. Cleaning. Grocery shopping at the nearby market. These were the tasks that occupied all of my time every day since I tendered my resignation as a counselor in 2014 to care for my growing family full time. There wasn't much variety in my daily tasks, aside from the monthly Toastmasters gatherings I attended at Jauhari Bilingual Toastmasters Club. A platform to harness the ability to speak confidently in front of an audience, I did not see the need to harness that skill when I attended it. In my mind, I only saw it as a respite for me from the mundane affairs I faced and the 4 walls I confined myself to every single day. The Club also offered good refreshments for break time. I was there for anything else except for the actual purpose of a Toastmasters Club; speaking. Nothing about my lifestyle prepared me for what was coming my way in 2018.

It started with the club's speech contest, held annually in December. A petite club, we didn't have many members to participate in the contest. But since every club had to be represented at the next level of contest, the Area level, the club often nominated a member to step up and speak for 5-7 minutes, regardless of their level of preparedness. That December, I was the chosen one.

Day of the contest. I had my barely-a-year-old 3rd born child in my carrier. By the time we arrived, most of the audience had entered the room, leaving only the contestants outside to be briefed on the contest rules. I blended in quietly. We drew lots to determine our speaking order. I was the last speaker. Cool! I could practice and put my baby to sleep.

While waiting for my turn to contest, I paced in front of the contest room door to practice my lines. In my hands was a recycled notebook from my college years. It had had barely enough blank pages left for me to scribble down what I wanted to say, which I only started thinking about while on my way to the venue. In my mind, I only thought of just completing this given task of mine minimally and moving on with the rest of my day. I'm a full-time housewife. I had nothing particularly captivating to talk about, much less inspiring.

My turn came. I passed my baby to my husband just before I stepped into the room. "Just for 5 minutes. I'll be back.", I told him. I opened the door. That was the first time I saw the room, the audience, the judges. I relished the coolness of the air blowing from the air-conditioner. I'd been standing in the heat before this. "Contestant number 5, Wiwiek Najihah, Time (the title of my speech)" bellowed the contest chairperson.

My speech was based on the movie In Time, featuring Justin Timberlake. I saw the audience resonating with my speech and responding whenever I involved them in my speech. We had so much fun, the time flew by so quickly. The next thing I knew, I saw the red light, which signaled my final 30 seconds to speak before I ran overtime and was disqualified. I eventually was barely 5 seconds shy of the maximum qualifying time of 7 minutes 30 seconds.

The relief I felt after that was intense, I didn't know how I missed the weight of contesting before this. I buckled my baby back into my carrier and stayed outside the room again until the end of the contest, returning back into the room only during the announcement of the results at the end of the contest.

"In first place, Wiwiek Najihah!" The announcement was met with energetic cheers from the audience. I was pleasantly surprised. For a stay-at-home-mom, this win was a treat. I was going to treat myself to sushi at my favorite place. But that happiness was replaced with shock when I heard the next announcement. "The winner of this contest will proceed to the next level, the Division contest. The date will be announced as soon as possible." What? There's another round? Right after the announcement, people started peppering their congratulatory wishes with "We're counting on you" and "Make us proud" as they shook my hand. I had to do this over and over again, writing my speech, practicing it, presenting it. All with a baby, 2 pre-school children, and endless housework to juggle at the same time. The audience chose me. Backing out on them felt like an act of betrayal. Hence, I hoped for a more natural end; losing a round and not advancing thereafter.

That end didn't come. "And the winner is… Wiwiek Najihah! She will be advancing to the District contest in March." My husband, a more seasoned Toastmaster, said "That's the national level already. Nobody from our club has reached that level before. Fly the flag high." I found myself writing and practicing on repeat. As I advanced, the preparation demanded more practice time. My husband helped me book more speech slots in various clubs for me to practice my speech. I almost felt like a circus act, making her rounds across the country to entertain the people watching me. My casual housewife outfit slowly changed into a more sophisticated, more professional look to fit the expectations of the contest level I was at. I felt like a hamster in a running wheel, constantly chasing for an end that didn't come.

"The winner is… Wiwiek Najihah. She will be representing us at the World Semifinal round in Chicago." Oh my god! I'm flying to Chicago!

As I prepared for the big stage, I increased my practice runs. Almost every other evening, I'd be practicing my speech in front of a fresh group of people, receiving their feedback at the end of the speech. Every night, after putting the children to sleep, after completing all the housework, I'd turn on my laptop and work on my speech. I even had 4 past champions of this contest helping me refine my speech at various times throughout the preparation. Rinse and repeat. I could feel lethargy and overwhelm flowing through my veins. Something in me was screaming for help. But I could not find the Stop button. This draining process has become automated, making me devoid of control over it.

Eventually, the audience saw my fatigue. The lines were forced. The emotions of my face were lifeless. My speech had lost its luster. Fernando, a Toastmaster with many years of experience to his name, approached me after one of my practices. He kneeled down like a father trying to help his daughter with her shoes and said in a gentle calming voice "Avoid over practicing. You're burning out." His words soothed me like a blanket on a cold rainy night. I know I had to slow down. Detach myself from it. But I was so overdriven, I have lost all control over it. In the whole process of upholding people's hopes and expectations, I didn't realize that I had lost myself.

The Plunge

"I can help you find your center again", Carolyn told me one day after yet another speech practice session at a club. Everything was a complete blur by then. I was simply going through the motions, following whatever that was written on my schedule, driven from one club to another like a celebrity being sent around to be displayed to others. Sure. Why not? I thought. What's another engagement? We agreed on a day and time before parting ways that night.

On our drive to meet Carolyn on that day, Hubby and I imagined what the session would be like. "I heard your darkest deepest secrets can be revealed when you're hypnotized. Do you have anything embarrassing that might come out?", Hubby asked me. Worried, I thought long and hard about my past. It was a very colorful one, to say the least. Anything could come out, and that would be the end of my good name. "Don't worry. I'll stay with you during the session. The moment you start spewing nonsense, I'll cover your mouth and slap you back to reality." Very assuring; his words.

As we reached the place, I scanned the building to have a sense of what was to come. It had a clean but old façade. Location: Town. The rent must cost a bomb here. Several offices lined the corridors of the building. So many people are trying to build their dreams, I thought. I imagined their resilience, their resourcefulness plastered all over their office fronts. Where do I stand in comparison? An imposter struggling just to write a speech. My legs felt heavier as I got closer to the office.

Carolyn was already there, waiting for me. We hugged. She invited me into the office. "We have an hour in this space", she said. Oh? She rented this just for me. My heart sank at the thought that I have just inconvenienced someone. What if the results in Chicago don't justify the effort she's invested in me? The guilt I'd feel. The disappointment I'd bring. Those thoughts ran uncontrollably in my mind like a derailed bullet train, zooming towards its doom.

I think the thoughts in my mind were too loud, because it seemed like Carolyn heard it all. "Just trust me, love. Focus on my voice and let everything else go." Why not? I'm already here. She directed me to the only comfortable chair in the room. Hubby sat on the rather worse-for-wear office chair behind me; Carolyn on another office chair in front of me. And the session began.

"Close your eyes. Listen to the sound of your breathing. I am going to count down from 10 slowly. With each number, I want you to imagine taking a step down a staircase." I listened to every word she said, forcing my mind to focus hard on just her words and releasing everything else.

"Imagine the colour. What material is it made of? Be as detailed as possible. Feel yourself going down that staircase". I chose white. Metal steps. Wrought iron decorative railing. Stairway to heaven. After a long struggle, I felt a sense of weightlessness setting in. I felt as if I had been transported to another world where my body and I were one but separate at the same time. I was just about to enjoy the freedom from this sense of detachment when I realized that she was nearing the end of the countdown. I was running out of steps.

"Three... Two... One. Let yourself go." My feet suddenly slipped into a deep dark ocean. Nothing. There was nothing around to swim to. Everywhere looked the same, I didn't know which way was up. I turned my head up, expecting to see the stairs I just built. It wasn't there. If there was a shark coming for me from underneath, I'd be dead.

Everything about the situation were definite triggers for me to feel overwhelmed and drown in fear, except, this time, it didn't. While I was finding my footing in the deep end, I heard Carolyn's gentle voice. "I want you to keep breathing. Be in the moment. Wherever you are.", she said. That made the difference for me. Instead of drowning in my fear and panic at my loss of bearings, I began to embrace the darkness. I looked down into the deep end and appreciated the beautiful shade of black. I realized I hadn't taken a breath since slipping down from the steps, but I wasn't struggling for air. Soon after, I laid down as though I was lying down on the bed and I saw, above me streaks of light from the sun, penetrating through the water. "Oh. What a beautiful emerald green.", I thought of the color of the water against the sunlight.

By then, Carolyn started calling me back. "I'm counting back up to 10. With each number, I want you to take a step back up the stairs. 1, 2, 3, 4..." Just like that, the stairs reappeared above me. I didn't want to leave. This feeling was very new to me; embracing deep uncertainties and not being consumed with fear. I felt empowered, in control of myself. With every step I took up the stairs to heaven, I glanced back to the deep end. "Thank you for the swim. I will not forget you." I uttered, as though leaving my mark there for me to go back to next time. "8, 9, 10. Slowly open your eyes. Welcome back, Wiwiek."

I beamed with joy. With my eyes open, the sense of calm from that swim in my personal pool remained. Carolyn walked me through with me how to find my way back to that state of calm whenever I feel overwhelmed again, as though handing me the keys to my pool of peace. I will be flying off to Chicago very soon. This key is definitely going with me.

The World Stage

Location - Chicago, backstage at the venue of the semi-finals and finals. Me, waiting for my turn to go up on stage. Out of the 10 finalists, I was the 4th to go as per the tightly-managed ballot. I looked at the script of my speech. It was so basic. I hadn't managed to clock in as many practice hours for this speech as the first one which had landed me in the final 10 two days earlier. For the finals, the speech must be totally different from the one delivered at the semi-finals. There I was vying to be World Champion Of Public Speaking. Listening to the cheerful and tickled responses from the audience towards my fellow contestants' speeches dimmed my unspoken speech even more. I could feel my heart racing. I was breathing so fast, my chest started to hurt. My palms were clammy. I broke into a cold sweat. I wanted to run away. The weight of the competition pulled me down once more. I tried conjuring up ways to avoid the contest. Maybe just don't go up on stage when they called for me. Maybe faint. Maybe just tell them to take my name out. I didn't realize that by then, I was so overwhelmed, I was drowning in my mind.

"What are you doing?", asked Kwong Yue Yang, one of my fellow contestants; a veteran. He must have noticed my awkward behaviour. His question snapped me out of my downward spiral. I realized then that I wasn't in a good state. I had to regain myself. That's when I remembered the swimming pool. I closed my eyes, inhaled slow deep breaths, and counted to 10. The pool appeared again. I was floating. In that pool, the noisy convention hall fell silent again. I thought to myself "My speech is not perfect, but it's still important." The speech I had put together for the eventuality that I might need it - should I make it to the finals - was about the empty nest syndrome parents feel. "I want my speech to at least shine a little bit of light on this part of the circle of life, even for a while." My parents' faces, my 2 children left behind in Singapore for this contest, my husband and my littlest one, waiting for me outside the hall- their faces came to my mind. "I'm going to do this for them. Just give it your best shot, Wiwiek. If you can remember your lines and do not go overtime, you're a winner. "

"Wiwiek? It's your turn next." I counted myself back out of the pool, slowly opening my eyes. I stepped onto the stage and went on auto mode with my speech. During my speech, I could see the audience's lackluster response. It was expected. My speech wasn't perfect. But I felt calm. My speech came out of my mouth smoothly. I managed to gain a few chuckles from the audience where I had planned. That was a bonus for me. I ended my speech just when the timer turned red. I made it within time! I did it! I took a bow and left the stage.

I didn't win, of course. The top 3 winning speeches were far better than mine by leaps and bounds. After the prize ceremony, I took my things and headed for the exit. My task here was done. Now, I needed to go back to my hotel room and pack for my flight home that night. As I walked out of the hall, strangers from the audience came to me. "Congratulations for getting this far", "Thank you for representing us moms", "Your speech made me miss my mom". These were the things said by these strangers to me as I walked my way out of the hall. I was caught off-guard. My speech did make an impact after all. I smiled, nodded briefly and continued walking. Very soon, tears rolled down my cheeks.

"Thank you. I will remember this." I said to myself.

About Wiwiek Najihah

A professional in counselling and special education since 2009, Wiwiek Najihah now dedicates all of her time in raising her children. Since then, she goes by her personal brand Momazing, as she believes that the hand that rocks the cradle rocks the world too. Through her brand, she aims to shine the spotlight to the value stay-at-home-mothers bring to the community. She brought this mission with her when she presented her speech at the 2018 World Championship of Public Speaking in Chicago.

There Is No Such Thing As Overwhelm

By Morag Shaw

I agreed to write a chapter for this book on a bit of a whim. It happened when I was on a high from writing my contribution to Authenticity and Us and wanted more of that same feeling. I had no clue what I was going to write but since overwhelm was something I had experienced often, I felt sure that I would have something valuable to say on the matter. What I hadn't expected was to end up doing some real time and last-minute experiential research into the topic of overwhelm!

There is no such thing as overwhelm

What? You can't say that! This is a book about overwhelm, so if it doesn't exist, why does everyone have so much to say on the topic? Good question, and one that, ironically, seemed to create at least some of my overwhelm during the course of writing this! On one hand I fundamentally believe in my statement that there is no such thing as overwhelm, and yet it is something that I have experienced on far more occasions than I would like to admit. How can that be? How can something that doesn't exist cause so many problems and so much upset to so many people? How can I write a whole chapter in a book about something that doesn't exist?

This apparent contradiction is what I invite you to explore with me as I share some of my own experiences. My goal is to point you towards the truth of how our experience of overwhelm (and everything else) is created and how this understanding allows us to see things very differently and live life with greater ease and satisfaction.

The group chat

One of the things I love about being involved (in my small part) in the creation of this book series, is the wonderful community of people I have been introduced to. To aid communication and make sure everyone knows what is happening, there is a Messenger group chat. Wonderful, supportive people all willing to help each other out when required and yet I found myself hiding from this group and ignoring notifications. Just when I needed the support of this group more than ever, I withdrew from it and isolated myself.

What looks completely illogical only makes sense when I tell you that I believed that the group chat was adding to my feelings of overwhelm. Too many people, too many notifications, potential for new things to do and the possibility of letting others down. Everytime I heard a notification on my phone, I felt an increased level of overwhelm, so I switched off notifications. Then every time I looked at my phone and saw there were new messages (that I hadn't been aware of after silencing notifications) I felt my overwhelm levels spike. When I plucked up the courage to open the app to see what I had missed and saw 53 unread messages, my overwhelm hit a new record high and I quickly closed it down without even reading all the messages. It really looked to me that the group chat was creating my sense of overwhelm, so avoiding it seemed like a good approach.

But it wasn't. If anything it made the problem worse, because now I could only imagine how many messages and what important information I had missed, and believe me when I tell you that I have a very good imagination!

Cause and effect

The idea of cause and effect is something that most people are familiar with. Here are a couple of examples just to be clear:

- You push a domino (cause) and it falls and knocks over the rest of the dominos (effect)

- An accident on the road causes a traffic jam (effect)

When I was feeling overwhelmed in relation to the group chat, I was seeing that as a cause and effect relationship, or several related cause and effects:

- The group chat is causing me overwhelm
- The notifications are causing me to feel overwhelmed
- The unread messages are causing me overwhelm
- The content of the messages is causing me to feel overwhelmed

But if any of these cause and effects were actually true, then my solution to simply avoid the group chat would have solved my problem, but it didn't. So what is the real cause and effect that is at play here? Well there is a clue in the fact that the problem got even worse the longer I stayed away and let my imagination blow things out of all proportion.

Illusion versus reality

When I was a young girl, there was a tall conifer tree outside my bedroom window. Sometimes I would wake in the night and see the shadow of the tree swaying in the wind silhouetted on my curtains. Except that is not what I thought I saw. I saw the shadow of a spy! Yes, I probably watched too many James Bond movies thanks to my older brother's love of 007, but whatever the reason, my brain processed the visual information and came up with the illusion of a shady character in a hat and raincoat. It freaked me out and I wouldn't be able to get back to sleep until I had got up and looked out of the window to check there was nobody there!

You will probably have your own examples where you have experienced something made up as if it was real. Perhaps it was a monster under your bed when you were a child, or the intruder in your house that was just the cat.

We all tend to experience this same effect when we go to the cinema. As adults, we know that it is just a film but we can still get completely caught up in the emotion of what we are watching on the screen. We get nervous when the hero has to make that impossible looking leap and then feel relief when they land safely on the other side. We cry when Andy gives away all his favourite toys to Bonnie at the end of Toy Story 3 (or maybe that was just me) because we can feel how much it means to both of them.

In all of these examples we accept that what we are experiencing as real, is actually coming from an illusion or made up reality. This is the same thing that happens when we experience overwhelm. The experience feels real but all the things we think are the cause are illusions.

What appears to cause our overwhelm

There are many different things that appear to cause us to experience overwhelm. Some examples that come to mind for me include:

- Quantity of work
- Complexity or difficulty of work
- Lack of time
- Conflicting priorities
- Different opinions from other people
- Too many choices
- A cluttered environment

I am sure you will have your own favourites to add to the list!

Most advice on how to cope with or reduce overwhelm tends to deal with the apparent causes. Stop multitasking, get better at time management, get clear on your priorities or create an organised workspace are just some examples I have come across. There is nothing wrong with this advice and I do believe that most of it can be helpful in the right circumstances. However, none of these helpful suggestions are addressing the true cause.

The one true cause

One day last year I got a phone call from my Dad at 7.30am. I didn't know what it would be about, but I did know that a phone call at that time in the morning was not going to be good news! He had fallen on the stairs and (he thought) dislocated his knee. The reason he was calling me rather than an ambulance was that the doors were still locked and he wanted me to come and unlock the door before he called them. I live at least 20 minutes away plus I had my youngest son still in the house and not due to be dropped at school until 9am.

If circumstances, conflicting priorities and emergency situations cause overwhelm then I should have been in a complete state by now! Luckily, whilst a little anxious, my mind was relatively clear and I called the neighbour across the road from my Dad, who I knew had a key, and asked her if she could go and unlock the door. Once that was confirmed, I called my Dad back and told him to call the ambulance now. Next came the problem of what to do with my 8 year old. I could have taken him with me, but then he would miss school and might get upset seeing his Grandad in pain, so I called the breakfast club at the school and arranged to drop him there at 8am. From there I headed straight down the motorway to my Dad's house to discover that he had just left in the ambulance and the neighbour had already locked up the house.

It turned out that he had broken his knee so badly that he needed 2 metal plates and several pins to put it back together and was in hospital for several weeks. It was during these weeks that my experience of overwhelm took hold. Now that the immediate emergency situation was over, I had time to reflect on how much worse it could have been, how he was going to cope when he did finally get home, how much work was required to make his house suitable for him to live in and how much more he was going to rely on me. Despite the fact that it took very little of my week to visit him in hospital and make a start on tidying and reorganising his house, it consumed almost all of my attention. I felt completely overwhelmed by the situation.

And yet it wasn't the situation that was overwhelming me. My feelings of overwhelm were being created by my thinking, and the more I thought about things, the more overwhelmed I felt. This is the one true cause of every single experience of overwhelm that anyone ever has.

How we respond to overwhelm

Overwhelm is a form of stress, so it makes sense that the fight, flight, freeze reactions to stress also apply to the experience of overwhelm, but are not very helpful. Just as freezing at the sight of a stick because you believe it to be a snake is not very helpful, reacting to overwhelm as if it were real is not the best plan either.

Many people go into fight mode in the face of overwhelm. They work harder and longer, thinking that the only way to conquer the overwhelm is to do battle with it. This can lead to a classic case of burnout as they reach exhaustion from their efforts and become emotionally drained through the lack of reward when the battle is never won.

Some people run away from overwhelm and simply avoid taking on new challenges and situations. If those people are happy with this approach and the life that they lead, then good for them, but sadly many of these people will find themselves full of regret at some point for not taking opportunities that appeared for them.

My own personal response to overwhelm tends to be to freeze. I don't run away from potentially challenging situations, but when feelings of overwhelm start to appear and I don't see them for what they are, I stop taking action and get stuck. This can lead to a less well known form of burnout that I call a slow burnout. Because I am not doing battle, I don't experience the physical exhaustion of my fighting friends, but I stay in the fire for much longer because I am not moving and end up with the same emotional exhaustion, cynicism and inefficacy as seen in the more well known form of burnout.

When we can see overwhelm as a stick and not as a snake, then we are free to continue along the life path that we want to walk without having to fight, run away or stand still.

How this helps us

On the day of my Dad's accident, I had a lot to deal with and yet I did not experience overwhelm. The reason for this is that I was focussed and present to what needed doing in that moment. We are built for reality and when our attention is on the present moment, rather than made up scenarios and dramas about the past, the future, other people or mistaken beliefs about ourselves, then we naturally take the actions we need to take.

In the days and weeks that followed, I got lost in the la la land of my thinking. I was so detached from reality that the monster under my bed kept getting bigger and bigger instead of me being able to see it as made up. But there were moments where I dropped back into reality and my overwhelm evaporated, at least for a while.

On one visit to see my Dad in hospital, I had stayed for longer than I had intended and when leaving the car park it was dark and the traffic was queued outside on the road. My heart sank as I realised that the traffic would be like this all the way to the motorway and it would take me well over an hour to get home. I started to blame my Dad, the hospital, my poor time keeping and lack of ability to say "I need to leave now" and was getting cross and agitated when suddenly I thought "where do you believe your experience is coming from?". "Do you really believe the traffic or the time is causing your stress?". I laughed out loud as the illusion melted away inside my head and I realised there was no rush to get home and I could now listen to my audio book for longer!

If that sounds like a positive reframe to you then you are both correct and mistaken. The result was that I now saw my situation in a whole new light, but I didn't need to do any reframing, it just happened as soon as I saw my experience for what it was. An illusion, created by my thinking in the moment.

If we go back to the examples of made up things feeling real we can see how this works in different situations. When you wake in the night hearing strange sounds and believe there is an intruder in your house, you will most likely feel fear and anxiety. Those feelings will be identical to what you would experience if there really was an intruder, but the moment you realise it is just the cat, the fear disappears and is replaced by relief and possibly a touch of embarrassment at getting it so wrong. You don't have to do anything to get rid of the fear. It just disappears when you wake up to reality.

The same thing applies to overwhelm situations. As soon as you realise that the only thing creating your experience of overwhelm is thought in the moment, and not your todo list, or that impossible deadline, or your colleagues that never agree with each other, then you are able to wake up to the reality of the situation. Your mind will settle and clear and from there, the next steps become obvious. Those next steps might involve putting into action some of the advice usually offered for dealing with overwhelm, but now you will do this with a sense of clarity and direction rather than those very actions adding to your state of overwhelm.

Is there really no such thing as overwhelm?

I started this chapter with a statement that there was no such thing as overwhelm and yet I have told you a few stories of my own experiences and written a bunch of words on the topic. Hopefully you will be starting to see the distinction between something that is real and things that we experience as if they were real. The experience of overwhelm feels very real in the moment and can have a huge impact on our ability to perform and produce the results that we desire, but it is no more real than the monster under your childhood bed or the snake that you mistakenly see on the path that turns out to be a stick. Knowing this does not make you immune to ever experiencing overwhelm again (unfortunately) but it does allow you to see it for what it is (or isn't) much quicker and then you will find yourself being caught out less and less often.

For me, personally, it helps me to unfreeze much quicker. To go back into the group chat with my wonderful fellow authors and to start experiencing the friendship and support that I have been missing because I made up a problem that didn't exist.

About Morag Shaw

Following her curiosity about how everything is made and works, Morag started her career as a Chartered Chemical Engineer and had great ambitions to use these skills to make a real difference in the world. During a successful 20+ years in chemical and pharmaceutical manufacturing, she discovered a natural aptitude for developing both the processes and the people she worked with and enjoyed a reputation as a problem solver. However, she became increasingly frustrated with her perceived lack of influence and ability to create real impact. This led to a slow burnout and the loss of her enthusiasm and engagement with the career she had previously loved.

Her ongoing journey to get her bounce back led her to retrain as a coach and she is now committed to helping other technical professionals to realise their unfulfilled ambition and potential so that they can have the impact and influence required to create true innovation and make the difference in the world that she has always wanted to see.

Connect with Morag on LinkedIn or contact her directly at morag.shaw@outlook.com

Burnout And Me

By Ina Leitner

It was dark in the corridor. My feet were moving along quietly, my heart pounding so loud that I couldn't hear anything else. Slowly moving up the staircase in the dark, slowly feeling my fear growing. My every move getting slower and slower.

Moving even slower - both hands gripping the staircase, trying to stay on my feet. I know (deep in my heart) that this is now the end of a way too long journey.

I try so hard to think but my brain gives me nothing. It is just numb and dark. Nothing is in there. I take a deep breath and try to inhale as deeply as my (restricted) lungs will allow. I need to get in. I need to enter this place.

My feeling for time has gone, my will is shrinking, and I have the strangest feeling outside my body. Darkness and fear in a peculiar, numb body-that once was me.

In taking the next two steps, the closer I get to what should have been my home, the more I struggle to move at all. I finally reach the door(after what seems like forever) and search for my key in the darkness. My fingers still can't move to find it.

At last I locate it, slowly move it into the lock and turn it even slower. One more difficult step and I am inside.

My bag falls to the floor, my heart rate is up to the level of a marathon runner. My legs are shaking. No more thoughts on everything that happened this past week-my soul is screaming inside me.

I walk into the dark kitchen and realize no one is home - that helps, a lot! I walk towards the fridge, open it, stare inside for a long moment and close it again. No thoughts, no feelings – just complete numbness.

Nothing makes sense.

I go to the toilet, that's a safe place at least. It's quiet, no big windows, it feels private. I know this is the end of an era for me; the things that happened are still echoing to this day. But it needs to end today!

Sitting there - tears running down my face, I know I must leave. I know I have to get out. I understand that this goes deeper and deeper, every quarter of an hour.

I wake up on my sofa with no memory of how I got there; I get up and go to bed. I try to listen to music, but nothing makes a difference. I can't feel anything by now - no emotions, just darkness, fear and endless tiredness. So numb.

The next day things get even worse. There is no clear thought in my brain, my heart rate is up, and I feel like I'm drowning as my nerves vibrate in a storm of thoughts.

I asked 'that man' for help to bring me to hospital, to a psychiatric ward, knowing that I need help badly. He says ‘no’. I knew he would.

Then as a last resort, I beg him to bring me to the train station. I tell him I will go to my parents.

I know this will be the end of everything that was once my life. I push an armful of clothes into my suitcase and add my company papers (in a quiet minute of single, clear thought).

Then I descend into an even darker place. I can't feel myself. My balance is fading. My brain gives in, no clear ideas.

I stare out of the window in silence. I say, "see you," set off into the street and walk to the station. I try to walk, My body only cooperates at the speed of an eighty-year-old woman.

Nothing makes sense.

I stop and wait for my mind to clear (for just a second) to walk on; entering the station hall. I sit down on the nearest bench I can find.

I know I have to buy a ticket, so I walk along the square on the floor. I can't think. I walk up and down, and I have no idea what to do.

I'm waiting for another brief, precise moment from my mind to help me focus.

Suddenly, I see someone behind some wooden panels and realize that it is the ticket counter. I can now move and step up to the counter.

I hear a shaky voice naming the town I need to go to. I ask for a one-way ticket. I move back over the squares on the floor, up to the platform.

I hear the train and other voices; they all get mixed up in my head. I can't see what's around me, but I hear the destination and step in. I am sitting there observing things pass by. I know my world is crashing down.

I make it to my parent's house (with absolutely no memory of how I got there). I step inside, and my parents notice straight away that I am not okay. I cannot talk to them yet, so I go to my room, fall into the bed, and cry.

Days pass, turning into weeks. Nothing is functioning. My brain, body, and soul are shut down completely. Descended into a dark abyss, I feel like I'm gone, like I don't exist. I had to leave the life that took the last vibes out of my soul. Nothing remained.

I can assure you burnout leaves you with an empty soul, a broken spirit, loss of memory and pure black darkness. The endless darkness and zero energy is like you never existed.

Looking back now, I know about all the signs I had missed early on when there was still time to get out of it intact. I know that my journey was one of seven years within a toxic environment. How do we get into this state?

We depend on a life (or work) style that sets us at a low value. We constantly give more than we receive. We live in an environment of power and dominance. Within a space that is a proven soul-killing environment.

We cannot define a space for ourselves, and it is often found in relationships with a dominant or mentally abusive partner. Or in a file of our work (where we never get the feeling we can stop working, where the pressure is enormous).

The pattern of the surroundings plays a role. It matches our inability to set boundaries - the system doesn't accept boundaries. That's the fatal thing (and you can try as hard as you want) if you try to set boundaries for a narcissist, you will feel much worse post effort.

It starts small. It's not even noticeable initially. You start adapting. It gets a little more substantial over time (and a little more vital with any attempt you want to take for yourself). The more you try to define yourself, the more you lose yourself.

'You could have gone a long time ago'. This is what you tell yourself.

But! You keep finding excuses: for them, for you, for the situation. You stay and drown. No one notices. Your friends and family don't see. You don't even notice, until it's far too late.

No one noticed me until it was too late, until things got out of control. When I started losing everything bit-by-bit.

You lose your ability to think, act, 'step in'. No 'step in' = no action. Just silent darkness starting to spread slowly all around you, taking you in. Then negative thoughts start creeping in and piling up. You tell yourself what you heard over weeks - months - years.... And you go deeper. You vanish in a way, you dissolve. And you lose yourself entirely by the end of this horrible experience.

The strange thing is you can pull yourself out - it's possible! You may never come back as you were before you are broken, but can rebuild yourself from scratch.

Like your brain forgot that this is you - the funny, strong, playful you. You are profoundly broken; it's day one of a long path to define who you are again.

And you need help. I did...we all do. In the emergency of the psychiatric unit, they understood my words. I didn't show any turmoil on the outside.

One major thing that enables you to end up on such a path is that you don't show body language, or what you feel (to yourself or others). You deny that things are not feeling good, or you have learned that the negative feelings are the new normal. The rest is like only on special occasions-when you are having that rare, good day.

But nothing is straightforward; you change, you cannot go back to who you were. You have to create a new self in a way. It's not logical, but the subconscious mind is not rational enough to go together.

Let's look at what happened that day / back then.

My body was past its limit for a long time. My hormonal levels had shifted into a critical state, had gone into "stress mode”. When you have created this state, you cannot regulate your hormonal system, and it will be tough for you not to give up. It feels like being under an electric current, like you just totally overdosed on coffee. And you can remain in this state for quite some time (if you keep staying in a situation where you are under significant stress and pressure).

It can seem like an endless, impossible journey to the abyss- sleepless nights, headaches, weight loss, no appetite included.

At this moment, you don't feel like you can turn things around. You feel like you have to do more and more…until the system collapses. Until your whole world disintegrates around you. The hormones that steer your brain and body then make such a mess that you have (so to speak) deregulated yourself on a chemical level.

And…Bang! Here's the burnout.

And it takes a long time to bring everything back into balance. There is no magic pill. And it is not like you sleep a night (or two) or rest for a week and it regulates itself again. Nope! You will need months on end (sometimes even years) of hard work on yourself. It takes a sustained conscious process, because everything has been off-balance for too long. You didn't get here overnight, and the journey back won't happen overnight either.

Let's look at the official definition of burnout about work. *"Feelings of energy, depletion or exhaustion. Increased mental distance from one's job, or feelings of negativism or cynicism related to one's job. A reduced professional efficacy."* Courtesy of Wikipedia

We can be full-throttle passionate about our jobs (fulfilled, purposeful, motivated…)and still get burned out.

The more emotional we might feel about our job, the easier it is for us to justify the long hours (because we take pleasure and find purpose in what we're working on, or toward).

That drive, tenacity, compassion, and 'laser focus' are not a limitless supply — we must cultivate it. It's not only about our work surroundings it's whether the pattern you have in your life gets to the point of a breakdown. This pattern is found not only in our work ethics, but also in other areas of our lives (such as romantic relationships, or relationships in general).

Your behavior is no different when you close your office door. Imagine sitting in the office trying to do it all - to get a passable appraisal from your boss/team leader. Do you think your behavior is different when you step out of the office and go home to your partner? And it might even happen that the real problems are at home, and the job is just another place to show up? Nope! We have the same problem patterns reflected in all areas of our lives.

We cannot hide behind the job and expect to be seen; that's the main difference. You can have burnout from the pressure and expectations of your partner. And you can also have it from the expectations from the boss at your workplace or interactions with friends, colleagues, etc. But it is important to note that it has nothing to do with their expectations, but all to do with our need to be accepted and acknowledged.

It is all to do with our boundaries (or lack thereof). And it sounds logical that we experience this in every aspect of our lives- doesn't it?

It is time for us to look at the pattern itself-at how we get to become trapped in focussing on pleasing others, and how we allow ourselves to normalise working ourselves to death in jobs.

It is about physical exhaustion and mental burnout that manifests in body and mind. It's a lack of an ability to use self-care and put ourselves first. It's easy for us to put huge efforts into a task and then not have a clear "no" (as an appropriate answer) when we get to an unhealthy point. It is this exact mechanism that gets us out of function.

Looking at this pattern closely, we have slowly pushed ourselves into a critical zone and no longer know what a healthy balance feels like. We do not know how to feel relaxed, calm and confident. We have been operating with this pattern and allowing others to support that for far too long. The emphasis here is we allowed it(knowingly or unknowingly).

The burnouts I have seen (in my field as a therapist and business coach) have been ongoing for an extended time. Sometimes over a month or even years. There has been a constant pattern of behavior until an end phase appeared (where the fear suddenly took over and propelled us into some action). This state is a clear sign we have reached that final stage and need to change something right now.

Let me tell you more about that. I have been proactive in the workplace on burnouts for two decades and have observed many details on this matter.

Here is an example:

Martin entered the room, pale and shaky. A distracted look on his face. He sat down in the corner of the meeting room, fidgeting with his pen, with no awareness of what was going on around him. When I asked him how his project was, he said it was 'all fine'-but the eyes showed pure fear and discomfort. He didn't say much and sneaked out as soon as the meeting ended - zero chat with anyone. As usual,Martin stayed late on his task, but he started to do more functions (not executing). He didn't know when I was talking to him-he didn't know! He was unaware of his growing discomfort. He was putting in more and more hours and even worked on the weekend. Weeks passed and things moved on in this same manner; until I got a call from him one day. He told me he urgently needed to talk to me (I was his coach at the time). His voice was shaky. His sentences weren't coherent. As usual; he was beside himself and seemed very confused. He proceeded to tell me that he couldn't go to the client meeting the following Monday and freaked out on the phone. I calmly asked him if I could support him and his client in any way. He thanked me and said he would love my help-but had no idea what he needed help with. I offered an early meeting with him and asked him to take the weekend before off (so he could have a break). He didn't. E-mails-he kept emailing me. The weekend passed and Monday came. I offered to help him; he could call me at any time during the meeting (if it was not going well I could help him on the spot).

I know the signs; it's a natural habit of people who always reject help and any support offered. And the characters were clear; the fear was kicking in. It's the game-changer to ‘the dark side’.

Monday, my phone rang. Martin (early at 9 am). Just before his meeting. He was out-of-control, crying, telling me he couldn't go to the appointment and see his client. And the worst thing was that he was supposed to fly to the meeting's location and hadn't even made the flight.

I tried to talk to him about how he felt (to take the focus away from the current situation and his job). He was past the point of doing any work. It took us one hour of talking to get him to see this job was taking a toll on him and he could not continue like this.

He finally accepted the situation, and I advised him to go on sick leave and see a specialist. He agreed to this and I promised him I would take care of company communications (which is a stressful part of the job).

We also decided that he would inform me when he would get help, any progress in this matter, and not to return to work until he felt okay again (mentally and physically).

Martin was one of the lucky ones and has managed to avoid a complete breakdown. He found a good therapist who helped him learn how to change his pattern. It took him quite some time (we all know it's a process to work on our wellbeing). He was back six months later and made a series of correct decisions that took him out of the type of work he couldn't bear and wasn't able for.

He learned that he didn't want to be responsible. And here comes one of the hints where the root cause lies...Martin was one of the few people who acted on time. He came back to his job again – with new boundaries in place. Most of the others I have observed never return to the same position again or even the same field. They break down completely and never come back.

As I was trained beforehand to spot these things as they happen, I was able to see he was on the road to burnout. I was able to help him turn things around and take action when there was still time.

What is also really important is that he was able to accept that he needed help and was willing to get help to prevent the worst outcome (even at the last possible minute).

So, root causes of burnout are not discussed in many companies at all. It should never be spoken about – a taboo topic. If someone has this problem, it's usually just brushed under the carpet.

Huge companies are playing the part of local psychiatry for their managers rather than looking at what causes the whole burnout theme. It's the culture of pushing people into a career, confronting them with high expectations, an overload of tasks and often with the added pressure of impossible-to-reach deadlines.

Our world can't accept prevention; how can you turn down this opportunity? It would be best if you were grateful you work for this great company-with no heed whatsoever for your wellbeing. It would be best if you were thanking them for overworking you.

Different roles and positions in a company are suited for other people. Not every job is for everyone. They are a form of life, and you have to want a particular job/position and embrace it. You must feel comfortable with the role's responsibility, size, power and expectations.

Some people who don't fit in their jobs avoid the burnout stage. These people have a particular personality and character with excellent coping skills. They are naturally very flexible. They can grow into positions and not drown. As mentioned a few times in this chapter, the same can happen in all areas of your life - at home, your personal life, career, family life, exercise….every place where you expect too much from yourself/at least more than you can handle. A good example could be an overwhelmed mother who has three children running around and one would already be enough for her level of coping skills.

People put themselves on overload and crash —often in public, or in front of others. The most significant difference in Martin's case is that it was identified in time and that the result happened behind closed doors, unseen.

Martin clarified what he wanted in life, what he cared about most, and how much energy he was willing to put into his career in the future. He decided he wanted a job with expertise, but not organizational / considerable responsibility. That's where we get to the point - when we choose how much responsibility is good for us, we can know when to say a clear 'no' when we get pushed into something too big, too strong, or too threatening.

There are ways (as mentioned above) the firm sets boundaries about what we are and not willing to do in a particular case (r.e. : the essential way to prevent the risk of getting burnout). Let me tell you what I think the most critical steps for burnout prevention are from knowledge and observation:

First - Learn to feel the level of hormones under stress. Know the ten key stressors you inhabit and take active action when triggered.

Second - Define how you want your life to look like, be very specific and if an opportunity arises; clarify if a shiny object caught your attention.

Third - Dedicate a maximum of nine hours per day to your job (or less if at all possible, especially if you are a mom with small children). You should make sure you have a private life the rest of the time - always a good idea!

Fourth - Make sure you have a best friend who is honest and supports you no matter what. Someone giving you a real talk and reality check when you start to act strange. Someone you trust, that is not a family member, someone who gives you feedback and helps you to create a clear action plan when you need help.

Fifth - Have a high level of fun and joy in everything you do. Focus on those things in life that matter to you most. Remember, you can't get burnout laughing. Giggles are always the best medicine!

So I will leave you now - with a big, quirky smile. As I giggle when things get wild, slow down when expectations arise, and know what I want in my life.

I know what I love. And I am sure burnout will never be on my to-do list anymore.

About Ina Leitner

"When we choose how much responsibility is good for us, we can know when to say a clear NO when we get pushed into something too big, too strong, and too threatening to ourselves. If we don't, we have a great chance to end up in a BURNOUT situation."

Ina is an online business coach and the founder of SheEO Success Society, located in Hamburg, Germany. She helps successful people to achieve a positive entrepreneurial mindset and measurable results in growing their dream business. Applying an individual approach for each person, she leads her clients to success through the air and step-by-step strategy. She works with all kinds of clients, from entrepreneurs to corporate leaders. They all value her elegant coaching style that maximizes client benefits in a relaxed, professional, and enjoyable way. Clients describe Ina as someone who stands up to big egos and respects her patience and the deep connection she builds with them. They also appreciate her straightforward, no-nonsense approach and her ability to find solutions for any circumstance, situation, or problem. Ina listens with an open mind and speaks in a down-to-earth manner as she gives the business owner a clear picture of the path to their success and dream life.

Squish Overwhelm

by Dianna Lane

1 Minute Trick to Combat Overwhelm

Overwhelm is a disempowering feeling that our challenges are bigger than us. The simplest and fastest mental trick to squishing overwhelm is to imagine that you are bigger than your challenges. Imagine that you are physically bigger, stronger and entirely capable. Breathe and mentally command that you shall overcome your unique set of challenges.

Game On

There are multiple ways to conquer overwhelm and here are 5 categories we can dive into. Chances are that we already address overwhelm using a few methods in particular categories. It is good to build our muscles in each category so that we are better able to squish overwhelm in the bud.

- Physical
- Environmental
- Tidying up our spaces and digital devices
- I'm Marie Kondo-ing as I write this
- Oh and yesterday I organized my cupboard . Feel so good
- Physical Body

- Grounding – Go barefoot; walk or sit on the ground
- Immersion in Nature – waterfalls, sea, forests
- Exercise – Variety of aerobic, stretching and strength building
- Massage – Book an appointment or massage yourself
- Sleep – Unwind and get to sleep ideally before 11pm
- Salt Bath or Shower – Cleanse the physical body
- Drink Structured Water
- Eat Fresher Foods
- Guided Fast
- Emotion
- Ask "What is the lesson that overwhelm wishes for you to learn?"
- Ask "What needs, wants and desires are not being met?"
- Sit with your emotions and talk to them as you would a friend
- Mental
- What are the root causes of my overwhelm?
- What strategies can I apply to reduce overwhelm?
- What action plan can I design to reduce overwhelm?

- Spiritual
- Dance, Sing, Laugh
- Meditate, Pray, Connect
- Read spiritual literature or watch spiritual movies to gain insights and strength
- Social
- Seek wise counsel or Play
- Spend time with friends who nourish and uplift your spirits
- Be your best friend and high 5 yourself in the mirror. Cheer yourself on.

If life were just a game, let's play it well and play to win. You've got this.

Practice And Life

By Majero Bouman

In this chapter I explore how and why somatic resources support us in overwhelm. After talking about 'tells' (the things that let us know we are in overwhelm), we will slow down a bit. We will explore how shifting our mindset from "no pain, no gain" to the more positively framed "no pleasure, no treasure" enables us to reconceptualize daily life. Somatic practice is different from talk and behavior-based therapies; so I'll talk about the how and why of resource-based movement practice. And finally, we'll celebrate the little things.

My Kitchen

I glance over at the kitchen. It's not good. The counter is full of dishes that need to be put in the dishwasher. I have no idea if the dishwasher is full or empty, just that there are piles of dishes on the counter. The sink, too, has unwashed pots in it. The coffee maker has overflowing grounds around it. I try not to look. And when I need to go there to make food for the family, I navigate around the dishes, focusing only on the thing I am doing. It's kind of like tunnel vision. I can make food. I cannot face the dishes. When this situation is the case, it is a clue that I am overwhelmed. The condition of my kitchen is one of my tells. Knowing my tells is important; because the truth of the matter is that when I am overwhelmed, I am not always aware of it. As I struggle more and more to keep my head above water, my ability to think around and through what is going on reduces to a pin prick in which I just do, or don't do what needs to be done. Instead of being creative and having the ability to zoom in and out of my situation, I get stuck close-in, and everything becomes sharp.

Sometimes, when I have an article to write, the opposite thing happens in the kitchen. It miraculously goes from dirty to clean. Dishes are washed and put away; counters are wiped clean; depending on the intensity of the project, the stove might be clean and the cupboard doors may have been washed. This is not a tell that I am near overwhelm. It is a strategy of procrastination. I really believe in the value of procrastination. It is a time of processing and planning, much of which occurs at unconscious levels. The cleaning and ordering of my outside world contributes to the ordering of material that is happening on the inside. In this I trust. And I know that when I finally sit down to the project, it will have been processed to the point that it can proceed well enough.

The dirty dishes kitchen that persists is not about procrastination. It is something else. It speaks to what I am capable of in the moment, whether or not there is material that needs internal processing. For the time being, I am not able to face the work that needs doing head on. It exists on the periphery of my vision, letting me know that my nervous system is experiencing very intense activation. I love my kitchen counters for alerting me to the condition of my nervous system.

All too often, we silence the alerts that cue us to how we are doing. We normalize accumulating stress and choose coping mechanisms that numb physical sensations of discomfort. We take sleep aids, wake aids, anti-inflammatories, pain meds for headaches, things that end in "pam" for anxiety … And all the while, accumulating stressors continue to impede our functioning and comfort. My kitchen is the antidote for all my many coping mechanisms that dull the physical sensations of overwhelm. My kitchen lets me know that I might need to slow down and do some in-tending. It lets me know it is time to inquire into what might be moving below the surface of things for me. It tells me it is time to pause, and take stock.

Overwhelm is not just about the current events in our lives. It is also about how these resonate with past experiences. Imagine an existing fault line deep below the surface of the earth. If a bomb goes off at the planet's surface, that surface explosion activates the pre-existing instability. The two sites of disruption meet and amplify one another, creating schismatic disturbance across many layers. At this point the conscious part of us is hostage to reactive patterns that might serve a dual function of letting off pressure on the one hand, and coping with the condition of overwhelm on the other. And fair enough! What else can we do when we are being overwhelmed by an event or situation that is out of our control?

There is nothing wrong with being overwhelmed. You are not broken inside. Experiencing overwhelm is not a problem with you that needs to be fixed. Life gets intense and we have every reason to be and feel overwhelmed in it from time to time… sometimes for a week and sometimes for decades.

What is Your Tell?

Take a moment to consider certain details of your life that might indicate how you are doing. Your tell might be the condition of your inbox, the state of your laundry, your bathroom, your hair, or even the amount of exercise you are getting. Consider whether there is something in your life that gets passed over when things are getting a bit much. It is time to stop feeling bad about it and start feeling grateful for this tell. Embrace your special place of disorder as the cue that lets you know it is time for some compassion and some softening regarding your surface explosion or underground fault line. What might be going on either at or below the surface for you? Can you meet your tell as an invitation to open your heart to yourself?

From Pain to Pleasure: Tuning into Sensation and Changing Your Mindset

If you, like me, live in a patriarchal, capitalist, colonial, or racist society (yes - they all belong to the same interconnected web), you have an enculturated habit of numbing and hiding any tremors and instabilities below the surface for the sake of maintaining high levels of productivity. Held hostage in the urgency of doing, we dissociate from the discomforts of stressful activation. When the tremors have been ignored too long, Overwhelm can hit like a tsunami. All of a sudden we suffer a situation that causes a shift within our autonomic nervous system: gone is the ventral vagal calm; activated is the sympathetic fight, flight, or fawn response, or sometimes, the dorsal vagal flop and freeze of collapse and depression. To some extent, we embrace the self-abusive rollercoaster of overwhelm, collapse, catharsis, and re-emergence. In a warped way, it satisfies the ideal that great achievements require suffering and discomfort.

Consider the phrase and philosophy 'No Pain, No Gain.' How many situations in life do we apply it to? Work, fitness, even pleasure: Work hard; Play harder. These messages imply that there is a fierceness in the impetus to push past our limits. We live in a culture that celebrates effort, pushing, activation, and stimulation: stronger, faster, harder, longer. Where does this narrative lead, if not to overwhelm, collapse, catharsis, and re-emergence? And how do you opt out of the ride?

Meditation, pause, and mindfulness offer the option of sitting with the witness in you. They may invite detachment from, or awareness through, the sensory. Sitting for 20 to 40 minutes a day is wonderful if you can do it. A lot of us can't. And that is ok. The best thing one of my teachers ever told me was that 1 second, one breath, one moment is enough. It is enough to return. The practice of meditation is the practice of returning, again and again, without making a story about it. Just return, and when you remember, return again - to presence, sensation, this infinite moment, this breath. Whew! Ok. That I can do. But is that going to support me when something happens and I flip into overwhelm?

Resource-based somatic practice offers some nuance that, with practice, rewires the brain and nervous system. In place of reactive habits like lashing out (fight) and / or numbing (flight or flop), somatic practice enables our capacity to regulate our own nervous systems, co-regulate others who are in overwhelm, and make responsive choices. The new ideology that is hitting fitness regimes and fueling success is 'No Pleasure, No Treasure.' Let's do a simple somatic practice with each of these phrases.

What sensations occur in your body when you read 'No Pain, No Gain?' Where are they located? Take a breath to return to neutral, and then notice what sensations occur in your body when you read 'No Pleasure, No Treasure'. Where are they located? There is probably a different activation for one phrase than for the other. Each somatic activation might articulate a stance and an "affective mode." An affective mode is the energy of an emotion. The somatic activation and affective mode might articulate a mindset.

For me, I feel 'No Pain, No Gain' in my low gut. If I stay with and follow this sensation, it feels hard, like I'm going to power through. The whole of my front body braces for impact, tightening and leaning in. It feels tough. If there were words to it, they would say, "I can take it." My jaw is set. My mode is aggressive. Beneath that, hiding in the shadows, are insecurity, inadequacy, and weakness. Simplifying these emotions to their primary mode, I have anger on top, and underneath it, fear. Fear often wears a coat of anger to protect itself in the world. Vulnerability often arrives armed with a hard exterior. And I lean in. I can take it. At some level I tell myself I want the suffering. It satisfies the complex presentation of my insecurity and sense of inadequacy, and rewards my aggression. 'No pain, no gain' opens the avenue of catharsis, which is the release of strong and/or repressed emotions. As I power through, I not only risk injury to the surface physical body of me and my environment; I also risk retraumatizing those deep fault-line wounds, and entering a dance with depression.

There is something missing in the sensation/affect/thought cascade described above. This mindset does not foster an ability to recognize and respond to the complex layers of emotional and mental activation it has triggered. It can not engage with the negative patterns of hurt, vulnerability, exposure, and shame that come from meeting the world with force, and so it keeps us cycling through the rollercoaster of highs and lows.

Let's next explore a somatic consideration of 'No Pleasure, No treasure.' Making an effort not to assume and think my way through here, I focus on the sensations that are alive in my body, and do not expect them to make sense. Sensations happen in the physical body. We are most familiar with the sensation of pain, then maybe pleasure. But there are also temperature, rhythm, pulsing, weight, bubbling, shakiness, emptiness, fullness, tightness, butterflies, tension, clenching, softness, release, spaciousness … and so many more. Finding a vocabulary for what we are feeling inside our bodies can be challenging at first. It can help to start by making a list of familiar sensations, and building it as you learn to differentiate and describe more nuance in what you are sensing.

We are so familiar with either assuming what is going on or just pushing through it, with or without numbing aids, that we seldom take time to really feel the sensation. Sensations are both faster and slower than thought. They arise faster, but it takes time and practice to actively tune our awareness into them. Developing sensation vocabulary is a valuable step in the awareness practice of becoming sensitive to what is actually happening for you and within you. When we numb out, we are often running away from sensations and shutting them out. Building a list of sensations as you learn to feel and recognize them is an act of curiosity. It is a step away from conforming to ideals and expectations; a step toward your Self. I capitalize Self here because I do not want to conflate it with what we think we know about ourselves. The Self is a many layered multiplicity, much of which escapes the reticulations of language and thought.

Sensations do not need to make sense. Often, when we do experience sensations, we defer very quickly to Story. In this move, we name and tame sensation with the formal and temporal logic of beginning, middle, and end. Because the experience of being in a body is amorphous and difficult to quantify or measure, we can lean into Story as a means to contain it. This practice of storying gives sensation reason and edges: cause and effect. So I encourage you, in this invitation toward sensation, to resist the instinctual urge toward story. Begin by just being curious about your sensations, and bringing awareness to the amorphous, edgeless expanse within. The invitation to become aware of sensation can be alot. If this is true for you, designate a specific body part, like one hand, in which you will notice sensation. Having your feet flat on the ground will support your nervous system. Hint: numbness, nothing, darkness, and 'I don't know,' are just fine when it comes to sensation. More than fine! They are sensation descriptors that offer us information about how we are feeling in our relation to ourselves in the given moment. And it's true that with regards to sensation and movement, things change moment to moment..

What do I feel when I follow my somatic awareness of 'No Pleasure, No Treasure'? Sensation rises from my solar plexus and spreads across heart and lungs.There is heat in my rib cage. Opening across my collar bones, I notice my shoulders relax as my shoulder blades drop and spread across my back. I feel impulse moving from back body to front body. There is curiosity in that impulse and opening toward: a lightness that snatches at the sides of my eyes. I sense my mind bending around the question of treasure, even as my body opens toward pleasure. If there were words here, they would be "yes?" Simplifying to the core emotions, curiosity relates to happiness.

The Freudian "Pleasure Principle" explains our tendency toward pleasure and away from pain. This is being utilized by coaches and motivation experts who recognize that grit and resilience are built through pleasure. We follow through from pleasure, not pain. And in this spirit, I challenge you to embrace the messiness of your secret tells, instead of beating yourself up about them. They are a gift, inviting you home to your Self.

Learning our tells and becoming sensitive to physical sensation are strategies that can mitigate major overwhelm. By major overwhelm I mean the kind that hits like a tsunami. Somatic awareness strategies help because they enable us to better track how we are doing under the surface of our doing. They alert us to the condition of our nervous systems, and thus open the possibility of pause, as well as other somatic interventions that help us to return to embodied presence in whatever situation. Of course, upheavals and unexpected things still happen. A loved one gets sick or dies; we have to change our living situation; we lose jobs, there is war and climate crisis. We can connect with our capacity in the moment by being in a practice that builds relation with our nervous systems, and with our sensing/feeling selves.

From Tolerance to Capacity: Recovering a Sense of Self in the Small Things

During overwhelm, we are reduced to basic survival. Popular author Dan Seigel describes a zone that he calls "The Window of Tolerance," in which we are best able to function effectively. He explains that overly intense or high arousal shifts us away from this effective zone into hyperarousal. We become less effective in hyperarousal because the body reroutes energy from the complex thought of the frontal cortex and to the more instinct-focused limbic brain, which governs basic life and death survival choices like fight, run, or fawn. Survival choices are faster than thought. They are physical chemical charges that leave little to no room for consideration and creative engagement. We may oscillate between hyper-vigilence and exhaustion. From this place, Siegel's choice of the word "tolerance" makes sense. The nervous system wants to return to a more tolerable zone, where it can regain a more nuanced state. Overwhelm occurs as we near and reach the line that differentiates the tolerable zone from the zone of hyperarousal. This is the point at which the autonomic nervous system is overwhelmed. When it shuts down the relaxed parasympathetic mode, it instead switches on the sympathetic nervous system. For as long as this second mode stays engaged, our bodies are super charged with survival chemicals, and we lose the ability to respond mindfully to whatever situations arise. We yell at kids, lose patience with partners, and generally overreact to all kind of stimuli.

Trauma doesn't just interfere with a person's capacity to tolerate distress. Language has power. Words carry energy. Labels matter. Elizabeth Dennison changed Siegel's word 'tolerance' to a more inviting concept, 'presence.' Tolerance is our ability to endure in the face of hardship or challenging circumstances. Presence is the ability to be where we are and with what is happening. Even while presence is more inviting than tolerance, both "window" analogies represent a hierarchical image that focuses on distress and fails to account for a person's curiosity, creativity and pleasure.

In 2021, Cathy Malchiodi developed a different image: The Circle of Capacity. In her therapeutic work she became aware that people struggling with trauma suffered "an absence of enlivenment, play, curiosity, laughter, and self-compassion." This insight brought her to the fact that recovery required not just an expanded window of tolerance, but a retrieval and fostering of positive experiences for mind and body. In her circle model, the goal of increasing capacity displaces the tolerance of distress. The road to this increase is paved with somatic skills. When we identify and practice embodied experiences, we can replace the experience of hyper- and hypo-arousal. The idea is to consider the small things and to ask yourself, "What am I capable of, in this moment, that might elicit an experience of liveliness, pleasure, playfulness, and / or self-compassion?"

Faced with the condition of my kitchen during an episode of overwhelm, the question isn't 'Can I tolerate this mess?' (No), nor is it 'Can I clean it? (also No). Rather, I might ask myself, "What am I capable of, in this moment, that might bring an experience of joy and accomplishment into my day?"And the simple answer might be to locate the nice mug that feels good in my hands and make a cup of tea to drink while staring out the window. Or, it might be that I can eat a cookie, bake a cake, or have a kitchen dance (let's be honest - is there anyone that doesn't sometimes appreciate a good dance in the kitchen?!). The practice is to take the time to really experience whatever it is you might be capable of, noticing the various channels of the thing:

- Sensory Channel - physical senses of sight, sound, touch, smell and taste,

- Relational Channel - solitude, partnership, belonging, environment
- Affect Channel - emotional charge
- Neurological Channel - sense of safe/not safe
- etc....

In this way, I focus my experience and practice, becoming sensitive to the small things that I do have a capacity for, and that enliven me to curiosity and pleasure. The energy of growing my capacity returns me to myself. The action of making tea and drinking it replaces the tizzy of inaction that happens when we are facing everything at once. It reduces the impossible task of everything at once, to one manageable small enjoyment. Half way through my tea I may make a list of things that will help me to parse the overwhelming situation I find myself in. And, I may not. The important thing is that both are ok. Making and drinking tea may not look like what we think of as a somatic practice, but it is. We are movement. The key is to inhabit the movement that we are with awareness. Then we are in the realm of embodiment and somatics.

From Tool to Resource: Discovering the Dance you Already Are

Being overwhelmed doesn't mean you are broken. You do not need the right tool in order to be fixed. The framework of having and using a tool suggests that there is a piece of you that doesn't work right, and that without fixing you will remain broken. The reality is that things are happening to you, to me, to all of us that live on spaceship Earth. Death, war, sickness, isolation, fear, frustration, anger, work, futility… Overwhelm in a field of multiple crises is not a sign of being broken. We do not need tools for this and in fact there are no tools we might wield on our own that could fix it. Furthermore, workshops that sell you "take-home tools that you can use" tend to teach to the wrong part of the brain. They provide intellectual information, which I love. Don't get me wrong. I am all for understanding how to do something as well as why and how it works. It is why I write! But no amount of learning is going to enable you to pull out the right tool when you are in capital 'C' Crisis. Remember that around that high edge of activation we are shifting into survival reactions. Considered thoughts, reflection and response are not available in this place. Either we catch ourselves before this happens, or/and we need something that is automatic for when we have flipped into fighting for our survival. We need something that is hardwired into the nervous system. And the only way to get that, is through practice.

A resource-based practice like Open Floor Movement Practice, which I teach and work with, is something that we practice by doing and repeating and exploring in and through our embodied awareness. Learning it once and remembering that it works is not the same as being able to do it when in overwhelm. It takes hundreds of practices to embody a practice, and thousands for it to become hardwired. Do not let those numbers scare you. For one, resource-based practice does not shoot you into overwhelm so that you can practice resourcing yourself there. Retraumatizing and catharsis based practices are a different cup of tea, and not ones I'd recommend for building capacity; Nonetheless, catharsis can feel really great for temporary relief of pressure.

Open Floor Movement Practice centers on familiar everyday movement patterns like toward and away, ground, expand and contract, and dissolve. We call these Core Movement Resources. They are not magic; they do not require mastery, nor do they require memorizing. We are always moving toward something and away from something else. We can always connect with our weight on the ground. We are always expanding and contracting - not only as we breathe, but as we enter and leave relationships, thoughts, and emotions. We dissolve when we fall asleep or orgasm or disappear into work, a story, art, music... What Open Floor Movement Practice does is practice these movement patterns through the body and with awareness. We enter a particular context for movement, and then explore the permutations and play that arise, allowing the movement to become what it already is, the dance of body, heart, mind and soul in their multiple relations and layers.

And let me tell you something - you are already in practice if you've bounced to a favorite song in the kitchen or had your tea while staring out the window. Each of these is a dance just asking to be noticed and explored. Bouncing activates the body and settles the nervous system. We know to bounce babies when they are distressed because we know it works. Most of us were bounced. This is the Core Movement Resource of Activate and Settle. We know to take a deep breath when we are angry or frustrated and need to focus. This is the Core Movement Resource of Expand and Contract. Explore it. Get curious about what in you is expanding as you breathe in; what in you is contracting as you breathe out. Only your body can give you clues to the practice. Your embodied exploration will invite emergent relationships and insights. You might expand your arms to the sides and drop them on the out breath already. What if you exaggerated that? Did it differently? What if you lifted your arms on the out-breath and dropped them on the in-breath? What if you opened and closed your mouth, expanding it big and wide, and sucking while shutting it tight? Can you add sound to that? What else can expand and contract like this? A single hand; both hands, your whole body. These are all possibilities for exploration. Don't think too hard about it. Don't over-complicate it. Don't worry about being pretty or correct. Get messy. Make mistakes. Try to stay with the sensations in your body. Notice what thoughts and images come up in the practice. Don't try to shut these down. Mind is integral to being a body. A Resource-Based Practice does not ask you to give up thinking, nor to stop or silence your thoughts. It will ask you to get curious about what thoughts arise, and invite you not to get wrapped up in making a story about it. Just notice the dance that is happening in this embodied mind as you explore physical movement. Similarly, get curious about any emotions that arise and where they are rooted in your body: sadness as you expand and contract a left hand. That's ok. Sadness is part of this dance for you right now. When you keep moving, sadness too will move. Moment to moment you are exploring and making patterns with your body, heart, and mind. Maybe anger comes up in your face. Maybe throat tightens. Ahhhh, contraction. Interesting. What expansion can partner with this? Trust the process. It doesn't have to make sense. Somatic processing is different from linguistic meaning. No amount of talking or sense-making can take its place.

If you make the choice to practice, you cannot get it wrong. Stay curious. Get creative. Give it a minute. Give it two hours. Practice it a thousand different ways. There you go. You are on your way to making real change. Not just in your understanding, but in your body: in your neural pathways; in the very wiring and firing of the nerves that make you you.

Sometimes there is nothing to be fixed. Sometimes shit is happening and you are in it, struggling for your life just to keep your head above water. You are not broken. And you cannot fix what is happening. It just is, and it is wildly, violently dysregulating. You've been practicing. Quicker than thought, you shake out arms - big shake with a big breath in, and a big settling bouncing shake with the outbreath. A few more times as you rock from foot to foot. You are not thinking this. You are just doing it. It is a part of you. Your practice has enabled nerves that have fired together to wire together. And while your practice does not fix or solve what is happening, it does provide you with the self-regulation necessary to tolerate the discomfort, the ability to return to presence and meet the situation just as it is, and the capacity to be creative in responding to it. With practice, we have the capacity to be both overwhelmed and resourced at the same time.

Celebrating the Little Things

"Life gets lifey," as my friend Shorty says. On the journey, celebrating the little things by bringing your full awareness to experiencing the moment is a gift. Taste the sunset, wish on a star as you feel the night wind, eat a piece of chocolate with your tea. Find your dance. It is the one you are in right now. And live it if you can, even if that is just a sip at a time. Trust in the practice. Get out of your way. Be silly. Get curious. Get it wrong. And when you remember, trust that this too shall pass, and that this is not all of me.

About Majero Bouman

Majero is a poet, a cultural theorist, a mother, an artist, and a life-long dancer. She merges the intellectual with the inspirational as an Open Floor Teacher. Her work is in service to cultural transformation, community responsibility, and self-awareness. She believes that movement practice can connect us deeply to ourselves and others - in service to communion - making the intangible visible. Her students appreciate the grit, substance, and inspiration she brings to her work. She is committed to making dance/ movement accessible to people from all walks of life: the ordinary and the unconventional, those who dance and those who never knew they could. Find out about Majero's publications, research, classes and workshops at www.openfloor.ca And for more about the practice, check out Open Floor International at www.openfloor.org

Dichotomy of Overwhelm

By Gail Costello

Why did I choose to name this interlude Dichotomy of Overwhelm? Dichotomy is a division of an idea or a thing into two different or opposing parts. That is why I apply it to an overwhelming emotion. My thoughts are that you can be overwhelmed by something that is, or becomes, a negative emotion, or you can be overwhelmed by something that creates a positive emotion within you. To put it into very simple terms, you can be overwhelmed with grief or it's antonym, the emotion of joy.

Sometimes, we can feel both emotions, although not exactly at the same time. I have written a poem, which is shared in this interlude, that conveys the emotions that I felt whilst dealing with the cycle of life; birth, life and death, but not in that order. This began with the death of my mother, followed by the birth and life of my first daughter.

The death of my mother, when I was in my early 20's came as a huge shock. The emotions were overwhelming and not easy to comprehend at the time. It took me some time to get over this bereavement, but a few years later, when I found out that I was expecting a baby, the excitement eased my pain just a little, or at least distracted me from it.

During the birth of my baby, which was a difficult and protracted labour, I went onto the 'danger list' and went through a 'Near Death Experience' (NDE). I remember the journey, during which, I encountered my mother again and other deceased loved ones. It was the most peaceful and wondrous experience and I was filled with overwhelming joy, love and gratitude to see my mother again. I remember wanting so desperately to stay with her, but that was not to be.

I have uploaded a spoken poem specifically about this deeply moving experience, onto You tube. Here is the link to it: https://www.youtube.com/watch?v=OXmR7BCLcbc&t=2s

The poem on You tube helps the listener to ponder on something beyond this existence that we cannot fully comprehend. I shared my emotional journey so that it may provide comfort to those that are bereaved and also to provide reassurance for others that there is something wonderful awaiting us beyond this mortal plane.

After having been through this overwhelming experience, it was a struggle for me to get used to being back in this world.

Raising a baby without my mother's help was incredibly difficult, especially as my baby was constantly ill and my husband was away on business a lot. I felt very alone for much of the time.

I often felt overwhelmed and tearful, but I wanted to do the best that I could for my baby. I also knew that she really didn't have anyone else, besides me, to care for her. My daughter didn't smile for some time; people remarked upon this. Looking back now, I guess it was because for a while, I didn't feel that I had much to smile about, and my joyless expression was all that she had as her example.

However, the miracle of life and the captivating developmental milestones that my baby achieved, activated the proud maternal instincts within me and I began to enjoy life with a baby a little more.

I still missed having a mother to turn to, but my little toddler kept me too busy to spend time ruminating. She was a very active child, rarely ever had naps and needed constant stimulation and entertainment. Life was hectic with a toddler who was now walking and talking. It was so difficult for me to find brief moments to even cook or clean.

One morning, I put my daughter into her room with some toys, wondering if I would be able to snatch a few minutes to simply be able to change the bedsheets in my room, before she demanded my attention again. I suddenly realised that she was unusually quiet and I went into her room to check on her. I witnessed an incredible moment observing my daughter conversing with someone, who was not visible to me. The conversation ended when I asked her who she was talking to. From my daughter's description of 'the lady' that had been talking to her, I realised that this was not an imaginary friend, but that this was indisputably my mother's spirit.

This prompted a huge mix of overwhelming emotions for me at that time. I no longer felt quite so alone, as I realised that my mother was watching over us and had spent some time with her granddaughter to help me out when I was in need.

It is my aim that the following poem conveys the depth of overwhelming emotions that I felt during this period of time in my life…

Dichotomy of Overwhelm

By Gail Costello

Without indication, no warning, no chance to say 'I love you';
The manic desperation of disbelief that this was true,
You were torn from your loved ones, way too young in years;
I was submerging and drowning in the torrent of my tears.

I couldn't extinguish the burning deluge of my pain;
How could I function, when it had massacred my brain?
This despicable grief, this descending black cloud;
Smothering and squeezing, becoming my sad shroud.

Acceptance dawns…time to celebrate and appreciate that life;
Gratitude and love to heal wounds slashed with sorrow's knife.
Fond memories and smiles that shift to stress's hysterical laughter;
A dimorphous response to remember hereafter.

It is said the miracle of new life begins as
another soul departs,
A generation that may not be known, casts a
shadow on our hearts.
An innocent progeny's expected arrival
stimulates tears of elation,
Easing past trauma and providing
consolation.

Unconscious with deadly exhaustion;
labour's last life energy spent.
A euphoric sense of weightlessness, floating,
content
to behold the celestial welcome committee
of beloved familiar souls; sweet silent
recognition -
dissolves into despair, as destiny halts this
expedition.

Compulsive, irresistible observation;
enraptured by the infant's formative years.
The genetic uterine bud unfolds;
prompting delightful dew of tears.
Experiencing the enchantment of each newly
acquired skill,
And the developmental milestone of a
bodacious self-will.

Generational cords transcend physical realms
and senses.
The intangible apparition readily accepted;
engaging and exquisite conversation
commences.
Forever grateful for your spiritual sojourn;
your soul's eternal imprint of maternal
devotion.
The memory of that metaphysical love
chokes me with emotion.

My diverse life experiences led me into studying counselling, in order that I could help others that go through difficult life challenges. This, together with the knowledge and experience that I have acquired in Hypnotherapy, EFT (Emotional Freedom Technique), and Reiki, enable me to support others in a holistic way. I use powerful methods of healing the mind, body and soul with both individuals and groups to bring about positive changes in people's lives.

The Journey Of Healing

By Jenny Schmal

A comprehensive explanation of overwhelm reads like this: If used in the context of emotion, emotional overwhelm is a state of being beset by intense emotion that is difficult to manage. It can affect your ability to think and act rationally. It could also prevent you from performing your daily tasks. Emotional overwhelm may be caused by stress, traumatic life experiences, relationship issues, and much more.

"Life is short. Stop worrying about what might happen. Live in the moment. Follow your heart. Be with good people. Forget what hurt you – but never forget what it taught you."
Karen Salmansohn

Dear Reader

As I sit with myself and have been for the past few weeks trying to write this chapter., overwhelm has been my constant companion. The dialogue went something like this

Overwhelm: Not sure why you said yes Jenny

Jenny: I said yes because I am committed to sharing a valuable chapter for readers of the book

Overwhelm: Really! Well up to now all you have is a few ideas and a couple of sentences that may not even resonate with anyone

Jenny: I will continue after I make a comforting cup of coffee

Overwhelm: another cup of coffee

Jenny: oh please could you shut up?

You may be smiling reading this, yet this is simply me sharing my heartfelt overwhelm with you, the reader. It's easy to say 'Yes! I am in! I want to contribute, I have something worthwhile to share' yet it's another thing altogether putting pen to paper ..

"Joy is overwhelming fun - fun so big that it overflows your mind, heart, body - as if all of life and love were spilling into you and you were spilling out."

Bernie De Koven

Let's get started.. the beginning may be a good place to look at for where my overwhelm began, a few origin stories may give an inkling to what started the path of overwhelm for me… notice it's only my interesting point of view of the events of my life and may have contributed to my overwhelming resistance to sharing parts of my life in publishing , yet and I sincerely hope my sharing them may be also be a blessing in disguise for you the reader.

It was planned to be a day of fun. I was 13 years old in my first year of high school and myself and a group of girls were leaning over the balustrade of the first floor balcony looking down on a group of matric students , yes you guessed correctly they were indeed "boys". We were giggling and being what some would call silly, we were trying to get their attention. One in particular for me was a tall young man with blue eyes and black hair named George. I knew his name as his sister was in my class .. she called out to her brother and using hand signs pointed to me and he waved at me … I went into fight or flight mode, bright pink cheeks my boldness disappeared and in its place: disaster.

We had just come from sewing class and I had in my mouth a pin, yes a straight pin with a red bobble on the top.. I have no idea why I did, but when he waved my shyness my anxiety turned into embarrassment and overwhelm. Needless to say, I swallowed the pin, caused a huge scene, the school nurse was called for as were paramedics. I spent a few days in a local hospital under doctors' scrutiny and a few scary moments of possible perforation of body parts … lucky for me I survived this ordeal and every time I saw George after that I froze .. overwhelm became my bodyguard.

George was the catalyst to an experience of immense anxiety, sadness and deep pain. Some 6 months later, he took his life and left myself and many young people at school overwhelmed with grief. His death was my first taste of the downward spiral of my senses and feelings of despair and apathy.

As a teenager this threw me a curved ball of not quite knowing how to react or behave so I self-isolated to comfort myself. My protecting myself from feelings of embarrassment, humiliation and apathy kept me disassociating from the real world at school to such an extent that I took the decision much to the disapproval of my parents not to continue with my studies and escape into the grown up world of business.

Being employed by a banking institution I felt safe secure and independent and far from the pain of the overwhelm of dealing with grief and authority of teachers and my parents

To be honest, in retrospect I was certainly setting myself up for failure of believing my overwhelm had miraculously dissolved.

A few years later my parents informed me they had decided to get divorced and I remember looking at them in disbelief and not being able to open my mouth to speak, the proverbial rug had been pulled out from under my feet and my life as I knew it was shattered. I made the decision to leave home, leave them and move in with my granny as a safety net.

If I wasn't at home their divorce would not affect me . Overwhelm had other ideas .. I continually fed myself so that anger, pain, humiliation and hate could be silenced and this continued for the next few years . I was on autopilot. I did not let my feelings overshadow my need to be strong, resilient and determined.

My life continued as if nothing was wrong and nothing bothered me. Except it did.

I was only 20 at the time: a well disguised, apathetic young lady.

So many things happened in the following years; marriage, children, my own divorce and recovery - a story on its own. The reason I am sharing with you, dear reader the following is that overwhelm can be joyous (the births of my children) - ecstatically so. For a few months to a few years the wounds and scars are not visible .. We manage overwhelm; we believe that we know how to appease it and yet it keeps lapping at the edge of our psyche, always present never letting us believe I am free of the scattered debilitating effects of overwhelm.

Let's continue: my life moves on and even a disastrous divorce and having to go out into the business world again after many years of being a stay at home mom does not sway me . I manage my life. I am courageous, bold and spontaneous. I grab life with both hands and at the age of 56 I remarry. I am his princess. Life is good. I am feeling safe and secure; significant.

The next part of the story is life shattering. Just when life was sailing along calmly and the days passing by filled with love, laughter and enjoyment. My overwhelm is far away from the surface of my celebration of life, it's a shadow of distant events which even when thought of don't touch the surface memory of trauma until 3 events that change my existence forever.

Life is cruel too. In the space of a few years - about 3 - I lost 3 of the most important men in my life.

First the father of my children died of prolonged cancer. Now this shocks me as even when you have been divorced for many, many years and are not in daily contact with the person you may think it will be easier to deal with .. no it was so painful. One never loses the close connection of having been in a relationship that births 3 beautiful children .. I was feeling off kilter, like a bad dose of vertigo and unbalance and scared internally and a sense of foreboding clouded my mind .. I loved him yes and he played a huge part in my life .. I tried to hide my pain from my husband and friends. They expected me to be ok with chirps of "well you two had been apart for a long time" and "you will be ok" .. overwhelm had other ideas! I really worked on myself to stay focused in the present moment so that I could go about life with integrity and appreciation.

The next year after a very short marriage of 18 months my husband left the tea table with " sweetie just going for a walk on the golf course", a kiss on the cheek and off he went. Barely 5 mins later I received a call to hurry. He had had a heart attack and died on the golf course that bright sunny day.. The paramedics told me it was instant and I sat down next to him, his head on my lap and spoke sweet nothings to him - without knowing how long or who was listening about how he was loved until they pried me away as it was necessary to move the body .... In that moment I knew that my overwhelm was back... I searched the faces around me as if to say "help me!"

As it happens everything happens as it should. Doctors & family assist and speak words you don't hear, they give hugs you don't feel, they make food you don't taste, you go to the funeral as if it's not you; rather someone observing you at someone else's funeral. You pray that this is just a bad movie not your movie .. you go home and as you get into your bed to sleep, overwhelm arrives.. surreptitiously it's back. Your skin crawls, you shiver you shake you get up and then get back into not being able to focus angst heart wrenching pain and an assault on your senses ensue.

Exhausted, you sleep and when you awake you feel unbalanced, nauseas, headachy and not in control. It's back in full force. You pretend you're ok. You say the right things. Only, deep down you can feel the churning in your stomach. You spin into an eat-sleep-angst state of being. Off kilter. Day by day you notice your behaviour and attitude to life changes. You are either in overdrive to get things right, or, you isolate, surrender and compensate in many ways to pretend to yourselves and others it's ok.

You know you have to make a plan to steer your life in a direction and to do this you look for something that is bigger than you. A new skill perhaps?

"Spend time with people who bring out the best in you. Not the stress in you."
Unknown

For me, I had realised, to stay sane and recover from the grief and loss and to bring some semblance of balance to my life, I would take a life-coaching course, which kept me busy. I was not only learning how this would benefit others, it would be a lesson on how to heal or coach myself. Overwhelm receded into the background. Maybe I had found a miracle to heal my secret of being afraid, insecure and out of control at times, although not visible to others.

Dear reader, a year later:

Just when I had discovered and realised my purpose in my dream job, was fully certified and had started to self-coach myself, working on inner-life skills needed to be equal to my overwhelm and making progress on staying grounded, centred and balanced, tragedy reared its ugly head again and the saddest day of my life arrived.

This news hit me energetically like what I can only say felt like a tsunami. My son was murdered. No parent should ever have to go through this! It's the wrong way around! It's not how life is supposed to work!

This overwhelm, this overpowering emotional onslaught, took over my life, my very being. My saddest goodbye and my highest mountain to climb. Why me?!?

You may understand dear reader, if as a mother I am not able to share the painful details of the months that followed, except to say the minutes, the days, were too long and fighting my overwhelm this time was like being submerged in a tidal wave. Unable to reach the surface of emotional composure. The pain, the angst, being afraid to wake up and afraid to go to sleep. Too afraid to drive my car. Not wanting to speak, then speaking too much. It was a dark, sad space of apathy and yet I noticed with practice of healing modalities, which I will share with you, I noticed an awareness of subtle shifts in my mental health, and yes psychology says we go through the process of healing in stages and we do. It's not easy, it's not pretty and it's necessary to get to the space where joy resides, where laughter and happiness are ours once more.

My healing included pushing forward and enrolling in more higher education to add to my coaching , and my focus became relationships with self and others. Having something to hold onto for me, was the memory of these beautiful men that had died and yet were my biggest teachers and blessing as my relationship with overwhelm had become a distant memory.

How? You may ask

There is always a way to become equal to your fears, your anxieties, your emotions. Yes they are real, and so are the tools that are available to assist you. Even if it is you learning the art of Self-Love or engaging with a Coach or Councillor of your choice, your life will surely change as you do the work. In closing, you never walk alone. Talk to somebody, they will hear you and assist you to overcome your overwhelm.

About Jenny Schmal

Jenny is an experienced and expert Relationship Coach, who guides her clients to a space of pure joy in all areas of life. Jenny has led a full life and has gained immense wisdom over the years, as she has triumphed over tragedy, including the murder of her son. She is an accomplished author of two brilliant books, including the aptly named: "Finally find the love of your life… at any Age". During a coaching session she uses great humour, insight and compassion to dismantle the defence mechanisms of the mind. Jenny is extremely intuitive and knows exactly when to push and when to be more gentle. Her ability to assist the client to switch to more empowering perspectives, can truly feel magical to say the least. Ultimately her coaching style is that of being a wise mirror and a lovely friend. Jenny is joy itself. The generosity which she transmits is so powerful, that her clients find themselves living their full potential before they even fully understand what happened to them. Jenny can be reached at jenny@rejener8.com

Four Factors Of Overwhelm And Four Keys

By Rachpal Kaur Tulsi

The last 18 years of my life as a freelancer have been exciting. One of the biggest thrills of the choice I made to move out of full-time employment was that I could choose when I worked and when I played.

Before that, I struggled for 7 years to report to work at a fixed time whilst working from the same office. I struggled with having to comply with rigid protocols. I struggled with having to squeeze in my housework, exercise, grocery shopping, laundry in those few hours after work and on the weekend. And by the time we got to Monday, I was starting the week exhausted.

Eighteen years on, and I'm feeling that way again and I don't like it. This time it's not just a struggle. It's a feeling I've got too much to do – it seems like I'm working non-stop. And housework just seems to pile up and I've got documents all over my dining table. Then there is the social obligations of meeting up with family and friends that I just don't feel I have time to myself.

And when finally, I do have a pocket of free time, I feel guilty that I am not doing work or that I am not attending to something that my family needs.

And perhaps the biggest nightmare of all - the endless chat groups – work, family, friends, interest groups – with videos and posts that may not be relevant or lists of things to do. More ANALYSIS and MORE DECISIONS to make!

By the end of the day, I just feel this DESPAIR, the feeling that so much is not accomplished, so much that is still not done. I carry with me a heaviness in my chest, lots of thoughts racing through my head, feelings of sadness and anger.

Every day I just feel like there is a long list of things I need to do and the list of things that have yet to be done just gets longer and longer. Does this sound familiar?

Overwhelm And The Fatigue Trap

If your life sounds very similar to mine, chances are you're in a state of overwhelm caused by being stuck in The Fatigue Trap. We often don't realise how much of our daily actions contribute to the fatigue that we feel as we're constantly engaged - either we're interacting with someone in real time or we're hooked on something online.

In a poll that I did on Linkedin , the following reasons were reasons cited for being fatigued:

- Working hours - 33%
- Time spent on the internet - 11%
- Lack of sleep - 11%
- Zoom fatigue - 44%

Pause: Put this chapter down for a few minutes and ask yourself this question:

What are the reasons I am fatigued?

Let's Look At Four Of The 'Usual Suspects' Of Overwhelm

First - Fatigue

CNA Lifestyle recently reported a piece of research by a UK bedding manufacturer that Singaporeans are the most fatigued people in the world. Are you surprised? Have a quick check on how you spend your 24-hour day. Every time I've done this activity the results are alarmingly similar - almost 12 hours (half the day) is spent on work or work-related activities. And the 4 to 5 hours of free time cannot be accounted for. Some people say they do chores, some say they tend to their children or help with their schoolwork, while others say they're exercising. But the biggest time-stealer has to be the time spent on electronic gadgets - be it attending to work, attending to the various chats, or scrolling on social media.

It's a vicious cycle - your brain is so active that when you go to bed, you have difficulty settling down and then you wake up tired and you push yourself hard the next day and then you're tired. And this repeats everyday.

Second - Not Quitting

When I know I've done everything I possibly could,

When I know that I've explored all options,

….. and nothing seems to be working,

I walk away, for my own mental health and wellbeing.

When you know you've done everything you possibly could, when you know that you've explored all options and it's still not working, I say give up for your own mental health and wellbeing.

Some day down the road, you may have the resources to complete what you left mid-way.

Third - Hankering For Closure

Closure is Overrated. In struggling to get closure for so many demons of the past, I've only succeeded in making myself more miserable.

Meaningful life balance for me meant that I liberated myself from the chains of the past, by not mulling over closure, but accepting that the past happened, had a reason for happening, what's the lesson to learn, forgive and carry on.

I often meet people seeking closure and have difficulty in doing so because the other subject in that situation has moved on, died, or is no longer connected. That ex-boy/girlfriend, that awful boss/colleague because of whom you quit the job, a family member you had a difficult relationship with died before you could resolve issues.

Instead of closure, seek acceptance.

I know that this is probably the hardest bit to do and I'm going to leave this here for today. Just one question - If I could accept what has happened, instead of seeking closure, what benefit would it bring to my life?

Fourth - See Burnout For What It Is

Long before you hit burnout, the writing was on the wall. You just didn't read it.

Work that was once exciting was starting to feel like a chore. The lunch-time or pantry conversations that once lifted your day, started feeling like mindless gossip. Clubbing, partying while once made you feel that you were living the life, now suddenly seemed pointless. Preparing meals for the family, doing the household chores, which you did with love and enthusiasm, now weigh you down.

The writing was on the wall.

Perhaps it was written in fine print or cursive and you missed it.

The writing on the wall was signalling you that your life has a new purpose.

That the old purpose had run its course and that it was important for that part of your life.

Time to move.

Read the writing on the wall again.

What is it saying to you?

What do you need to let go of so that you can bring new meaning and purpose to your life?

Tangible Steps To Get out of Overwhelm

It's so easy to get overwhelmed with the multitude of responsibilities that we juggle at work and our personal lives. You may have experienced the situation where you get started on a task and then you cannot stop until you complete the task and as a result, everything else gets held up or delayed? For example, when you finally decide to clear your Inbox of unwanted emails and as you scour through the history, you easily manage to delete some obvious ones and then there are those that you need to read and decide if you need to keep them or not and next thing you know, 4 hours have passed!! This is very true for all MUNDANE TASKS - they're annoying but if you don't get them done, it just adds to your agony in the long term.

Here are 5 steps to reduce overwhelm while attending to mundane tasks

Step 1: Choose the Time of the day when you're least productive

Step 2: Set your Timer for 15 minutes (maximum 2 rounds)

Step 3: Start the Task

Step 4: STOP when the timer goes off

Step 5: Repeat everyday

When was the last time you did something for yourself? In the busyness of work, household chores, perhaps part-time studies or raising children, have your needs been overlooked?

How do you refuel when all your energies have depleted? For me, a walk by the beach or one of the many nature reservoirs in Singapore does the trick. Sound of the waves, the birds and the greenery is always a welcome break.

Love to hear what you do to recharge.

Early this year (2022) my motto was New Year, New Beginnings and I happily announced my latest coaching programme Nature-based Coaching.

You've probably heard the term "nature heals" - from sages who wandered off to the jungles for months to meditate to modern day executives going for holistic retreat in a spa set in a nature reserve. Humans turn to nature when life overwhelms.

Nature has done wonders for me this past 18 months of the pandemic. I recall in the first lockdown we had in April 2021 that lasted 2 over months, it came to a point that I felt miserable and sad - from having to stay home, not meeting my family and friends. Finally after 3 weeks of being cooped up at home, I put on my running shoes and headed out for jogs and walks every evening for about 2 hours every day. While I've always loved being outdoors, my work schedule for the past 20 years limited the amount of time I had outdoors and when the pandemic descended upon us, I suddenly found myself with little else to do. It was also then that I reaffirmed my assertion on the Healing Power of Nature.

Flowers bloomed, fruits emerged, leaves flew off their twigs and new leaves emerged. Birds, bees and other creatures went about their daily routine - oblivious to the fear that had shrouded the world.

How has nature healed me these past few months? For one, I've learnt to not fret the small things. Learning "acceptance" (though I have some way to go on this) has been a big one. Some things I cannot change like the weather or when a flower is going to bloom. Rather than be miserable that nature didn't meet my expectations, I've learnt to look for the beauty even on stormy days.

Perhaps the biggest healing was finding joy in the discoveries I've made this past year as an "urban hunter" in search of wildlife in the nature reserves and parks. I'd make multiple trips to Sungei Buloh to see the crocodile and when I recently saw on a friend's post that there was an iguana on the prowl, I just had to go see it for myself. It took me 2 days before I finally spotted them (I was lucky to see them both). On the second day, I jogged up and down the path in the midday heat, bargained and then pleaded for Divine Intervention for them to emerge. And when they finally did, I couldn't believe my eyes! Every trip into nature is a new discovery of the environment and myself.

And for all of you who are reading this and can identify with it, I say - YOU HAVE A CHOICE. If you are tired of being tired, then time for you to look at what's happening in your life, what are your activities and what needs to change.

Oh and get out in nature first chance you get!

About Rachpal Kaur Tulsi

Rachpal Kaur Tulsi has over 25 years' experience in training, customer service, organisational development, mentoring and coaching. As a Consultant, Rachpal has had extensive experience working with top management to conceptualise strategies for communicating the organisational mission and vision to its employees and the successful immersion of new employees to the organisation.

Rachpal is nationally known speaker and an expert on change, health and wellbeing and workforce trends. Having survived 4 major crises in her career – 1998 Asian financial crisis, SARS in 2003, the global financial crises of 2008 and now the Covid-19 Pandemic, Rachpal is an expert on how to remain agile and pivot in uncertain climates. Rachpal specialises in delivering training programmes for developing personal and organisational leadership through changing beliefs and mindset. Organisations that have engaged her services include Fortune 100 Company and a wide range of sectors such as health, marine, oil and gas, network and telecommunication and financial services.

Rachpal has extensive experience in coaching both Senior Management and High-Potential Executives in reviewing their performance and coaching them on areas for development using 360-degree feedback, performance management standards and other tools. Have a look at www.rachpal.com

A note to us all

By Maybelline Tan

Maybelline Tan has been a part of every book.
This time she had this to share :

As some of you readers know, this period, my dad is at the brink of death, and I just have a newborn.

I am shuffling between the hospice with weight and sadness, and coming home to look after my baby with joy and anticipation.

It is really showing me the full spectrum and paradoxical events of life. It is indeed the feeling of being overwhelmed and I want to write it but nothing comes out. I thought it might help to let you know how overwhelmed I am as an inspiration for you.

Now What?

Your journey with *Overwhelm And Us* doesn't end here. Whilst we've introduced you to different modalities for dealing with overwhelm, this isn't the end of the story. Come and join the private Facebook group where you can meet the authors, ask questions, download resources to accompany the book - and much, much more!

www.bit.ly/AndUsFacebookGroup

About Carolyn Street

Carolyn is a type 7 with a lot of 2 Enneagram. Her MBTI is 'advocate' except she doesn't like to be labelled 'introverted'. She advocates for extroverts who have misplaced guilt and fear of offending voyeurs - oops - introverts as well as for introverts who get overwhelmed and offended and (seriously) cannot get a word or look in edgeways. Seriously, she helps extroverts, introverts and ambiverts like herself to be the public speakers and sharers they know they can be. Combined with that is her drive and desire to get people on the path of finding their audience and sharing their messages. This book is part of that purpose.

This series is her most major work to date.

Carolyn's 'niche' is anxiety-related projects (in JSJ we say projects not problems) and she believes that healing comes with self-expression and the ability to know and trust oneself. She offers a bouquet of healing and empowering modalities. Clients call her 'happy pill-ar' because she brings an attentive, deep listening awareness, lightness and spaciousness to her work. Clients see her as a stabilising and grounding influence and appreciate her joy and appropriate, interestingly fun vibe.

Recent clients have had breakthroughs in public speaking, being published authors, leadership, AD(H)D, hyperhidrosis and getting pregnant naturally. She attracts gay singles and couples and misfits and kids who have been bullied whether by other kids or their teachers and -sadly- parents.

Carolyn has had an awareness of energy emitting from her hands similar to reiki since she was a child. While on her own search for answers to various questions and existential queries she discovered she had the double whammy of polycystic ovarian syndrome (PCOS) and hypothyroidism.

In 2003 she discovered JSJ, short for Jin Shin Jyutsu. While experimenting with JSJ self-help she went for a routine ultrasound which showed that the cysts had cleared from her ovaries. JSJ also cured severe back issues and averted serious surgery. JSJ is invariably part of her work with clients. NLP usually also features Perceptual Positions and the 'Swish' technique.

In 2017 Marisa Peer who developed Rapid Transformational Therapy (RTT) caught her attention and Carolyn used RTT to initiate some significant weight loss and improvements in her vision. She became an Advanced RTT therapist and was cured of the hypothyroidism (hormone levels normalised and remain normal) and had significant improvement in many aspects of her life.

The bouquet also includes Tapping, Access Bars body processes and clearings. Carolyn is currently enjoying working with the Compassion Keys by Edward Mannix and will soon add that to her bouquet of offerings of which this is a small posy.

Carolyn's hobbies are keeping the LITandUs facebook group going, reading, travelling (virtually these days). Not to mention public speaking and making books like this one. She is an active and selective Toastmaster enroute to her third Distinguished Toastmaster award (all that admin - who'd have it? smile). She lives in the east of Singapore with her mum Shanta, Steven Rennie, her SpouseGrouse, and recently adopted cats Cue and Hugo.

Carolyn is contactable at carolyn@litconsultings.com or via Facebook messenger @ Facebook.com / carolyn.street

About Youier Media

"What we want is not more little books about Christianity, but more little books by Christians on other subjects - with their Christianity latent."
- CS Lewis

Youier Media is the publishing arm of Youier, aimed at helping authors write and publish books in a way that honours who God created them to be. In essence ... Youier!

Established in 2015 by founder of *The Blue House*, El Edwards, the goal then was quite simply to "scratch an itch" and that's as true today as it was back then.

Those itches or niggles to write a book? What if they were God's way of trying to get your attention? (Spoiler alert: If something's important to you, it's important to Him!)

Whether you need group accountability to get your first draft finished via the *The Rainbow Room* or you have your book "done" and you're ready to take the next step towards getting it published, Youier Media is here to help! Youier.com to find out more.

Copyright © 2022 by Carolyn Street

All rights reserved. This book or any portion thereof may not be reproduced or used in any manner whatsoever without the express written permission of the publisher except for the use of brief quotations in a book review or scholarly journal.

First Printing: 2022

ISBN 978-1-8382248-7-5

Youier Media
The Blue House
Queen Victoria Road
Llanelli, SA15 2TH
YouierMedia.com

Printed in Great Britain
by Amazon

80287167R00243